Contents

IRISH FOREIGN POLICY AND THE EUROPEAN COMMUNITY

A Study of the Impact of Interdependence
on the Foreign Policy of a Small State

PAUL SHARP
Institute for International Studies
University of Minnesota, Duluth

Dartmouth

Published by
Dartmouth Publishing Company Limited
Gower House
Croft Road
Aldershot
Hants GU11 3HR
England

Gower Publishing Company
Old Post Road
Brookfield
Vermont O5036
USA

British Library Cataloguing in Publication Data

Sharp, Paul, 1953–
    Irish foreign policy and the European community:
    a study of the impact of interdependence on
    foreign policy of a small state.
    1. Ireland (Republic). Foreign relations, history
    I. Title
    327.417

ISBN 1 85521 018 5

Acknowledgements

My thanks go first to a number of public figures in Ireland who readily gave of their time to share their experiences and opinions regarding the conduct of Irish foreign policy. Similarly, many officials in the Irish foreign service were very helpful, and I am particularly indebted to the Embassy in Ottawa and the Permanent Mission at the UN for the use of their library facilities. Finally, this book would not have been possible without the assistance of the Royal D. Alworth Jr Institute of International Studies the professional advice and encouragement of my colleagues there: Dr Douglas Nord, Dr John Kress and Professor Walter Baeumler, and the secretarial support provided by Mrs Bonita Drummond.

Paul Sharp
University of Minnesota, Duluth

Introduction

My purpose in this book is to study certain aspects of Irish foreign policy. In particular, I am concerned with two sets of questions: why, and with what consequences, did the Irish government pursue a policy of international role-playing after Ireland became a member of the UN in 1956; and why, and with what consequences, was this policy continued after Ireland became a member of the European Economic Community (EEC).

The focus here is the foreign policy of one particular country. However, I shall argue that the questions posed cannot be satisfactorily answered without examining two themes of significance for the study of foreign policy in general. The first concerns questions of intentionality. What do the governments of small states believe they are trying to achieve with their policies? This has been a neglected aspect of foreign policy analysis, partly because of the methodological difficulties inherent in the concept of intentionality, but primarily because the main approaches to understanding foreign policy behaviour are concerned with explaining outcomes in the international system. This concern has led to an emphasis upon either the foreign policies of the great powers – those capable of making a sustained impact on the system – or the processes by which the international system itself may be said to determine the positions and policies of most of its members.

It is clear that most small state foreign policy is largely determined by external factors. Typically, small state governments are confronted by decisions taken external to their borders, for example, concerning trade policies, international security or cooperation on functional issues, to which they have to respond. This being so, their policies may be understood primarily as exercises in managing the impact of the external environment on the internal affairs of the country. They respond, however, not only to a succession of substantive demands. The governments of small states are also concerned with the implications of these daily demonstrations of the limits to the independence which they enjoy for their internal legitimacy. I shall argue that it is in these terms that the Irish policy of establishing a distinctive national identity through the performance of actions associated with a specific role – that of 'international good citizen' – should be understood. It was and is a prestige policy which, although it may be regarded as having, at best, only a minor significance for outcomes in the international system and, at worst, as a mystification of the real external circumstances of the country, is extremely important to those charged with practising it. This is because its objective is to demonstrate that Ireland is a distinctive country which possesses a capacity for independent external activity on that basis.

The significance which the governments of small states attach to such policies is of great importance for the second theme. This is the proposition that, as relations between states and between states and other actors become increasingly characterised by interdependence (mutual need), so the character of their foreign policy behaviour will be transformed from the pursuit of national interests within an anarchy to the management of collaboration within an increasingly rule-governed environment. Conventional wisdom has assumed that the governments of small states are either not, or ought not to be, concerned with the projection of the power and the prestige of the state as a state. To this, interdependence theory has added that such policies should become even less important as interdependence increases. This is so, they have argued, because the governments of small states will find such policies both harder to undertake and less necessary as they exploit the new opportunities for more effective action provided by rule-governed international regimes in which the importance of traditional forms of power has been considerably reduced.

This has not been the case as far as Ireland's experience with the EEC is concerned. Irish governments continue to pursue opportunities for international role-playing, and although they are certainly now more deeply involved with the international system, they do not seem to enjoy many advantages from these new arrangements in terms of the effectiveness of their foreign policy. Rather, EEC membership has provided both the need and the opportunity for an extension of the role-playing approach to foreign policy. The reasons for this are not to be found in the peculiarities of the Irish. They lie, rather, with major weaknesses in the arguments of the interdependence thesis, in particular with the claim that conditions of complex interdependence have an equalising effect upon the capabilities of states in the international system.

x

I shall argue that this line of reasoning rests on several false assumptions, namely, that increasing interdependence brings with it an imperative to cooperate, a tendency to depoliticise issues, and an erosion of the importance of national identity for those involved in such relationships. These observations have a prescriptive value at best, and in the case of Ireland and the EEC, there has been no great equalisation of the ability to produce intended effects among the members. The status quo between the strong and the weak in traditional terms is preserved in conditions of increasing interdependence. Thus, any gains made by the Irish have been derived not from any qualitative transformation of international relations in Europe, but rather from shifts in the distribution of power, primarily as a consequence of Britain's decline.

Ireland, I shall argue, remains a weak, dependent actor within the EEC, but with one important change in its external environment. Membership of the EEC has made it impossible for Irish governments to maintain a distinction between economic and political affairs, a posture attempted with increasing difficulty between 1955 and the late 1960s. The consequences of this difficulty may be seen in the controversy and debate which has surrounded the question of Irish neutrality. The latter is still the basis of Ireland's distinctive foreign policy, but now is also potentially an obstacle to securing special consideration from the other members of the Community increasingly interested in political and security cooperation.

To date, the EEC has shown little sign of developing in such a way as to provide any Irish government with clear incentives for abandoning the traditional and popular assumptions upon which Irish foreign policy has been based. However, it does provide them with considerable opportunities for asserting an independent and distinctive national identity through the performance of a number of international roles. I shall show below how these have been variously regarded by Irish governments as a contribution to the Community, a compensation for the failure of the EEC to provide more tangible rewards for Ireland, and, increasingly, as a device for mobilising popular support in the face of both internal and external economic and political difficulties.

The book is divided into three parts. First, I offer an historical account of Ireland's foreign policy and its domestic significance, principally for the reader who may not be familiar with the subject. I also develop my theoretical arguments here regarding small state foreign policy and increasing levels of interdependence. In the second part I attempt to reconstruct the way in which key members of the Irish political elite interpreted and explained the purposes of its foreign policy after Ireland was admitted to the UN in 1955–6 and in the context of this, look at two particular areas of Irish policy: UN peacekeeping activities and the management of Ireland's economic relations with Britain. Finally, in the third part I examine the impact on its foreign policy of Ireland's membership of the EEC between 1977 and 1983, looking particularly at Irish perceptions of the EEC, the strategies adopted in their dealings with it, and their success – or otherwise – on a number of important policy issues. The conclusion also offers a brief postscript of events from 1983 up to the Irish ratification of the Single European Act and their accompanying declarations regarding regional imbalances and Irish neutrality in 1987.

1 Ireland in international affairs

The Irish Free State was established by the Anglo-Irish treaty of 1921. This brought to an end a period of direct rule by England which had been maintained, with varying degrees of effectiveness, for some 800 years. The Free State consisted of 26 of the 32 counties of Ireland, although this was considered to be a temporary arrangement, certainly by the Irish negotiators and possibly by their British counterparts. The Free State became a member of the British Commonwealth, an arrangement which left the monarch and, hence, the British government with an unspecified but contested role in its constitutional, external and security affairs. The Free State's position as a dominion was clarified by the Statute of Westminster in 1931, and the ties to the British monarch established by the treaty of 1921 were all but removed by the new constitution of 1937. This constitution asserted that the 'whole island of Ireland, its islands and the territorial seas' were the 'national territory'.[1] The Anglo-Irish agreements of the following year saw the removal of British naval bases permitted under the original treaty and, in 1948, a republic was declared, thereby formalising Ireland's departure from the Commonwealth and severing the last constitutional ties with Britain. In 1961 the decision was made to apply for membership of the EEC and, eleven years later, following a national referendum and the necessary constitutional amendments, Ireland became a member.

The history of Irish foreign policy may be conveniently, if not altogether satisfactorily, divided into five phases: the pre-independence and first Dáil

1

period; the period of the Cumann na nGaedheal Free State government, 1922–32; the de Valera era from the early 1930s to the Second World War; the post-war period from the late 1940s to the late 1960s; and finally, the current phase, commencing with membership of the EEC. Both in official mythology and academic treatments, this division of the subject is based on distinct stages in the emergence of an independent Irish republic as a full participant in international life. While it is correct to say that Irish foreign policy has been about much more than achieving international status, and that much of it cannot even be related to such preoccupations, this theme, more than any other, characterises the activity, and certainly seemed to be central to the way that practitioners of Irish foreign policy have presented it until fairly recently.

'Foreign policy' during the independence struggle, for the most part, consisted of fund-raising and propaganda trips abroad. It was only with the establishment of the first Dáil (Irish parliament) in 1919, by Sinn Fein parliamentary candidates who had abstained from the London parliament in order to create their own one in Dublin, that one may note the development of what Patrick Keatinge, in his study of issues in Irish foreign policy, calls 'a foreign policy in embryo'.[2] Instead of merely seeking financial help from any quarter, the 'diplomats' of the 'Republic' focused their effort on attempting to secure a hearing from the victorious allies at the Paris peace conference. De Valera's fund-raising tour of the United States also involved an attempt at defining a possible future security relationship between Britain and Ireland.[3] Finally, and perhaps this is one of the surest signs that a nationalist group senses its proximity to power, a debate developed as to whether the weight of the first Dáil's diplomatic effort should be behind an appeal to the established powers, or to the nationalist movements and newly-established revolutionary governments in positions as tenuous as their own.[4]

The importance of the pre-independence period for Irish foreign policy lay in the way that, in the minds of the nationalist leadership, it linked the achievement and maintenance of Irish independence with the course of events in the world outside. In the light of common perceptions of Ireland as an international actor which occupies a position on the geographical, social, economic and political periphery, 'an island behind an island',[5] this link, and the fact that it continues to exist today, cannot be overstressed.

The connection can be seen to have operated in two ways. First, the attainment of Ireland's independence was seen to be dependent, in part, on the course of events outside the country. The external environment of the future state was seen as a potential source of help and, hence, a target for efforts to secure that help. However, the practical effort to secure help from other nationalists, the Irish overseas and the enemies of the British empire, also developed into the need to take an interest in European and world politics. For those who desired a complete separation from Britain, this was based on the premise that England's difficulty was Ireland's opportunity. For those who wanted a measure of Irish self-government within the Union or the Empire, the objective was to demonstrate a capacity for responsible cooperation with Britain in its struggle against Germany.

Secondly, the Irish question came to be regarded as a specific instance of a broader conflict between the system of empires and the principle of national self-determination which increasingly was to occupy the attentions and concerns of the international community. The success or failure of the Irish struggle could be seen as important to others besides the Irish themselves. Thus, while the attainment of Ireland's independence might be dependent, in part, on external help or external developments such as the outcome of the Great War or Wilson's Fourteen Points, it also had an external significance which was crucial for nationalist perceptions of the future identity of the state. If its independence was to be preserved, Ireland would obviously need a foreign policy to conduct it through a world composed of elements and actors variously supportive or hostile to the cause of Irish independence. Their conception of that independence, however, embodied the need for a foreign policy which went beyond self-preservation to playing a part in the world which was based upon the external significance which they felt that Irish independence possessed.

The Anglo-Irish treaty of 1921 essentially created the major substantive concerns of Irish foreign policy for the future, namely the partition of the island in which the six counties of the north-east were retained by Britain, and the character of the Anglo-Irish economic and security relationships. These did not, however, dominate the attention of the Free State government which was in power between 1922 and 1932. Rather, the latter was concerned with more symbolic and formal objectives that its members and others felt they had failed to achieve in the negotiations with the British.

Their major problem was the extent to which the government's constitutional ties with the Crown, set out by the terms of the treaty and implied by relationships which the other dominions had with Britain, permitted the latter to intervene in what the government considered to be purely Irish affairs. As Collins had argued in the Dáil debate on accepting the treaty, Ireland had gained freedom, 'not the ultimate freedom that all nations aspire and develop to, but the freedom to achieve it'.[6] As a consequence, foreign policy was directed at obtaining external recognition of the Irish government's interpretation of what these constitutional ties involved. They did this by declarations and demonstrations of independence, and substantive actions designed to minimise the right and the capacity of the British to reserve to themselves, or participate in, areas of decision-making in which they could have no competence if Ireland was to be a fully independent state. Much of the struggle for status consisted of attempting to acquire some of the ordinary attributes of statehood, such as the right to issue passports or to fly the national flag from merchant ships.[7] But other, more constitutional, preoccupations, such as the effort to obtain the Irish Great Seal used in confirming legislation from

3

London, were crucial to the strategy of excluding the British government from the Irish policy-making process by obtaining direct access to the monarch.

The two principal platforms for Irish foreign policy during the period were the Commonwealth and the League of Nations. Within the Commonwealth, but especially at imperial conferences, Irish representatives worked with their Canadian and South African counterparts, not so much to broaden the scope of dominion powers, but to ensure that those powers and rights that already enjoyed formal recognition would also be recognised in practice by the British. It was in the League, however, that the first Free State government operated most successfully to emphasise its claim to a conception of independence going beyond dominion status. It did so by using the League to demonstrate that Ireland's Commonwealth commitments and agreements were similar to other such agreements and commitments undertaken by fully independent states, and not special arrangements of significance only within the British system.

In accordance with this policy, the 1921 treaty was registered as an international agreement under Article 18 of the Covenant. A Free State representative stood over British objections for one of the non-permanent seats on the Council of the League in 1926, presenting himself as an 'anti-group' rather than as a Commonwealth candidate. And in 1929, the Minister for External Affairs signed the 'optional clause', Article 36 of the Permanent Court of International Justice, thereby accepting the compulsory jurisdiction of the Court in all international disputes to which Ireland was a party, including those which might occur within the Commonwealth.

The foreign policy of the first Free State government is significant for two reasons. First, it demonstrates the continuing external dimension to the concept of Irish independence held by members of the government. The importance attached to foreign policy persisted, despite the fact that they were confronted by the major internal problems posed by a civil war and the establishment of the organs of government. There was no simple separation between internal and external problems permitting the latter to be shelved while the government put its own house in order. The problems of internal dissent and disorder were intimately bound up with external matters, which, in their turn, revolved around the extent of the continued British involvement in Irish affairs.

While it might be argued that external matters were thrust upon the government, however, the second major point is that it is with this government, and not with de Valera as is often supposed, that the importance of an active foreign policy was clearly established. The rationale behind such a policy is clearly seen in a memorandum from the first Free State Minister for External Affairs, George Gavan Duffy, to his successor, Desmond FitzGerald. In it, he argued that the global distribution of the Irish people, their history, traditions, values, reputation, the strategic location of Ireland and Irish knowledge of the English and Americans, all combined to place Ireland in a position of 'international

4

importance quite disproportionate to the size and population of this island'. Ireland's attributes gave it parts to play. Played well, these would enhance Ireland's world position, and 'the bigger our world position becomes, the more increasingly difficult it will be for England to attempt any undue interference with us'.[8]

Since the scope for independent action on issues of substance, such as Partition or the British bases in the Free State, was severely limited, however, Irish policy was focused on the politics of constitutional practices and international organisations. The pattern was established by which Irish representatives stood as candidates for positions which they knew they had little hope of winning. They signed renunciations which they stood little chance of ever violating (e.g. the Kellogg–Briand Pact) and they participated in conferences on matters of no direct concern to them.[9] They did this, in part, to help strengthen international law and security. They did it also, however, in pursuit of status, to be seen to be taking part in international conferences as a sovereign equal, since acceptance of this would imply recognition of the government's claim to be acting on behalf of a fully independent state.

The third period in Irish foreign policy may be broadly said to run between 1932 and 1948. It is dominated by the figure of de Valera, the force of whose personality in general terms was aided by the fact that he held the offices of both Taoiseach and Minister of External Affairs. There were considerable elements of continuity in Irish foreign policy between the period of the first Free State government and the first five years of the de Valera period. De Valera, however, introduced new elements into Irish foreign policy which were important in defining, now that Ireland had 'a place among the nations',[10] just what sort of place Irish governments felt it to be. In doing this, he also underlined the limitations on what an active foreign policy focusing on substantive issues could achieve for Ireland.

Changes in Irish foreign policy after 1932 were quite likely for a number of reasons. First, it was clear that there was little left for the multilateral approach within a Commonwealth framework to achieve. The Balfour Declaration of 1926 had established the co-equal status of the dominions. The Statute of Westminster confirmed the full international status of the dominions in 1931. More importantly, perhaps, a foreign policy, the criteria of success for which were defined in terms of the way a British role within a British system was successfully exploited for Irish ends, held few attractions for de Valera and the rest of his party, Fianna Fail. They, after all, were the parliamentary successors to the losers of a civil war fought, in part, over the acceptability of such a status. Hence, in addition to the continued distancing from Britain pursued by constitutional means and, after initial hesitation, the pursuit of an active League of Nations policy, the de Valera government attempted to make progress on the more substantial issues of Partition and the economic and security relationships with Britain.

With regard to Partition, de Valera's policy initially followed that of the previous government. He excluded a role for the armed force in any solution to the problem and stressed the importance of obtaining 'for the people of this part of Ireland such conditions as will make the people in the other part of Ireland wish to belong to this part'.[11]

Nevertheless, by a series of interventions in the political life of Northern Ireland, and by presenting Partition at the top of any agenda for Anglo-Irish discussions, de Valera laid the foundations for a policy which was to move away from the conciliatory approach to the northern Protestants embodied in the retention of the Commonwealth links for external matters and other concerns of joint interests. Instead, Partition was tackled on three fronts: by approaches to the British government directed at drawing their attention to the treatment of the nationalist minority by the government of the province; by public advocacy in the United States, British newspapers and international fora stressing the injustice of Partition; and by the claims set forth in the 1937 constitution.

In terms of the stated goal of ending Partition, de Valera's policy was a total failure. While it is hard to conceive of alternatives which might have been more successful in that respect, it may also be argued that, if anything, by emphasising the existence of the border, his approach made the achievement of Irish unity more, rather than less, difficult. Further, not only did the policy fail to achieve a basic goal of all Irish governments, but it also created new problems where resources had been mobilised to support it, namely in Ireland's economic and security relations.

With regard to the question of Ireland's security in the international system, the watchword of Irish nationalists and governments alike had been neutrality. Neutrality, however, had taken on a particular meaning in the context of the struggle for Irish independence. It was not a legal concept on the Swiss model and it had few of the later connotations of non-alignment: it meant not having to fight in Britain's wars. As such, the ability to refrain from participation in such wars became a measure or test of the reality of Irish independence. Under de Valera, however, and particularly after the start of the Second World War, the neutrality policy came to be viewed as a response to Britain's refusal to grant concessions on Northern Ireland. In linking neutrality to the maintenance of Partition, it has been argued that the Irish government did much to cut itself off from the main international currents of the post-war period. To be neutral in 1940, in what was still recognisably a British war, was, perhaps, sensible. To keep out of what, by 1945, had become a United Nations effort against fascism, while principled, did little to serve the Irish pursuit of international status.

Similarly, attempts to mobilise economic levers in support of the Partition policy based on conflict with Britain proved costly. Economic policy under Fianna Fáil was directed at achieving self-sufficiency through protection and restrictions on imports and foreign investments. While this was justified on the

6

grounds of economic autarky being the precondition of true independence and de Valera's idiosyncracies regarding the desirability of a certain material frugality in Irish life, such a policy was by no means out of step with prevailing trends in the economic policies of more wealthier states after 1929. Economic policy, however, became closely linked to the National Question in 1932 when the Irish government stopped paying annuities to Britain arising from pre-independence Land Acts. The British retaliated by placing tariffs on imports from Ireland and in the ensuing 'tariff war' which was not fully settled until 1938, the value of Irish export earnings was considerably lowered.

De Valera's policy appears to have been based on the assumption that Ireland had already achieved, or was in the process of achieving, the place among the nations which would provide the basis for independent actions directed at achieving Irish objectives. By attempting to pursue goals of substance, however, and mobilising other issues in support of them, the Irish government succeeded in pulling Ireland out of one forum of multilateral diplomacy – the Commonwealth – and rendering it ineligible for membership of another – the UN, established at the end of the Second World War. This isolation, however, was not entirely of the Irish government's own making. As Lyons points out in his history of Ireland, just as the country's place in the pre-war international society was fully established, that society was dissolved by the rise of Fascism and the outbreak of the war.[12]

Further, de Valera's policy was not without its successes. The constitutional ties with Britain were further weakened. The 1938 agreements with Britain, in addition to resolving difficulties which might have been avoided, also achieved the removal of the British naval bases from the territory of the Free State. Ireland's policy in the League of Nations was marked by institutional successes, and principled stands on the major international issues of the 1930s. Finally, the neutrality policy contributed to sparing Ireland the horrors of warfare to which most small European states were exposed during the period.

To assess de Valera's foreign policy in terms of its lack of success in achieving substantive external goals, however, is to miss much of its significance, or rather, what became significant in the process of external failure. The policy of the Free State government had revolved around achieving and then demonstrating a degree of international status, both to international and domestic opinion. It was conspicuously successful in terms of its limited objectives and the external projection of them, and yet it failed to achieve much domestic recognition. In contrast, however, de Valera's policy, while failing to achieve external goals, in the process of trying, demonstrated the reality of Ireland's political independence and established the main components of Ireland's international identity for domestic opinion. While demonstrating that it could not force its more powerful neighbours and friends to do what Ireland wanted them to do, it also showed that Ireland did not have to do their bidding in order to continue to exist.

The post-war period 1948–69 is characterised here by the policy of selective international involvement through the UN. For the first six years, however, the foreign policy preoccupations of the Irish government were scarcely distinguishable from those of the previous period. This is mainly attributable to the isolationist consequences of de Valera's foreign policy which left the new government with few other options. However, the coalition character of the government, containing as it did some fairly radical and republican elements, also helps to explain the continuity in policy.

The Inter-Party government, as it was known, made its contribution to establishing the formal status of Ireland by repealing the Executive Authority (External Relations) Act in 1948 and passing the Republic of Ireland Act the following year. From this point on, Ireland's status was that of an independent republic with no formal ties to Britain or the Commonwealth. The question of Ireland's broader international involvement, however, remained tied to the issue of Partition. UN membership was excluded by Ireland's wartime neutrality and Soviet interpretations of the same, although Irish diplomats were active in some of the specialised agencies of the UN. Ireland became a member of the OEEC and accepted a £40.8 million loan under the Marshall Plan. More typical of its foreign policy at this time, however, was the restricted use which Irish diplomats made of the Council of Europe for airing the issue of Partition, the so-called policy of 'raising the sore thumb'.[13] In addition, the question of Partition continued to be cited as an explanation of why Ireland retained a neutral posture in general and would not join NATO.

By 1955, however, domestic and external circumstances were altered sufficiently to permit the elaboration of an external policy less immediately linked to the requirements of the National Question. Most importantly, as a consequence of the 1955 arrangement between the USSR and the United States, Ireland was finally permitted to become a member of the UN. In addition, the composition of the government was such that it was capable of elaborating the principles of an Irish foreign policy less immediately linked to the requirements of the Partition question. The 'three principles' then enunciated by the Minister for External Affairs: a commitment to uphold the UN charter; the maintenance of a position of independence from the major blocs in the UN; and the characterisation of Ireland as a country whose values were both Christian and Western,[14] have remained the reference points for formal statements and political debate about Irish foreign policy ever since.

From this point on, Irish foreign policy became increasingly involved with the UN. This involvement took, and has continued to take, several forms. At New York, Irish delegations have participated in the day-to-day bargaining processes of UN politics in accordance with a certain image of themselves as constructive neutrals, and they have worked with a considerable degree of success for the occupancy of institutional positions within the various organs of the UN. But Irish foreign policy became associated at home, and known abroad, for actions taken mainly under the guidance of the Minister for

External Affairs, Frank Aiken,[15] in support of UN efforts to improve international security, through arms control, disarmament and peacekeeping operations, notably in the Congo and Cyprus.

Behind the rise to prominence of the image of Ireland as a successful and major participant in the activities of the UN, however, was what Keatinge calls a 'pragmatic and deliberate fragmentation of the foreign policy field'.[16] By this he means a division of labour in which different issue areas became the responsibility of different parts of the government. But almost as important as 'who did what?' was the concomitant question of how specific issues were handled and presented to the public. In part, this division of labour had its origins in the practice of distinguishing between constitutional matters, often referring to Partition and relations with Britain, which were considered the preserve of the Taoiseach, and the rest of foreign policy. This was a residual category which was the concern of the Minister and the Department of External Affairs. What changed, however, was the way in which issue areas formerly closely tied to the pursuit and demonstration of Irish independence, that is, relations with Britain and the question of Partition, became increasingly lumped together with Ireland's bilateral, chiefly European, contacts, as economic, technical, 'functional' issues, the details of which were to be the responsibility of the appropriate economic departments.

The main reason for this was the decision to abandon the strategy of consolidating independence through self-sufficiency and protection, and to aim for growth made possible by foreign investments, loans and the earnings of new industry geared towards the export market. The consequences of this for Irish foreign policy were not immediately apparent because the major external objective of the Irish government in the context of such a shift of strategy, the decision to apply for membership of the EEC, was aborted by its being made conditional on the success of the British application made at the same time. The substantive acts of foreign policy which seemed to flow from this change, therefore, were restricted to the EEC application itself, deciding to join the GATT, discussions on improving economic cooperation between both parts of Ireland and the negotiation of the Anglo-Irish free trade agreement of 1965. The latter, in particular, while presented by the government as a step in the direction of free trade, also underlined the extent to which the Irish economy was still tied to its British counterpart.

The final period in this brief review of Irish foreign policy, that between 1969 to 1983, is the most difficult to characterise. On the one hand, Ireland became a member of the EEC in 1973. In Ireland, as in other countries that have joined the EEC, the case against membership stressed the diminution of national sovereignty and scope for independent action on the part of the government which it would involve. The case for membership was frequently made in economic and, indeed, 'bread and butter' terms. It should also be noted at this point that the various procedures by which the EEC provides Ireland with money are, taken together, regarded by many Irish people as *the* Common Market issue.

Nevertheless, joining the EEC was also presented as a major act of national assertion and, as such, has been regarded by governments and commentators alike as fitting into the theme of Ireland's emergence into international life. Whatever derogation of national sovereignty EEC membership was seen to involve is usually considered to be more than outweighed by the increase in 'real' independence to be gained from diversifying Ireland's external relations beyond the Anglo-Irish pairing. Further, the EEC has been viewed as a second UN, a regional rather than a global platform, but a platform nevertheless, for the pursuit of a distinctively Irish policy. As a consequence, Irish policy within the EEC has attempted to go beyond the quest for a larger share of Community finances and advocacy of the measures that would facilitate this. Irish governments have also devoted considerable efforts to making a contribution towards the Community's policy towards the wider world, for example, on the Middle East and in the preparation of the Community's position in the negotiations for the Lomé conventions, and towards dealing with the Community's own-internal problems.

However, in the same year as de Gaulle left office and, hence, the major obstacle to Irish and British membership of the EEC was removed, Partition re-emerged as a prominent issue. At the moment of crisis in 1969, the 'functional' approach established by Sean Lemass when he was Taoiseach, which emphasised cooperation on economic and technical matters in talks with the government of Northern Ireland, disappeared. It was replaced by a hurried sifting through of military and political options which ran from direct intervention by the Irish army and providing the northern IRA with arms, to appealing to both Britain and the UN for the introduction of an international peacekeeping force into Northern Ireland. While highlighting the fact that Irish governments could still do very little about Northern Ireland, either on their own, with Britain or by efforts to internationalise the problem, and while precipitating a crisis within the Irish government in 1970, the impact of the immediate upheaval upon Irish foreign policy was not lasting.

The major impact of Northern Ireland upon Irish foreign policy was not in the specific actions taken as a result of it. Rather, what it did was to emphasise the extent to which the legitimacy of the state continued to rest on the Republican tradition and the extent of the gap between the conception of an independent Ireland in this tradition and the concept of independence upon which Irish policy had been built in the late 1950s. By the 1970s, therefore, one could see the emergence of two competing images. One was that of modern Ireland making its contribution to international security, economic cooperation, aid and development, struggling with the best to attract foreign investment and increase its exports. This view was particularly strengthened by the initially positive experience that membership of the EEC provided. On the other, was the enduring failure to end Partition, protect the minority in the

North or bring about any significant progress in national, or even provincial, reconciliation. Irish policy on Northern Ireland has been largely confined to responding to outrages, participating in a number of efforts to reformulate the constitutional context of the problems there and, latterly, offering its own initiative of this kind.

By the end of the 1970s, economic difficulties both within Ireland and the wider systems of which it was a part could be seen to have ominous implications for the first of these images. Internally, unemployment, inflation and the amassing of a large foreign debt, without the establishment of a level of industrial development and employment which these loans had been partly intended to secure, made the internal projection of a modern Ireland more difficult to sustain. Externally, the difficulties confronting Ireland became crystallised in the government's disappointment with the EEC. As a consequence, as we shall see below, Irish foreign policy was increasingly thrown back on securing and reasserting the traditional components of Ireland's status as distinctively independent sovereign state, rather than using these as the instruments of other policies within the EEC.

It is possible to identify two major schools of interpretation with regard to the context within which Irish foreign policy is made and, hence, should be interpreted. The first follows closely and, indeed, has fed the official myths of a virtuous activism by which Ireland has achieved its place among the nations and an international status in excess of that suggested by its size and power.[18] In this view, Ireland's foreign policy is significant for the positive contribution it has made to strengthening peace and fostering economic development in the international system, and because it has demonstrated the reality of Irish independence. The second school doubts very much if there is such a thing as an independent Irish foreign policy. In this view, UN activism and Irish neutrality are both so much posturing designed to obscure the fact that after sixty years Irish governments have failed to break a relationship of dependency with Britain and unite the country. This is explained either by treating the Irish state as the instrument of a dominant class, the interests of which are served by continued close links with Britain, or by reference to an historic failure of nerve on the part of Republicans negotiating the Anglo-Irish treaty which produced a Free State conceived in the sin of accepting Partition.[19]

The first school celebrates the emergence of the Irish Republic as a full member of the international community; the second denies that process has been completed. Between the two, however, it is possible to identify an increasing number of academic studies, the general purpose of which appear to be to present their readers with the sobering realities of Ireland's external circumstances so that expectations about what the country can achieve in those circumstances may be considerably reduced. The activism and, perhaps, the neutral posture celebrated by the first school are relegated to the pre-history of Irish foreign policy. Whatever their intrinsic worth, it is suggested, in a world concerned with economic development and characterised by increasing levels of interdependence, such policies can no longer be regarded as the central planks of a foreign policy. Indeed, Ireland may not even be able to afford them as peripheral eccentricities. The pursuit of 'independence' as it was traditionally defined must be regarded as a chimera.

However, the assumptions of the second school are also rejected by these writers. They disagree not so much over the objective evidence upon which the dependency case is made, but with the assumptions that the present situation is intolerable and that a radical, better alternative is realisable. Believing in the possibility of the latter necessitates a theory to explain why Ireland's governments have made so little progress in this direction, notably that they are actively concerned both with maintaining Ireland's dependent state and obscuring the fact of it. Since the academic approaches referred to here are extremely sceptical about the possibility of any radical transformation of Ireland's circumstances for the better, however, they generally do not impugn the reasons which Irish governments give to explain their policies. Further, while they accept (indeed, they are at pains to point out) that the freedom of action of the latter is severely circumscribed by their external circumstances, this is not the same as saying that Irish governments have no freedom of action at all. The important task is to map out the possibilities for action which do exist in the given scheme of things and the likely consequences of specific actions being taken or rejected.[20]

The story of Ireland's emergence as a full member of the international community remains central, in one form or another, to each of these perspectives on Irish foreign policy. This being so, none of them captures the tensions and contradictions of the social context within which Irish foreign policy is made and of which it is a product. The academic approaches referred to above come the closest to succeeding in this respect. Yet, as their pessimism about the future of Irish neutrality and independence policies suggests, their elaborations of the external constraints under which Irish governments must function are impregnated with specific assumptions about both the character and the primacy of the latter.

There certainly is a practical force to these assumptions. Ireland is a small country which is becoming increasingly involved in an interdependent international system. However, Ireland was also once enmeshed within a network of relationships presided over by the British empire and, whether it was a 'practical' proposition between 1916 and 1922 or not, it did become an independent country in something more than just a formal sense. This is an important point because it forces one to view the contemporary Irish social context, not as a frozen moment in the Irish part of a general march of progress towards economic development, here retarded by peasant cunning and religious conservatism, there accelerated by Irish wit and resourcefulness. That context is, rather, an uneasy assemblage of the experiences, compromises and objectives of different classes in Irish society. To grasp the character of this assemblage, one needs to keep three things in mind. First, Ireland was a colony

12

for a very long time. Secondly, the measure of political independence it currently enjoys was achieved by a successful anti-colonial struggle. Thirdly, this struggle and the state which was created by it came to be dominated by the representatives of classes who conceived of revolution in terms of national and political liberation rather than social and economic transformation.

The significance of Ireland's prolonged colonial status may be demonstrated by a brief review of its economic history and the demographic consequences of that. Ireland under the British enjoyed, at best, highly uneven economic development. Prior to the Industrial Revolution its land was regarded as a source of rewards for non-Irish nobility and commoners who might exploit it by the extraction of rents or by direct settlement. Except in the specially favoured north-east, native industrial development was heavily discouraged and Ireland's role in the British empire became that of a source of agricultural produce, surplus labour and soldiers. The result in the nineteenth century was an extremely vulnerable society, unempowered to solve its internal social problems and dependent on others to satisfy the material needs of its people. In the space of six years, between 1845, just before the start of the Great Famine, and 1851, the population of Ireland fell from approximately 8.5 million to 6.5 million: some two million people either died or emigrated. A further million had left by 1855. The population continued to decline until 1966 when the census of that year showed an increase of 62,411 over the previous count. Between 1966 and 1981, the population of the Republic increased from 2.8 million to just over 3.4 million. In the island as a whole, there are now a little under 5 million people.[21]

Since independence, Irish economic policy has been directed at trying to break free of the colonial legacy of an underdeveloped and mainly agrarian economy, high levels of unemployment and emigration, and a low standard of living in comparison to other western European countries. Apart from the early years of the Free State and until the late 1950s, this was done by attempting to 'achieve self-sufficiency through the development of native industries behind high tariff walls'.[22] Self-sufficiency, particularly during the de Valera period, was seen as both the precondition of independence and, at times, as taking priority over the quest for material prosperity. From 1956 onwards, however, Irish governments became increasingly convinced that whatever political independence this policy procured was being bought at an unacceptable price in terms of the sluggish performance of the Irish economy relative to its booming international counterpart.[23] As a consequence, the priorities in policy shifted from self-sufficiency to promoting expansion of the economy by domestic reforms, the removal of tariff barriers, increased government borrowing and the encouragement of foreign and domestic investment to finance the development of industry geared to the export market. In line with this shift in policy, the Irish government decided to join the General Agreement on Tariffs and Trade in 1960, signed a free trade agreement with Britain in 1965, and successfully negotiated membership of the EEC in 1972.

13

As a consequence of this latter strategy in particular, the Irish economy has undergone considerable change and development. For example, the importance of agriculture relative to industry has decreased markedly and industrial production is increasingly concentrated in high-technology areas such as electronics and pharmaceuticals.[24] Despite the efforts of Irish governments to correct them, however, certain problems have remained broadly constant since independence. First, the Irish economy has manifested a high degree of openness in terms of the relative importance of cross-boundary financial and commodity flows to those which take place internally.[25] This in itself is not necessarily a bad thing but the government failed to alter this characteristic of the economy with an autarkic policy which lasted for some twenty-five years. What was intended as a strategy for consolidating political independence amounted to a policy of marginally reducing Ireland's dependence on foreign trade by depressing domestic consumption.[26]

Since the mid-1950s, Ireland's economic policies have shifted from trying to minimise the consequences of openness to maximising its effectiveness as a performer in the world economy on that basis. As a consequence, the impact of the outside world upon Ireland has been considerably increased, most simply in the sense that when the world economy is flourishing, then Ireland's economy also performs well. This simple relationship is, however, complicated by the fact that some of the benefits Ireland has received from an expanding world economy have produced problems within Ireland and, indeed, turned into problems themselves when the world economy contracted from the late 1970s onwards. Specifically, the effort to promote growth through foreign borrowing has left Ireland with an unevenly developed, capital-intensive export industry that is particularly vulnerable to depressed foreign markets, high interest rates or demands abroad for protection. The earnings of this industry are unable to cover either the original debts or the costs of maintaining the expanded infrastructure of social programmes and policies which were put in place in the late 1970s.

Further, this kind of development has done little to ease the unemployment problems that have been a feature of Ireland's economy since independence, with the possible exception of the five years between 1960 and 1965. Between 1948 and 1965 the unemployment rate dropped from 9.4 to 5.6 per cent, but it began to rise again in 1966, and by 1982 was standing at around 13 per cent. Ireland's unemployment problems are complicated by two factors. First, the age structure of the population is such that there have been increasing numbers of young people entering the labour market and so the economy needs to grow merely to maintain the current levels of employment. Also, pressure on the labour market is increased by the fact Britain and the United States are no longer able to provide the safety valve of jobs abroad to the extent that they did in the past. Only the highly educated, that is, those on whom Ireland has expended considerable resources, have a strong chance of finding employment abroad. Secondly, while high unemployment should be a problem for any country, in Ireland it has particular significance for the legitimacy of the state because of the long history of emigration and the claim that only an independent Ireland could provide its people with the means to a livelihood denied to many of them under British rule.[27]

A final constant has been the continued, if declining, dependence on Britain and British economic policy. Between 1926 and 1978–9, imports from Britain as a percentage of total imports declined from 75.7 to 49.8 per cent (although they have stayed around 50 per cent for most of the period). During the same period, exports to Britain expressed as a percentage of all exports fell from 96.3 to 46.8 per cent. While the decline is marked, the continued importance of Britain as Ireland's major trading partner is also evident. This trading link is reinforced by a broad network of political, social and cultural links and patterns of interaction which have worked to maintain a strong and generalised British 'presence' in Ireland. However, membership of the EEC has enabled Ireland to diversify its trading contacts and loosen some of its close ties with Britain. For example, the Anglo-Irish free trade agreement of 1965, and a number of reciprocal arrangements regarding residency and employment rights, have been absorbed in similar agreements applying to all the members of the EEC. More importantly, the relative weakening of the British economy has contributed to reducing its role in Ireland, most notably in terms of the declining British share of foreign investments in new manufacturing enterprises and the declining proportion of British exports to Ireland made up of manufactured goods.[28]

The consequences of Ireland's former colonial status may be seen in the uneven character and socially distorting characteristics of a late, for Western Europe, and externally generated economic development. While Ireland exhibits many of the structural features of a Third World country, however, it is clearly a part of Western Europe. This is so both in the sense that it has been a participant in and contributor to Western European history and culture, and in the sense that it obtains the benefits of proximity to the centres of power and wealth in the area. Moreover, the political elites which have governed Ireland since independence have defined their answers to Ireland's problems primarily in terms of the achievement of national independence, not a radical transformation of internal, social relations. Without political independence, Ireland was doomed to remain exploited by and dependent on Britain. With it, the country could develop into a modern European state. When asked, Irish politicians and diplomats frequently identify Denmark as a model for Ireland's future development.

The form of government in Ireland is that of a parliamentary democracy. Since independence, Irish politics have been dominated by two large and one small political parties: Fianna Fáil, Fine Gael and Labour, respectively. Between 1923 and 1981, Fianna Fáil was in power for a total of 39 out of 58 years. The origins of the two major parties are to be found in the split in the republican movement known as Sinn Fein over accepting the treaty with

Britain in 1921 and the ensuing civil war. It is frequently commented by outsiders that their differences over this point in history seem to distinguish them from each other more clearly than any set of policies or identifiable source of electoral support. Certainly, as one writer in *The Economist* has noted, neither party shows any great inclination to set about redistributing the wealth of the country.[29]

Fianna Fáil was founded by de Valera and those members of Sinn Féin who had rejected the Treaty when they finally decided to enter the processes of constitutional politics in 1926. It was originally supported by small farmers and the small bourgeoisie but under de Valera it was able to broaden its electoral appeal and claim to be the authentic voice of Irish nationalism and republicanism. Fianna Fáil has been a very successful political party in the sense that it has been able to adjust its policies in response to changes in both Ireland's external circumstances and its social structure and yet retain and, indeed, mobilise a broad range of support for its own pursuit of power. The party in government has presided over industrial development strategies variously based upon protection and import-substitution, free trade and export-led growth, expansion through extensive foreign borrowing and demand-stimulation and, most recently, fiscal restraint and severe deflationary measures.[30]

Fine Gael is the heir to Cummann na nGaedheal, the Sinn Féin faction which accepted the treaty of 1921 and governed the Free State for the first ten years of its independence. It has been regarded as the party of larger farmers, big business and the professional class although it too, like Fianna Fáil, derives its electoral support from a wider area. In contrast to Fianna Fáil, however, Fine Gael has struggled to find an identity with which to appeal to the electorate. For example, while traditionally regarded as the more conservative and 'pragmatic' of the two parties, particularly in regard to the conduct of relations with Britain, for a time in the 1960s there was a failed attempt from within to transform it into a social democratic party. Further, the party has never won a clear majority of the votes in any election and, hence, has only held power in conjunction with electoral allies with which it has enjoyed no easy coincidence of interests, for example, socialists, farmers' parties and radical republicans. Until recently, Fianna Fáil has presented itself as the party of the nation, attempting to foster economic development and resolve domestic difficulties through populist policies designed to preserve a broad coalition of support. In contrast, Fine Gael has claimed that it is the only party capable of making the hard economic choices (cutbacks in government spending) necessary if both taxes and the nation's debts are to be reduced.

The third party, the Labour Party, has its origins in the Irish socialist intelligentsia and the support of agricultural workers from the south and west of the country. While it has produced excellent critiques of government policy when in opposition, its own policy record is somewhat ill-defined because it has only been in government as a junior coalition partner, and then only with

16

Fine Gael, the major party with which it might be expected to have least in common on social and economic policy.[31] With regard to foreign policy, the major differences between Fianna Fáil and the other two parties in coalition are not usually over their positions on specific issues when they are in power. The Labour Party campaigned against EEC membership but dropped its opposition once Ireland joined. There are differences of approach between the two major parties with regard to Northern Ireland. In the 1970s, for example, Fianna Fáil favoured direct dealings between Dublin and London whereas Fine Gael stressed the importance of bringing the two communities in the North closer together as the first step in any improvement of the situation.[32] However, a broad consensus exists on Ireland's basic foreign policy orientations: a commitment to the UN; neutrality; and a generally pro-Western, pro-EEC stance. Whatever preferences may exist in some sections of the parties for non-consensual policies, for example, a more militant line on the North within Fianna Fáil, or for membership of NATO in Fine Gael, are held in check by the electoral costs expected as a consequence of voicing such preferences. Party differences usually take the form of exchanges between the government and the opposition with regard to the extent to which specific actions taken by the former accord with the opposition's conceptions of the basic principles upon which the foreign policy of the state is supposed to be built.

The most important of these principles is the idea of republicanism. Since independence, all the major political parties in Ireland have been committed to the development and maintenance of a capitalist system of production and exchange which primarily serves the interests of the national bourgeoisie. *Within* this context the parties may represent the interests of particular constituencies, but it is this context, and changes within it, that set their priorities for other issues of policy. For example, Fianna Fáil played a leading role in responding to the redefinition of the interests of the national bourgeoisie in more international terms and managing the structural consequences of this change for the country as a whole. However, this priority, which is shared by all three major parties, exists in a permanent tension with republicanism, the radical nationalist ideology of the armed struggle to establish an independent, united Ireland. This ideology and its associated symbols are the focal point for claims to legitimacy made by Irish governments and other aspirants to political power. They must show that they are the worthy heirs of the patriots of 1916 and that their policies and vision of Ireland are worth the costs and privations of the independence struggle and beyond.

This tension is enduring for a number of reasons. First, one can observe the discomfort of a political elite that wants its country to be a modern, stable location for investment and production and yet that owes its own position to the acts of violence of its predecessors, both against the British and against internal opposition, and that exists in a culture which continues to celebrate the historically more remote and less ambiguous episodes of that violence. Secondly, and more specifically, there is the problem of reconciling the legitimation requirements of a capitalist state expressed in terms of national identity, sovereignty and independence with the objective requirement of the capitalist order for the increased integration of the national economy into its global or regional counterpart. This has always been a problem for Irish governments because most of the close economic ties with Britain survived the achievement of political independence. But even today, when it is widely claimed that membership of the EEC has done much to dilute the British presence, this problem persists and, as I shall argue below, is becoming harder to solve. Finally, there is Ireland's specific problem. The demand for a united Ireland was, and is, built in to the republican tradition. For obvious reasons, this has allowed the legitimacy of the entire political system to be called into question, since the origins of the latter may be traced to the treaty of 1921, which accepted Partition, rather than to the uncompromising men and women of 1916.

It is as a product of this uneasy context that Irish foreign policy should be understood. Much of it has been directed at objectives of substance, for example, in the past, Irish unity, in the present, improvements in the North and managing the links between Ireland and its principal trading partners and sources of investment. However, the conduct of Irish foreign policy has also been intimately bound up with the problematic aspects of the legitimacy of the political order. Its primary use in the past was to demonstrate that, despite the compromised circumstances of the foundation of the state, Ireland was indeed an independent country. When Ireland was a member of the League of Nations and, more importantly, once it joined the UN, its foreign policy was also used as an instrument for deflecting the moral–radical component of the republican tradition away from the question of Irish unity and towards the projects of making the international system safer and more just.

Finally, since Ireland became a member of the EEC in 1973, its foreign policy has been used as a component of the increasingly explicit efforts since the late 1950s to redefine republicanism in terms of economic development and high standards of living, rather than cultural identity and national unity. This effort has been part of a huge, if unavoidable, gamble on the part of Irish governments regarding the benefits of increased participation in the international economy. Because of the specific difficulties, but also the political character, of the latter, the economic benefits of that participation have been uneven at best; the costs in terms of social dislocation and political legitimacy have been considerable As the extent of these costs has become more pronounced, Irish foreign policy has increasingly reverted to its original objective, demonstrating that the government does, in fact, act for an independent country.

18

Notes

1. Bunreacht na h'Éireann, Article 2.
2. Patrick Keatinge, *A Place Among the Nations: Issues of Irish Foreign Policy*, Institute of Public Administration, Dublin, 1978, p. 22.
3. See F.S.L. Lyons, *Ireland Since the Famine*, Fontana Paperbacks, London, 1973, p. 422.
4. Keatinge (1978), op. cit., p. 50.
5. 'Une île derrière une île', in Jean Blanchard, *Le Droit ecclésiastique contemporain d'Irlande*, Paris, 1958, p. 11.
6. Michael Collins (1890-1922), minister in the Republican Provisional Government, major supporter of accepting the treaty with Britain and key figure in the Irish civil war until his death.
7. See D.W. Harkness, *The Restless Dominion*, Macmillan, London,1969, pp. 70, 136, for this point and following discussion.
8. Ibid., pp. 31-2.
9. See, for example, the comments by a Japanese delegate to the Washington conference of 1937, to the effect that it had been a failure for all but the Irish who used it to assert their international status. Cited in ibid., p. 96.
10. This phrase indicates a recurrent theme in both Irish nationalism and foreign policy. It probably originates with Robert Emmet's famous speech from the dock about his epitaph. Both Parnell and Pearse also used it, however, and it forms the title of Patrick Keatinge's study of issues in Irish foreign policy (1978).
11. Cited in Keatinge (1978), p. 105. The account below rests heavily on this source, and Lyons, op. cit.
12. op. cit., p. 557
13. See F.S.L. Lyons, 'The Years of Readjustment, 1945–51', in K.B. Nowlan and T. Desmond Williams (eds), *Ireland in the War Years and After: 1939–45,* Gill and Macmillan, Dublin, 1969, for details of this period.
14. Liam Cosgrave, Minister for External Affairs, *Dáil Debates*, Vol. 159, 142-4 (hereafter in the form 159, 142-4) .
15. Frank Aiken (1898–1983), IRA Chief of Staff in 1923, Minister of Defence 1932–9; after serving in several other key positions he became Minister for External Affairs in 1951, held that position until 1954, and between 1957 and 1969. Also Tánaiste (Deputy Prime Minister) from 1965-9, he was the originator of, as well as personally closely involved in Ireland's UN policy.
16. Keatinge, op. cit. (1978), p. 210.
17. See *Sunday Times* 'Insight' Team's *Ulster*, Penguin, Harmondsworth, 1972; Keatinge (1978), op. cit., p. 117; and Roger Hull, *The Irish Triangle*, Princeton UP, 1976, p. 249-51, for details of the Irish reponse.
18. See, for example, Harkness, op. cit., p. xi; T.P. Coogan, *Ireland since the Rising*, Praeger, NY, 1966; T.A. Mulkeen, 'Ireland at the UN', in *Eire: Ireland*, Vol. 8, No. 1, 1973; and Basil Chubb, *Government and Politics of Ireland,* London University Press, London, 1970, p. 316.
19. For examples, see contributions to Austin Morgan and Bob Purdie (eds), *Ireland : Divided Nation, Divided Class*, Ink Links, London, 1980.
20. For excellent examples of this kind of work see Patrick Keatinge (1978), op. cit., and his other works, *The Formulation of Irish Foreign Policy,* Institute of Public Administration, Dublin, 1973; and *A Singular Stance: Irish Neutrality In The 1980s*, IPA, Dublin, 1984.
21. See Lyons, op. cit., pp. 44-5; and *Facts About Ireland*, Department of Foreign Affairs, Dublin, 1985, p. 248.

22. Lyons, op. cit., p. 600; see also Keatinge (1978), op. cit., p. 134; John Blackwell, 'Government, Economy and Society', in Frank Litton (ed.), *Unequal Achievement: The Irish Experience 1957–82*, IPA, Dublin, 1982, p. 43.

23. See Keatinge (1973), op. cit., p. 31. See Paul Bew and Henry Patterson, *Sean Lemass and the Making of Modern Ireland 1945–66*, Gill and Macmillan, Dublin, 1982, for an account of the role of Sean Lemass, leader of the Fianna Fail party and Taoiseach, in managing this major shift in policy.

24. Dermott McAleese, 'Ireland', and John O'Brien, 'Irish Economy Concentrates on High Technology', both in *Europe: Magazine of the European Community*, July/August 1986.

25. This definition is from T.K. Whitaker, 'Monetary Integration: Reflections on Irish Experience', in *Quarterly Bulletin: Central Bank of Ireland*, Winter 1973, p. 68, cited in Keatinge (1978), op. cit., p. 250.

26. See Keatinge (1978), op. cit., p. 129 for a table of trade dependence figures between 1926 and 1972.

27. For unemployment figures see the UN statistical yearbooks. The 1982 figure was taken from *The Globe and Mail*, November 1982. *The Economist*, 3 October 1987 estimates that 30,000 people will leave Ireland this year and that current unemployment rate is about 20 per cent of the workforce (250,000 people).

28. See Keatinge (1978), op. cit., p. 130, for the figures cited here. See Dermot McAleese, 'The Foreign Sector', in Norman J. Gibson and John E. Spencer (eds), *Economic Activity in Ireland*, Gill and Macmillan, Dublin, for comments on Britain's declining importance. See also Patrick Keatinge, 'An Odd Couple? Obstacles and Opportunities in Inter-State Political Cooperation Between the Republic of Ireland and the United Kingdom', in Desmond Rea (ed.), *Political Cooperation in Divided Societies: A Series of Papers Relevant to the Conflict in Northern Ireland*, Gill and Macmillan, Dublin, 1982, p. 310.

29. Nicholas Harman, in *The Economist*, 27 January 1981.

30. See Bew and Patterson, op. cit., for an account of Fianna Fail's success in making the great opening up of the economy acceptable politically in the 1950s.

31. See Chubb, op. cit., ch. 6; and Keatinge (1973), op. cit., pp. 247–67, for discussions of Irish political parties.

32. This distinction has now been blurred by FitzGerald's acceptance of the Anglo-Irish Agreement of 1985.

2 Small states, high politics and the theory of international relations

In the last chapter I offered an account of Ireland's foreign policy which interpreted much of it as a response to legitimacy problems confronting the political order. I suggested that the problems were caused by the particular and circumscribed character of the Irish struggle to achieve and maintain independence. These specific remarks about the case of Ireland are derived from a theoretical argument which will be developed in this chapter. I shall discuss, in turn, the foreign policy of small states, the place of 'high politics' in these policies, and the impact of increasing levels of economic interdependence upon the latter. I shall argue that contemporary international theory underestimates the extent of both the importance which the governments of small states attach to the legitimation function of their foreign policies and the problems which increasing levels of economic interdependence pose for their efforts in this regard.

Even though most of the states in the international system are clearly something other than super, great or medium powers, the study of their foreign policies remains largely neglected by most scholars of international relations. The reasons for this are straightforward. Most of these scholars live in rich and powerful countries, and even those who do not are understandably drawn to examining the consequences of the actions of the rich and powerful for their own people. Whether they conceive of the international system as a field within which more-or-less autonomous states interact, or as a structured hierarchy of political and economic relations by which the behaviour of most of the members of the system is determined, the shared concern of most scholars is with the systemic consequences of the distribution and use of power. It follows, therefore, that small state foreign policy, definitionally regarded as being either unable to make an impact in the international system or as being determined by the system, generally receives little attention.

As an exception to this, an upsurge of interest in the foreign policy of small states took place in the late 1960s and early 1970s. This attempt to develop the study of small state foreign policy as a sub-field, however, foundered on the problem of defining just what they are with some kind of precision.[1] Focusing on size *per se*, measured in terms of population, GNP, or defence expenditure involves making arbitrary cut-offs and yields little of great significance beyond the obvious regarding the characteristic behaviour of those states which happen to fall within the specified parameters. With this approach one may find, for example, that the external interests of small states tend to be regional rather than global in scope, that they possess a limited array of foreign policy means and are vulnerable to external pressures, and that their governments are often very concerned about safeguarding national independence.

As most of these writers were quick to point out, however, it is not size *per se* which is a significant determinant of state behaviour but size relative to that of other states, and combined with a complex of other factors such as resources, culture, position and relationships. The trouble with such a contextual approach, of course, is that it makes it very difficult to talk about anything specific to the foreign policy of small states. Symptomatic of this is the fact that the most important work in this surge of interest in small states focused on the success in power politics of 'abnormal' ones, what David Vital called the 'pocket battleship' states of North Vietnam and Israel.[2] Indeed, it was their 'counterintuitive' or 'surprising' success in power politics which provided much of the stimulus for investigation into the field.

Vital might not have agreed with Purnell's assertion that 'Small states, in short are great powers writ small. They behave as much like great powers as they can'.[3] But it was when they behaved so that they became interesting. According to him, the moment of truth for small states arrived when they came into conflict with a great power. Vital's work on the foreign policy strategies available to small states in such conflicts is very important.[4] Here, however, I wish to make two points about his work. First, it does not identify small states in terms of size, but in terms of characteristic foreign policy issues. The governments of such states are confronted by questions of national survival and the problematic character of the political independence which they presently enjoy. As Handel has argued, the concern, therefore, is not with small states but with the conduct of weak or weaker states in conflict with their stronger fellows.[5] This moves one away from sterile debates about whether

22

one can bracket Israel, Vietnam, Denmark and the Lebanon together, or when India 'fits', to a focus on something which, while admittedly more situational, is sufficiently common in the international system to permit an attempt at some generalisations about the foreign policies of such states.

Secondly, however, both Vital and Handel employ a 'realist' perspective on foreign policy which emphasises a power-politics view of weakness and strength. Small state foreign policy becomes interesting when such a state is confronted by a military–political threat to which it is both able and willing to respond. When small states are not faced by such threats, or cannot respond to them, then there is very little to talk about. In this view, while, in principle, the foreign policy of a small state ought to be about preserving or broadening the scope for autonomous action, in practice, mere survival as a national entity is often purchased at the price of 'political quiescence, compromise, or the sacrifice of political principles to economic necessity'.[6] In short, while the democratic forms of contemporary international society may offer a variety of opportunities for the governments of small states to 'look busy', and while occasionally a small state may become involved in a life-and-death struggle, most of the time, most of them continue to exist in a formal sense, because they do nothing and have no real foreign policy.

Such a view is a natural consequence of using the ability of a state to make an impact on the international system as one's main indicator of significance. For these purposes, weakness may be defined in terms of the quantitative and qualitative aspects of territory, population, economic resources and armed forces as components of the potential military power of the state. From the point of view of the governments of many weak states, however, the problem is neither one of how to achieve an impact on the international system, nor one of being ready to deter or defeat specific external military threats. Rather, it is the more generalised difficulty of maintaining both the internal and the external credibility of their claims to be acting for sovereign, independent states which are capable of ensuring the cultural identity and material prosperity of their people. For many weak states, particularly in the Third World, these problems take the form of domestic legitimacy issues resulting in political instability. Whether or not these problems may be attributed to primarily domestic causes, however, it may be seen that many of them are exacerbated by the increasing contacts and interaction which these countries have with the international system.

An important way in which governments of weak states may attempt to ease their legitimacy problems is by pursuing foreign policies which encourage popular identification with the nation and hence, they hope, with the state. It is common wisdom, for example, that governments may embark on a foreign adventure such as a war to distract the attention of their populations from domestic problems. Whether this is actually the case may be debated. It is certainly the case, however, that some governments commit considerable material resources to prestige policies intended to demonstrate national power.

The governments of several very poor countries spend considerable amounts on sophisticated military equipment for which little objective need exists, and the Gaullist foreign policy of 'grandeur' was explicitly directed at reconstructing the idea of France as a great and independent power in the aftermath of its failures in power politics.

There is also a series of actions, however, less drastic and more benign, which the governments of weak states may take in order to strengthen both their own political positions and the legitimacy of the regimes which they serve. I refer here, in particular, to the opportunities for activism, so-called 'middle powering', which have been provided for small states by the establishment of regional and international organisations such as the EEC and the UN, particularly in the post-war period. In substance, these opportunities are exercises in apolitical or technical problem-solving on issues ranging from health, economic development and communal violence in the Third World, to the non-proliferation of nuclear weapons globally. However, they take place within the context of organisations which reflect the ordering principle of international society as, primarily, a society of sovereign states. This being so, participation in the low politics of functional collaboration takes the form of activity by states and, therefore, necessarily takes on political connotations in so far as it offers their governments an opportunity to accrue some measure of substantial advantage or national prestige.

They seek the latter in two ways. First, and obviously, governments hope that the performance of good works under the auspices of an international organisation will procure them status and influence with other governments. Usually, they are not looking for rewards which are specifically linked to the international contribution which they make, for example, trade agreements in a region where one makes a peacekeeping contribution. What governments are seeking to create is a good standing for their countries in international society and a favourable disposition on the part of others towards them. Secondly, however, and following from this reputational aspect of the activity, they seek to create a high political foreign policy for their countries. By this I do not mean a policy designed to maximise national power and security in a narrow sense. Rather, what they seek to do is to present the foreign policies of their countries as possessing what Richelieu once called 'l'unité de direction', that is, embodying the national purpose in an integrated strategy of means and ends. Dorothy Pickles has referred to foreign policy in this high political sense as 'an explicit plan about a country's relationship with the outside world: a conscious image of what is or ought to be the country's place in the world'.[7]

There are, of course, practical reasons why coherence and consistency in a foreign policy should be valued, even if they are becoming increasingly difficult to achieve as international relations become more complex. However, a more ideological or psychological objective is also served by trying to pursue a coherent and consistent foreign policy. In so doing, governments explicitly attempt to strengthen the idea of the state as a national entity or

24

personality with which people may identify. Within international and regional organisations, governments have attempted to develop national identities through the elaboration and performance of international roles. In social theory, the role concept has been used to suggest a set of appropriate behaviours by which an individual takes on their social identity, and in international theory, role analysis has been used in attempts to explain the behaviour of both individual decision-makers and nation-states.[8] In both, the central assumption has been that the social defines the role in general terms and that the role shapes the behaviour of the individual who performs it.

As a power structure, the international system strongly determines the range of identities available to its member states. Theorists write of great, small and, sometimes, medium powers. As a society, however, it is distinguished by its weak character and this has permitted governments considerable scope in both choosing and defining roles for their states, that is, giving meaning to what they manage to do in their foreign policies. Thus, for example, Canadian governments and diplomats have elaborated the idea of Canada as a 'middle power' or 'helpful fixer' on the basis of their activities at the UN and within NATO and the Commonwealth. In doing this they were, in part, attempting to strengthen the idea of a specifically Canadian identity and national purpose in the face of both regional tensions within the country and the difficulty of defining themselves apart from the United States. It is a measure of the weakness of the social aspect of the international system, that in its heyday, the exercise of trying to define their own country as a middle power also involved an attempt to develop the idea of the international system as constituting an international society or community of states.

Interest in middle power activities on the part of both governments and scholars has declined since the heyday of the former in the 1960s. There are two explanations for this. The first focuses on the fact that middle-powering did not take off in the way that some of its practitioners hoped that it might. After an initial hesitation in the face of an activist UN Secretariat, the permanent members of the Security Council reasserted their control, or paralysis, of the UN's security procedures. Even many of the smaller members of the UN, the victims of power politics, decided that they would rather take their chances in such a world than have their sovereignty and budgets encroached upon by international civil servants. As a consequence, some of the strongest supporters of the middle power idea such as Canada, had to scale down their ambitions and, with not a little embarrassment, redefine international activism as an aspect, rather than the centrepiece, of their foreign policy. While these governments, for the most part, continued to practise activist policies within international organisations, they accepted the prevailing orthodoxy that power politics had triumphed over functionalism in the post-war international order and that, by inference, what they did was of limited international significance.

The first explanation of the decline of interest in middle power forms of international role-playing rests on the claim that the character of international politics as power politics between sovereign states did not change as a result of the emergence of international organisations in the post-war period. Some governments may continue to practise such policies, but as far as outcomes in the international system are concerned, they are not very important. The second explanation rests on precisely the reverse assumption, namely, that as a result of increasing levels of economic interdependence in the international system, international relations, and the opportunities for small states which exist within them, are in the process of being transformed. It is to the arguments which sustain this position which I now turn.

The history of human societies is, in one aspect, the history of the increased application of science and technology to their reproduction and the consequences of this for the ways in which they are organised.[9] Among these we may note the expansion of productive powers, the increasingly social character of production and the improvement of the material quality of life of large numbers of people. These material changes have also had their ideological counterparts. While not everyone has benefited in material terms, there has been a rise in expectations about the possibility of a better life in nearly all societies. One result of this has been the extension of the functions of governments from upholding the law and safeguarding physical security to fostering economic development and providing for the material well-being of citizens.

In their expansion, however, these processes of reproduction have both gone beyond and transcended the boundaries of the societies in which they were originally rooted and which were organised around them. They have so in the sense that countries, or the people within them, need raw materials, finished goods, services, capital, markets and labour which lie beyond their national boundaries, under the control or law, at least, of someone else, and in the sense that the application of technology to production within a society often has ecological consequences for others. Human societies, therefore, find themselves in objective conditions of mutual need and mutual influence which are increasing and which bring with them, it is argued, the need for new forms of social relations.

Here is the problem: there exists a tension between the development of interdependencies between societies and the way in which they are organised into an international political system of sovereign states. This system has remained stubbornly unchanged, if not in its objective structures, then in the subjective imperatives of its principal actors, since the age of mercantilism and autarky in the seventeenth century. As a consequence, governments continue to act as if wealth and power are finite and, hence, seek to maximise their own possession of these at the expense of others. This 'parochial tribalism' is practised in a world where, according to many politicians and scholars, economic developments have long since invalidated most the assumptions

26

upon which it rests and it continues to stand in the way of the effective management of projects and problems which are increasingly global in their scope.[10]

What is the relationship between the objective processes of interdependence drawing societies together and the subjective, fragmented political forms in which they continue to exist? This is an important question and a very difficult one to answer for those who focus on the processes of interdependence. For if the social forms of the present conform to the requirements of a logic of production which is now past, then the obvious question is why did they not disappear with the processes of which they were a function. The rhetorical answer is that things *have* changed. Morse, for example, has written of the 'complete transformation' of international relations, as a consequence of which the 'traditional paradigm' for understanding them has become 'obsolete'.[11] Put thus, the problem is one of educating or alerting people to the changes which have already taken place, and hoping that they are both clever enough and willing enough to adapt their behaviour. This is a very popular argument, but even Morse is aware that to present the problem as one of a collective, stubborn state of mind resisting change is an oversimplification. As he points out, increasing interdependence between national societies has been accompanied by a rise in domestic demands upon the governments of those societies. Hence, even as they are drawn together, their objectives become 'more and more incompatible'.[12] Nevertheless, this does not alter his position; the world has changed and the dangerous potentials of this change only make it all the more important that people be made to recognise it and act accordingly.

The trouble with Morse's position is that even if the continued existence of the state system is to be understood primarily in psychological terms as an atavistic predilection of governments and people, then it still has important material consequences for the forms in which interdependence manifests itself and the character of the international system as a whole. The international system which governments and people confront is still one of sovereign states *as well as* increasing economic interdependence. Stanley Hoffmann attempts to accommodate this fact by suggesting that the system can be conceived of as consisting of two ideal types, the 'diplomatic-strategic game' and the 'modern world economy' with a type of power and logic of behaviour appropriate to each. In the short term, governments are confronted with a choice. They may emphasise the diplomacy of military threats and manipulations of strategic balances, the foreign policy derived from what he calls the 'logic of separateness'. Or they may employ the 'more or less cooperative strategy' of maximising 'relative gain [while preserving] sizeable joint gain', that is, behaviour appropriate to the politics of interdependence. The statesman's opportunity to make a philosophical or ethical choice exists within a loaded game, however, for like Morse, Hoffmann asserts that 'the ultimate perspective is one of solidarity; the dynamics of the world economy, of world science and technology, is...a dynamics of integration.'[13]

27

Both Morse and Hoffmann prescribe a certain kind of foreign policy behaviour on the basis of identifying an important trend in the international system and treating it as dominant. In contrast, Nye and Keohane develop two competing models of international relations which they apply to concrete situations in order to see which one best explains what is going on.[14] Whatever doubts one may have about the claims of interdependence theory in its strongest form regarding changes in international relations, it is hard to object to Nye and Keohane's observation that much international activity and many foreign policy outcomes do not conform to the 'realist' model of international relations. In many situations, states do not act as coherent units and they are not the most important actors, the threat or use of force is both absent and irrelevant, and there is no clear hierarchy of issues, particularly in the sense military security concerns taking priority over economic or social affairs.[15] The realist model, for example, would not be able to tell us much about Canadian–American relations other than to say, perhaps, that they were not international political relations properly speaking.

The realist model fails where relations of a certain kind of interdependence exist. By interdependence, Nye and Keohane mean relations of mutual need where the costs and benefits of the relationship are not necessarily symmetrical, but where breaking the relationship would entail a significant cost to both parties. Of course, relations of interdependence in this sense exist all over the place; at one point, for example, the authors suggest that the strategic relationship between the United States and the Soviet Union could be characterised in this manner. They are particularly interested, however, in those which arise out of the conditions of what they call complex interdependence. Because of their complex, technical and multilateral character, increasing numbers of international issues can only be managed by creating 'procedures, rules or institutions' for the conduct of interstate and transnational relations with regard to them. One cannot manage monetary systems, ocean resources or, some would argue, superpower security relations, with the sparse mechanisms of classical diplomacy.

What we see, therefore, is the establishment of *international regimes*, procedures for regulating relations between a few states on many issues or between many, or nearly all, states on a single issue. Nye and Keohane are not clear as to whether it is political will and political power or the changing character of what international relations is increasingly about which is primarily responsible for the creation of international regimes. These regimes certainly can be broken by political or, *in extremis*, military action and this may well happen if the power structure within a regime becomes too divorced from the underlying distribution of state power conceived in realist terms.[16] The point of the authors, however, is that, as the benefits of regime-participation increase, then so too do the costs of breaking such a regime by the exercise of a more dominant form of power. This being so, international regimes may enjoy a degree of autonomy from the underlying distribution of power between the participating states. In so far as they do, then outcomes within them may be determined by a variety of factors, for example, the possession of issue-related attributes of power such as a large fishing fleet in negotiations about the conservation of fish stocks, or international organisation skills such as expertise on the issue or the ability to bargain or build coalitions successfully.[17]

Interdependence theorists like Nye and Keohane are struck by the way in which international regimes, once constituted, exert an influence on the behaviour of their members. Governments are drawn into them by considerations of self-interest expressed either in terms of positive benefit or avoiding loss. These regimes hold together and function, however, not merely because of calculations of immediate self-interest on the part of the members. They develop an autonomous existence and a capacity to shape the behaviour of their members, if not in the sense that they obtain their own means of extracting compliance, then in the sense that their maintenance becomes a positive value to the members for which they are willing to sacrifice other interests and their freedom of action.

Nye and Keohane, in particular, are aware that, because there is no central authority in the international system, the existence of these regimes is dependent to some extent upon fragile coalitions between governments and some kind of symmetry between the distribution of power within the regime and the underlying power structure. However, they give very little guidance as to the importance of this relationship except in the sense of after-the-fact. If a regime collapses, then the discrepancy between its internal distribution of power and the relative strengths of its participants must have been too great. As a result, they give no clear account of why regimes come into existence and provide no grounds for assessing their overall significance.

Consider, for example, the UN. While it was carefully constructed to the requirements of the governments of sovereign states, the UN has created its own imperatives on the behaviour of states, both as an environment and as an actor in itself. Member governments have on occasions become very angry at its activities and yet, to date, none has felt able to forgo participation in the organisation. Having said that, however, it may still be claimed that the important question with regard to the UN remains after over 35 years, not how this genie summoned up by the governments of sovereign states has contributed to the transformation of international relations, but rather, under what conditions they allow it to remain outside its bottle. A similar point could be made about UN Conference on the Law of the Sea; what is significant, the processes by which the new law was created and the content of that law, or the fate, perhaps temporary, of the agreement once the United States decided to defect from it.

There is no correct response to these points in any simple sense. Realists will take their bearing on the present from the past and argue that the existence of effective regimes depends upon the presence of a hegemon, a state, the government of which is prepared to enforce and pay the costs of sustaining a political order.[18] Interdependence theorists, however, do little more than refer to their projections about the direction in which the international system is supposed to be evolving to make their claim that it is the first interpretation in the cases above which is the more significant. Nye and Keohane, for example, even though they try to root their work in case studies from the present, are unable to make a clear distinction between the conditions of complex interdependence and the relations to which these conditions give rise. They describe both in terms of the presence of multiple actors and channels and the absence of issue-hierarchy and the threat of force.[19] In short, they provide a very good account of what politics within conditions of complex interdependence are like but offer little explanation of what those conditions are or how and why they come into being.

In general it may be said that interdependence arises out of the inability of governments to achieve domestic and external objectives without the cooperation of other governments and non-governmental actors abroad. The loss of autonomy which this entails is compounded by the form this cooperation takes, that is, participation in international regimes. The latter, according to interdependence theorists, also have some very specific consequences for the way in which governments conduct their foreign policies, the issues with which they deal and the outcomes of their dealings with one another and other actors.

First, it is claimed that as interdependence increases one will see an expansion of foreign policy. This takes place both in the sense that more and more government business will have, or be seen to have, a foreign policy or external dimension, and in the sense that the foreign policy establishment will have to expand to deal with the new business and the new non-state actors who are involved in it both at home and abroad.[20] This issue proliferation will also increase the economic content of foreign policy and this too will be reflected in changes in the foreign policy bureaucracy as the old generalists and diplomatists give way to economic and technical experts.

Secondly, theorists of interdependence have argued that as levels of interdependence increase, an equalisation of power between strong and weak states in realist terms also takes place. This is said to be so for a number of reasons. Stanley Hoffmann, writes of 'the *revenge* of the weaker' which appears to be a function of interdependence *per se*. He sees the latter in terms of a developing web of relationships characterised by mutual need and as such it engenders a series of new and paradoxical axioms about foreign policy behaviour, for example,

In an interdependent world, the more intensely you are my friend, the more I have to worry.

I pull on your thread, you pull on mine; I need you but you need me.

You and I may be so entangled that we do not clearly know where your power ends and mine begins.[21]

Others, notably Nye and Keohane, see this reversal of fortunes as enjoying a much more provisional status in that they regard it not as a function of interdependence *per se*, but of regime politics. As long as a regime holds up, however, the governments of small states are regarded as being in particularly fortunate positions. Because they have small policy processes and a narrower range of policy interests, it is argued, they will not be as vulnerable as their larger counterparts to the trans-governmental politics and issue-linkage strategies which characterise relations within regimes. By the same reasoning, they will also be less inhibited from exploiting such strategies.[22] Small states are also said to possess a number of other 'advantages'. It is easy, for example, for their governments to present an issue as one of national survival and, hence, to mobilise domestic resources and resolve and foreign sympathy in support of their policies.[23] Finally, it has been suggested by some, notably Mancur Olson, that because the governments of small states have less interest than their larger counterparts in the provision of international public goods, then they will be able to obtain the benefits of 'free-ridership' or extract 'side-payments' as a condition of their participation in joint projects.[24] (It may be remarked here that only those who live in a powerful country could see the saliency of national survival primarily in terms of its being a tactical advantage in negotiations or assume that small states have a relatively low stake in the establishment of international organisations and order.)

Thirdly, it is claimed that as levels of interdependence increase, then governments will become less interested in pursuing what Morse has called 'transcendental' foreign policy goals such as grandeur, security, international stature or 'role premises, like "mediator" or "balancer"'. For those who regard interdependence as an objective and presently existing fact demanding, primarily, psychological adjustments on the part of governments, there is some uncertainty about this prediction. Morse, himself writes of the emergence of a 'new transcendental politics...activity for its own sake' within the EEC as the member governments lost the political will to move in the direction of further integration.[25] Others, however, regard this loss of interest as a natural consequence of both the expansion of foreign policy into new issues involving new actors and the emergence of new opportunities for effective action on the part of small states.

According to these arguments, therefore, as a small state moves into conditions of increasing interdependence, its government will become less interested in pursuing a foreign policy of international role-playing of the kind outlined above. Such a policy of emphasising national identity will become increasingly futile in a process where the state and national society are increasingly penetrated along multiple channels by large numbers of state and non-state actors. Indeed, on occasions, such posturing with no substantial end in mind might aggravate those actors able to exert great influence over the country. Further, these activities will constitute a drain on the scarce foreign policy resources and diplomatic talents of a small state at a time when there is

31

both an expanding demand upon these and they could be put to use exploiting the opportunities of regime politics.

Interdependence theory and its arguments about what is happening to foreign policy have become a major reference-point in contemporary international theory. As a measure of its success, it may be noted that exponents of the other two major paradigms for understanding international relations, realism and Marxism, seek to engage it and may seem, at times, to enter into unholy alliance against it. In their efforts to stress the primacy of political conflict in the international system, whether between states or between classes, one finds that realists have now been drawn into discussing political economy and Marxists into discussing the autonomous logic of interstate relations. Interdependence theory, clearly straddles two critical dimensions of human behaviour.

Nevertheless, in the ensuing account of Irish experiences with the UN and the EEC, I shall endeavour to show that the problems with interdependence theory as I have summarised it above are considerable. In its worst manifestations, it may be said to constitute an argument about how governments *ought* to behave in accordance with a partial rationality derived from classical liberalism's hostility to politics and a particular historical experience, the defeat of the United States in Vietnam. The latter provided the emotional impetus and context for an elevation of the former into a claim that a process of transformation was actually happening in international relations. Even in its stronger forms, however, the writings of Nye and Keohane or those who have styled themselves as 'complex neo-realists'[26] for example, I shall endeavour to show that assumptions about economic rationality and political irrationality provide the critical, and unsatisfactory, basis for the claim that we are confronted by, in Nye and Keohane's phrase, a 'world politics in transition'. On the basis of such assumptions they offer a perspective which, at best, is profoundly unsympathetic to the kinds of problems with which increased participation in the international system confronts the governments of small states. At worst, they perform an ideological function facilitating a particular kind of international integration, by obscuring or ignoring these difficulties.

Notes

1. See Annette Baker Fox's review of Michael Handel's *Weak States in the International System,* Cass, London, 1981, in the *International Journal,* Vol. 37, No. 2, Spring 1982, pp.337-8. For attempts to offer 'definitions' of small states on the basis of 'objective' criteria, see Nils Orvik, 'Norwegian Foreign Policy' and R.P. Barston's introduction, both in Barston's (ed.), *The Other Powers: Studies in the Foreign Policies of Small States,* Allen Unwin,1973; and David Vital, *The Inequality of States,* Oxford UP, 1967.

2. See Vital, op. cit., and David Vital, *The Survival of Small States: Studies in Small Power/ Great Power Conflict,* Oxford UP, London,1971.

3. Robert Purnell, *The Society of States: An Introduction to International Politics,* Weiden-

feld and Nicolson, London, cited in Michael Handel, *Weak States In the International System*, Cass, London,1981, p.38.

4. Vital (1967), op. cit., pp. 121-2. He suggests the following: a passive strategy of doing nothing and hoping for the best; a defensive strategy of building up one's internal strength; and an active strategy of attempting to exploit contingencies in the international system. He admires the latter, but recommends the defensive approach.

5. Handel, op. cit., p. 11.

6. Barston, op. cit., p.19.

7. Richelieu, cited by Erling Bjol, in 'The Small State in International Politics', in August Schou and Arne Olav Brundtland (eds), *Small States in International Relations*, Wiley Interscience Division, New York, 1971, p.35. Dorothy Pickles, cited in William Wallace, *Foreign Policy and the Political Process,* Macmillan, London, 1971, p. 11.

8. For discussions of the concept of the role in social theory and international theory, see P.F. Secord and C.W. Blackman, *Social Psychology*, McGraw-Hill, NY,1964; and K.J. Holsti, 'National Role Conceptions in the Study of Foreign Policy', in *International Studies Quarterly*, Vol. 14, No.3, 1970.

9. See, for example, Edward L. Morse, *Modernization and the Transformation of International Relations*, Free Press, NY, 1976 ,for this perspective. It is also possible to offer a 'technological' interpretation of Marx's theory of social change. See, for example, G. A. Cohen, *Karl Marx's Theory of History*, Princeton UP, 1978.

10. See H. and M. Sprout, *Towards a Politics of the Planet Earth*, Van Nostrand, NY, 1971, and Stanley Hoffmann, *Primacy or World Order*, McGraw-Hill, NY, 1978, for discussions of international relations in these terms.

11. Morse, op. cit., p. xvi

12. Ibid., p. 20.

13. See Hoffmann, op. cit., pp.114-77 for this discussion. For a good example of the atavistic psychology approach, see p. 185. 'This is a world of active self-fulfilling memories: states that behave *as if* nuclear weapons and the increasing cost of conquest had not sharply reduced the positive productivity of military power and *as if* might were still the yardstick of achievements; and behaving this way, they carry the past into the present.'

14. Robert O. Keohane and Joseph S. Nye, *Power and Interdependence: World Politics in Transition*, Little, Brown, Boston,1977.

15. Ibid., pp. 23-5.

16. Ibid., p.57.

17. Ibid., pp.17, 5, 58-60.

18. See, for example, Stephen Krasner, 'State Power and the Structure of International Trade', in *World Politics* 28, no.3, 1976.

19. Ibid., pp. 24-5.

20. See, for example, Maurice A. East, 'The Organizational Impact of Interdependence on Foreign Policy-Making: The Case of Norway', in Charles W. Kegley Jr and Pat McGowan (eds), *The Political Economy of Foreign Policy Behaviour*, Sage, Beverly Hills, 1981; and Gordon Osbaldeston, 'Reorganising Canada's Department of External Affairs', in *International Journal*, Vol. XXXVII, No. 3, 1982.

21. Hoffmann, op. cit., pp. 124-6.

22. Nye and Keohane, op. cit., p.31.

23. Ibid., p.19, and Hoffmann, op. cit., p. 128.

24. M. Olson and R. Zeckhauser, *An Economic Theory of Alliances*, Santa Monica,1966, cited in Morse, op. cit., pp.133-6.

25. Morse, op. cit., pp.86-9.

26. For an example of this kind of work, see D.B. DeWitt and J.J. Kirton, *Canada as a Principal Power*, Toronto, John Wiley and Sons, 1983.

3 National identity, international roles and the construction of a prestige policy for Ireland

So far, I have argued the following. Problems of credibility with the claim to be acting for a sovereign, independent country dictate that the governments of small states become concerned with the pursuit of some kind of international status. For the governments of large states, status and prestige often accrue from the exercise or demonstration of their concrete attributes of power in pursuit of specific and substantial ends. For governments which lack such attributes, however, the pursuit of status necessarily takes on a more ideological character. It does so both in the sense that they have few material resources with which to support the exercise and, following from this, that the effort to create a national identity or reputation may become more or less an end in itself.

In the context of these propositions, I now wish to examine Irish foreign policy at the UN between 1956, the year of Ireland's admission to the organisation, and 1966, the year in which the Anglo-Irish Free Trade Agreement was negotiated. This chapter will examine the way in which an international role was constructed for Ireland on the basis of the attributes of its 'national identity' as these were articulated by members of the government. Chapter 4 will offer an assessment of how important this role was to the Fianna

34

Fáil government which was primarily responsible for defining it. Chapter 5 will be concerned with the relationship between Ireland's foreign policy of international role-playing and the conduct of its mainly economic relations with Britain.

I shall argue that Irish governments saw international role-playing as a political policy to which they were prepared to commit considerable domestic resources and on behalf of which they were prepared to face considerable criticism whether from home or abroad. This commitment, however, was dependent upon two things: the supply of opportunities for action from the UN; and, the maintenance of ideological and organisational distinctions between 'political' and 'economic' foreign policy. Over the former, Irish governments exercised little control. With regard to the latter, they were more successful, but even this was a function of the character of the international organisation in which their political policy was largely practised.

Ireland, along with several other countries, was admitted to the UN as a result of an agreement between the US and the USSR regarding how membership of the organisation should be expanded. Prior to that time, it had been kept out by Soviet objections based upon the fact of Ireland's neutrality in the war against fascism and the probability of its government adopting a pro-American orientation once it became a member of the UN. Because of this, and because Irish governments had linked their membership of NATO to a favourable resolution of Partition, Irish foreign policy between the end of the Second World War and 1955 had largely been restricted to complaining about the latter in the Council of Europe and cooperating on technical and economic matters with the OEEC. UN membership, therefore, was seen by political figures and commentators alike as heralding the start of a new period in Ireland's external relations. As a consequence, the Dáil debate on the 1956 estimate for the Department of External Affairs was largely devoted to an extended discussion of its implications and it may be seen that the terms in which this was conducted have largely defined the structure of public debate about Irish foreign policy ever since.[1] The government argued for accepting admission to the UN on two general grounds. First, as the Minister for External Affairs, Liam Cosgrave, argued, it provided Ireland with new opportunities for pursuing its old objective of international cooperation 'as a responsible member of international society'. Secondly, it was a 'proper and necessary consequence' of Ireland's 'membership of the family of free and independent states'. For Ireland to 'turn its back on such an organisation...would be tantamount to committing ourselves to a position of isolation and insignificance in international affairs'. Indeed, according to the Taoiseach, John Costello, the 'privilege of becoming a full member of the comity of nations' was one of the principal objectives of the independence struggle.[2]

National interests, national values and considerations of national status all dictated that Ireland should become a member of the UN and about this there was a general agreement in the Dáil. The rest of the debate focused, therefore, upon what Costello termed the 'basic principle' upon which Irish policy towards the 'outside world' should be based.[3] In fact, Cosgrave announced three 'broad principles'. First, he stated that Ireland should not only observe the terms of the UN charter but do all it could to see that its provisions were enacted in all situations where they were supposed to apply. In particular, he wished to counter what he described as a tendency to handle international problems by conferences and meetings 'outside the scope of the organisation itself'.[4] Thus, the commitment was to one particular international political process dominated by the institutions, rules and personnel of the UN, rather than simply to general principles such as the peaceful resolution of disputes or respect for international law.

Secondly, Cosgrave argued that Ireland should maintain a 'position of independence' at the UN, casting its vote or adopting an attitude to issues before the organisation in a 'just and disinterested way'. Few governments would claim to act otherwise, but in Ireland's case this may be seen as an attempt on the part of Cosgrave to translate the posture of neutrality, historically defined by reference to Partition, Britain and abstention from the wars of the latter, into something serviceable in the context of the political circumstances which would confront the Irish at the UN. He noted that at the UN, as in other international organisations, there was a tendency for some countries to form groups which would concert their actions on specific issues. While this might be inevitable, up to a point, he argued that Ireland should 'avoid becoming associated with particular *blocs* or groups as far as possible'. Rather, it would act independently, judging issues on their own merits, in accordance with 'national traditions and objectives', 'fundamental' 'ideas and beliefs' and without 'consideration of expediency or temporary advantage'.

Having proclaimed an 'independent' UN policy, however, Cosgrave's articulation of the third principle of Irish policy made it very clear from what position the government thought that this independent judgement would be exercised. It had to be both a 'constant concern' and a 'moral responsibility' of the Irish to do whatever they could at the UN, and in their foreign policy as a whole, to preserve 'Christian civilisation' and, thus, 'to support wherever possible those powers principally responsible for the defence of the free world in their resistance to the spread of Communist power and influence'. Geography, culture, tradition and national interest bound Ireland's national destiny to the 'great community' of states made up of the 'United States of America, Canada and Western Europe'.[5]

Cosgrave's speech in the 1956 debate outlined Ireland's place in the world as a small, law-abiding, independent country with Christian values and Western sympathies. The three principles which he outlined in it have remained the central reference points for government explanations of their foreign policies and public debate about them ever since. The speech, however, provided few clues as to what precisely Ireland would do, either at the UN or in the international system as a whole. Indeed, its lasting significance is probably attributable not to any guidelines which Cosgrave laid down but to the tension implicit in his claim that Ireland was both an 'independent' and a 'Western' country. The immediate task, however, was to decide what Ireland should do, given that a consensus existed in the Dáil in 1956 to the effect that the opportunity of UN membership should be used to pursue an active foreign policy.

The problem, according to Costello, was that the preoccupation with Ireland's struggle for independence had permitted no 'tradition of interest in international affairs to emerge'.[6] This was not strictly true, of course, but what had emerged was a circumscribed understanding of what such an interest should involve. The struggle for independence and the continuing problem of Partition had resulted in an approach to foreign affairs which consisted largely of making moral commentaries backed by a strategy of abstention and non-compliance as a political act of protest. At its worst, this approach harkened back to the pre-Independence practice of provincial newspaper editors thundering at the Russian czar or local boards of guardians passing resolutions condemning the latest British imperial adventure.[7] Its best was reflected in de Valera's role as President of the Council of the League of Nations in the 1930s when, according to O'Brien, the foundations were laid of the Irish commitment to 'the strongest possible international order', 'the acceptance of rules in the conduct of international affairs' and the willingness to sacrifice immediate self-interest in support of these principles.[8]

To the Fine Gael members of the Inter-Party government, none of this probably looked too promising as a prescription for how the Irish government should conduct itself in an international arena dominated by the concerns of the Cold War. This was particularly so as their sympathies were clearly directed to one side in that contest rather than to the non-aligned group of states, the governments of which were trying to steer a highly politicised and highly publicised course between the two dominant blocs. As it happened, however, the results of the 1957 general election entailed that it was Fianna Fail, rather than Fine Gael, which became charged with the responsibility of giving substance to Ireland's active role at the UN. As the party of de Valera and republicanism, they were not uncomfortable with either the foreign policy tradition outlined above, or with the opportunities for middle-powering at the UN which the governments of countries like Canada, India and Sweden had begun to develop in alliance with the Secretariat from 1956 onwards. While the model for Irish activity as a 'middle power' and the opportunities for such activity were being created 'out there' in the international system, however, it remained largely the task of the new Fianna Fáil government to explain why they applied to Ireland and what actions would follow as a consequence.

The starting point for thinking about Irish foreign policy, which transcended party divisions, was that Ireland had nothing to gain from an international system in which outcomes were determined by the actual or threatened use of force. It had, as Cosgrave put it, a 'vested interest in peace'. For example, in reply to the assertion that the leader of a small country had no business passing comments on the conduct of the Soviet Union or the struggle between the super-powers, Costello had stated that since the primary interest of a small nation is peace, then the conduct of the Soviet Union concerned Ireland as much as it concerned anybody else. Sean Lemass, speaking as Taoiseach in 1960 and defending the decision to send Irish troops to the Congo as part of the UN force, argued that while all states suffered from wars, their effects were particularly hard on small states like Ireland, which would have to suffer their consequences without being able to influence the course of world events. Small states had a 'special interest' in peace because they could gain nothing from war.[9]

It followed, therefore, that Ireland should be a strong supporter of the UN since, as Costello argued, it had been set up to secure the maintenance of peace and the rule of law and justice in international affairs'. According to Aiken, who became Minister for External Affairs in 1957 and held the position for the rest of this first period and beyond, the UN might have many shortcomings, but it offered the 'best hope' for safeguarding the interests of small states, and the 'best prospect for the evolution of a world order based on justice and the rule of law.'[10] In very general terms, therefore, Ireland was committed to a revisionist position on the way in which international relations were conducted, and its governments regarded a strong UN as something which they should support since it would be a major agent of any transformation which might be achieved.

Nevertheless, Ireland's support for the UN did not rest on the principled objective of transforming the international system alone. It might be regarded as an embryonic model for a better way of conducting international affairs in the future, but of more immediate importance were the several ways in which the UN, as an international organisation, was seen as providing an opportunity for acting more effectively in the present. For example, international organisations could, as de Valera argued in the 1956 debate, serve as a 'general representation clearing house' in which the smaller states, lacking extensive diplomatic networks, could come together to discuss their problems. Indeed, Jack Lynch, speaking many years later about Irish membership of the Council of Europe, stressed the sense of 'discovery' which the Irish had experienced in their encounters with the representatives of other small states with similar problems. In addition, according to Lemass, the UN allowed a small state to initiate policy on occasions without drawing too much hostile attention to itself.[11]

Implicit in these perceptions of opportunity, but rarely articulated, was the fact that Irish governments had some substantive external interests of a more immediate nature than the transformation of the international system, the pursuit of which might be facilitated by membership of the UN. The most obvious of these, one might suppose, was the objective of eventually uniting Ireland once again. Regarding Partition, Irish governments had attempted to negotiate with their British counterpart. They had attempted to appeal to British and international public opinion in a variety of fora, and they had refused to fight in the Second World War or become members of NATO partly because this would have involved cooperation with a country which continued to occupy what the Irish claimed as a part of their national territory. None of these measures had been successful in their primary objective and there were members of the Dáil who supposed that where they had failed, the UN might, if indeed it was such a great opportunity for Ireland, succeed. Anticipating the expression of such sentiments from the political opposition or other domestic sources, however, spokesmen for the government went to some length to explain that simply pleading the injustice of Partition to the General Assembly or Security Council of the UN would yield few results.

In so doing, they started to establish the idea of achieving objectives by establishing an international reputation for Ireland. In the 1956 debate, for example, Costello argued that one would not succeed at the UN by making demands or pleading. Rather, it was, as he put it, 'a question of timing, a question of discretion, a question of making friends, a question of doing good turns for other nations so that they will do good turns for us'. The official policy of the United States, he pointed out, was not to come between Ireland and Britain on the question of Partition. Therefore, the key to success was to play 'our part' at the UN, to acquire a 'standing influence' there. On the basis of such influence, 'powerful friends' would be secured 'who without any formal *démarche'*, would help Ireland in the struggle to end Partition. Speaking the following year as Minister for External Affairs, Aiken claimed that if he were to address nothing but Ireland's 'own troubles' when he spoke at the UN, then he would be as effective as the Dáil member who spoke about only the smaller cases in his own constituency'. Getting others to be concerned with one's own interests, 'in common with the interests of mankind', necessitated becoming concerned with 'the affairs and troubles of other countries'.[12]

This view of foreign policy as a process of exchanging favours and lending one's influence and help on the basis of a *quid pro quo* is a familiar theme to students of Irish political culture. Useful though this might be in that domestic context, however, in international affairs such an approach confronted obvious and major problems. First, and most importantly, Irish governments had very little to offer and, hence, very little influence to wield in support of such a strategy. Secondly, domestic purposes necessitated that in their foreign policy rhetoric, at least, Irish governments adhered to a principle of even-handedness and eschewed expediency in the conduct of their relations with other governments. This being so, they pursued what Hans Morgenthau called a prestige policy in that they worked to obtain recognition by others of the status they considered appropriate for their own country.[13]

In part, this continued the nationalist tradition of seeking recognition of Ireland's independence as an important end in itself. However, spokesmen for the government also argued that in raising Ireland's external status and prestige, they also increased its external influence and capacity to pursue its own goals effectively. Thus, in defending the work of Aiken and the UN delegation in 1959, Lemass claimed that through it they had secured 'increasing respect' for Ireland's viewpoint, indeed, they had 'secured recognition of the fact' that Ireland had a viewpoint and in so doing had increased Ireland's influence at the UN in a way which might be important to it in the future. Similarly, in explaining the following year why Ireland had not withdrawn from the UN force in the Congo after several Irish soldiers had been killed, he asserted that this displayed a 'maturity' which had been 'universally recognised' and which would 'enhance Irish influence in world affairs'.[14]

Prestige has traditionally been pursued by the performance of diplomatic ceremonial and displays of force. While the first, in a modern form, was of considerable relevance to the Irish case, the second, for obvious reasons, was not. Therefore, Irish governments sought to pursue prestige by two methods: through their performance of a series of international security functions, generally within a UN framework; and through the elaboration and proclamation of credentials which, they argued, were essential to an effective performance of these functions and which, they claimed, Ireland possessed. By taking appropriate actions when the opportunity existed for them and continuously projecting the credentials which they asserted were essential to effectiveness in this respect, the government attempted to create an external role for Ireland as a responsible member of international society, a 'good international citizen'.

After his retirement Lemass provided a useful summary of these functions undertaken by Ireland and a group of what he called other 'lesser powers at the centre'. The Irish, he said, saw their role as one of 'promoting compromise' and 'softening the extreme positions' of other governments who were parties to a dispute. Further, they thought that they could, on occasions, successfully sponsor resolutions on issues which they considered to be important and they had a function in 'helping to develop world public opinion'. Finally, according to Lemass, the Irish thought that they had a responsibility to contribute to the effectiveness of those UN agencies involved with reducing international tension. All these activities, he claimed, were facilitated by Ireland's 'recognised position of integrity in the Assembly' and its impartiality.[15]

Among the specific policies pursued in the context of this general statement of Irish activity between 1957 and 1966 were the following: extensive support for UN peacekeeping operation; the initiation of proposals on controlling nuclear proliferation and the disengagement of conventional forces in Europe; and initiatives on UN 'organisational' issues such as discussing the admission of the People's Republic of China and the methods by which the organisation and its activities should be financed. These actions in themselves, while important to Irish governments, were only part of the policy because they lacked the continuity, frequency or significance of the foreign policy of a great power. The other part of the policy, therefore, and the part with which Irish governments were more continuously involved, was the promotion of the national attributes which they claimed were the necessary credentials for such behaviour. Only by doing this could intermittent actions using highly circumscribed, if important, policy resources, be presented as a foreign policy which projected the status and identity of the state in a prestigious manner.

What credentials, therefore, did Ireland have to offer, according to its governments, for their efforts to construct a position of external influence? First, Ireland was a small, weak country. While this weakness, according to Aiken, entailed that small states like Ireland could not 'force any particular solution on the nuclear powers', it also meant that they were unlikely to have particular interests in most international disputes and were, hence, free to assist in creating 'the climate for fruitful negotiations between the great powers'.[16] It was this sort of 'acceptability', for example, which had resulted in Ireland being one of only two European countries (the other being Sweden) that the members of the UN could agree should provide troops for the Congo force.[17]

Secondly, Ireland was not only a small, weak state, it was also one which, according to its governments, enjoyed the reputation of being an 'independent' actor. As Aiken pointed out, such 'independence' resulted in many practical advantages. Speaking to the Dáil in 1961, for example, he recalled an occasion when Ireland's UN delegation had been sponsoring a resolution on controlling nuclear proliferation. During the process of negotiations which preceded the formal discussions, he said it had become clear that half the resolution would pass easily while the rest would fail. Aiken had simply withdrawn the unacceptable half, an action which he said would have been impossible if he had been tied to fifteen or twenty other delegates co-sponsoring the resolution. It was for this reason that he was against joining even the Non-Aligned group at the UN, for as he argued the following year in a debate on the implications of EEC membership for Irish neutrality, 'the best contribution we can make to the world and world peace is to keep ourselves as free as we can to make suggestions, suggestions that a member of a *bloc* could not make.'[18]

The third, and most distinctive credential which the government claimed that Ireland possessed was the fact that it was both a developed, capitalist, liberal democracy and an ex-colony which had fought for and won its own independence. Ireland's governments, it was claimed, spoke with the moral authority of a country whose only involvement in international affairs had been directed at the emancipation of its own people, and the practical authority of both success in this respect and achieving the kind of economic development which it was assumed most of the newly independent countries were trying to achieve. In so far as they did this, Irish governments went beyond the formula of justifying an international role on the basis of posited attributes of national identity to claiming that their own specific experiences made Ireland a model for other countries to follow.

Much of the 'model' component of Ireland's 'good international citizen' role simply consisted of describing Ireland's efforts on behalf of the UN and international peace and security in situations where a general policy statement was required, notably during the opening debate in the General Assembly. On occasions, however, Aiken would shift from speaking on behalf of small states or addressing them as a group with shared concerns on shared issues, such as independence and the freedom of other small states, to pointing out to them, for example, how while Ireland had a genuine grievance – the partition of its national territory – its government handled this difficulty in a responsible manner. Specifically, they did not threaten to create a more unpleasant and dangerous situation in order to get their own way.[19] The most notable example of this came in Aiken's contribution to the discussion of the Cuban crisis at the UN. In this he expressed his disappointment at the fact that, while Cuba had the right to exercise its sovereignty in choosing how to defend itself, it had done so by making itself a base 'for the prosecution of the cold war'. He contrasted this with Ireland's conduct during the Second World War, when its government had guaranteed that it would not let its territory be used for an attack on Britain. Small states had a major obligation not to allow themselves to become a cause of international tensions.[20]

On the basis of these components of Ireland's national identity as they were articulated, particularly by spokesmen for the Fianna Fáil government which came to power in 1957, therefore, an active, international role was claimed for Ireland at the UN. With regard to security, Ireland could provide troops for peacekeeping operations since these usually involved disputes between new countries and ex-colonies. With regard to diplomatic functions, while Ireland was a Western country, it was, as Cosgrave put it, impossible for its people to regard anyone's struggle for national self-determination without sympathy. Thus, it could take a leading role in the task of reconciling the aspirations of the emergent nations with the sensibilities of the old imperial powers. This, according to Cosgrave, was one of the most 'urgent needs' of the world because in the absence of 'specific formulas' there was a danger that the Western Powers might fall out among themselves and weaken the stand against Communism.[21] The Fianna Fáil government were not so inclined to express the significance of Ireland's independent standing in terms of the contribution it might thereby make to the solidarity of the Western alliance. Nevertheless, its significance could equally well be expressed in terms of the logic of preventive diplomacy and the emphasis of the latter on the dangers of local conflicts becoming global through the involvement of the super-powers.

Notes

1. See 159, 127-45 (3 July 1956).
2. John Costello, Taoiseach 1948-51 and 1954-57, speaking in the Dáil., 159, 613. Liam Cosgrave, son of William Cosgrave, the head of the first Free State government, 1922-32. Liam was Minister for External Affairs in the second coalition government between 1954 and 1957 and Taoiseach in the Fine Gael/Labour coalition between 1973 and 1977, quoted, 159, 140-1 and 138-9.

3. Ibid.
4. For Costello's presentation of the three principles of Irish foreign policy, see 159, 139-44.
5. 159, 144.
6. 159, 611 .
7. For example, *The Skibbereen Eagle* was a nineteenth-century newspaper known for its editorial comments on the high politics of European diplomacy. It is regarded as a symbol of a pretentious and unserious approach to the place of Ireland in world affairs which the country can no longer afford. See Keatinge (1973), op. cit., p. 218 fn., for a comment on this.
8. Conor Cruise O'Brien, private interview 1982. The policy of pursuing offices in international organisations was established at this time, e.g. de Valera himself and Sean Lester, the League's High Commissioner for Danzig. For information on the latter see, Stephen Barcroft, 'The International Civil Servant: The League of Nations career of Sean Lester 1929–46', unpublished doctoral thesis, Trinity College, Dublin, 1972.
9. For Cosgrave, private interview, but see also 208, 1085 (7 April 1964). For Costello, see 159, 612. For Lemass, see 185, 776 (7 December 1960).
10. Costello, 159, 612; Aiken, 164, 1215 (28 November 1957), and 194, 1315 (27 March 1962).
11. 159, 434 for de Valera talking about the Council of Europe during the 1956 debate. Jack Lynch was Taoiseach in 1966–73 and 1977–81. His comments on the Council of Europe were given in a private interview. Sean Lemass was Taoiseach between 1959 and 1966. His comments are to be found in his 'Small States in International Organisations', in Schou and, Brundtland (eds), op. cit., p.115.
12. For Costello, 159, 623, and for Aiken, 164, 162 (23 October 1957).
13. See H.J. Morgenthau, *Politics Among Nations*, Alfred A. Knopf, NY, 4th edition, pp. 69-83. The policy might also be said to be 'Morgenthauian' in that it emphasised the pursuit of means, rather than ends, as the important objectives of foreign policy.
14. 176, 661 (2 July 1959) and 185, 987 (13 December 1967). Ireland's decision to remain in the Congo force contrasted with the decision taken by several other providers to pull out when the operation became controversial and difficult.
15. 'Lemass', in Schou and Brundtland, op. cit., p.117.
16. Frank Aiken in the 17th Session of the First Committee of the UN General Assembly, 1262 meeting, 1 November 1982, cited in *Ireland at the United Nations 1962: Speeches by Frank Aiken,* Dublin, no date.
17. See 183, 1878 (28 June 1960) for Lemass's claim that selection for the Congo force amounted to recognition of Ireland's status. See 208, 1098 (7 April 1964) for his expression of similar sentiments regarding participation in the UN force for Cyprus.
18. See 191, 675-8 (11 June 1961) for Aiken's discussion of preserving Ireland's freedom of action at the UN. See 194, 1418 (5 April 1962) for his contribution to the EEC debate and his discomfiture with his own government's position therein.
19. See, for example, 214, 1040-2 (11 February 1965) for an account of such efforts by him.
20. Aiken during the 1023 meeting of the UN Security Council, 24 October 1962, cited in Aiken, ibid., p.25.
21. 159,145.

4 The internal commitment to international role-playing, 1956-66

Irish governments between 1956 and 1966 viewed Irish membership of the UN as providing them with the opportunity to pursue an active foreign policy. They constructed a role for Ireland as a 'good international citizen' which supported the efforts of the UN to reduce international conflict, and by performing this role, they claimed, Ireland would obtain diplomatic influence the better to pursue its own particular foreign policy objectives. To establish that the spokesmen for Irish governments said this sort of thing, however, does not in itself demonstrate that it was important to them or, indeed, anyone else for that matter. Talk, after all, even in the form of declaratory foreign policy can be cheap and may serve a number of purposes other than those implied by its own content.

Most of the public figures interviewed for this book were very aware of the other purposes to which foreign policy and debate about it might be put. One, for example, stressed that as often as not, 'Irish neutrality' became a 'political football' in Dáil debates which provided an opportunity for party political point-scoring rather than national soul-searching. Another suggested that Irish foreign policy, as an activity of a democratic government, should be primarily

44

regarded as an exercise in playing to what he called 'the domestic gallery'. He went on to say that the grand thing about the annual debate in the UN General Assembly was that it provided the opportunity for 'a series of speeches by political leaders to their home public' in which the domestic audience could see the whole world listening to 'our man and putatively hanging on his lips'.[1]

Nearly all foreign policy has some domestic significance of this sort, of course. Even the external actions of a powerful country like the United States are often undertaken with an eye to how they 'play' at home. One might expect, however, that, generally speaking, the weaker a state is, the more likely its foreign policy actions are to be accounted for in these terms. In the Irish case, it is clear that, at times, the primary purpose of some of foreign policy debates was to make the government look good – or bad – and not to elucidate the major operating principles of that policy. The point is, however, that if we are interested in the foreign policy of small states as such, then the fact that some of it is practised primarily for domestic political purposes does not diminish its importance. As I have argued above, there is a tendency among both the powerful in international affairs and scholars in the discipline to discount such activity because of its limited impact on outcomes in the international system. What is strange, however, is the way that, in the Irish case, both students of the foreign policy of the country and members of its attentive public have shared the attitude that if a foreign policy action is to be explained primarily in terms of its domestic significance, then this in some way discounts it as a genuine object of attention.

Further, even if they concede that the governments of small states may on occasions be concerned with issues of national identity, status and prestige, there is a tendency among scholars of international affairs to regard such considerations as both stupid reasons for actions and weak explanatory variables in accounting for behaviour. The former may be regarded as a legitimate tradition of ridicule arising from the experience of international disorder to which these considerations have contributed in the past. It does not follow, however, that because a cause is thought to be stupid that it is necessarily unimportant. With the major powers this is rarely a problem because their capacity to project power necessarily dictates that their pro-claimed reasons for doing so are attended to, and the capacity to project in itself constitutes an unambiguous demonstration of strength, status and prestige. To talk of small states in the same vein, however, is to entertain visions of Ruritania, 'Soccer Wars' and Peter Sellers in 'The Mouse that Roared'. It is, for example, the idea of Paraguay declaring war on Brazil, Argentina and Uruguay simultaneously in 1865, rather than the virtually complete destruc-tion of the male population of the country in the ensuing five years of conflict, which one associates with small state policies of grandeur.

Irish foreign policy was not, and is not, entirely free of some of the trivial, banal and ludicrous episodes commonly associated with small state prestige.

It is fair to say that one of the tasks of the Minister for External Affairs during this period was to communicate the fact, and the particular form, of Ireland's existence to foreigners, and to be seen to be doing so at home. A general preoccupation of Aiken's reports to the Dáil was with the listing of visits of statesmen, politicians and other notables to Ireland, and charting the efforts of his department to 'create a general interest in Ireland abroad', by the distribution of information and the sending forth of literary figures.[2] Such preoccupations are not unusual in themselves, but, as the opposition was quick to point out, it seemed at times as if Aiken considered these to be the central aspects of Irish foreign policy, in so far as he mentioned very little else in some of his general statements on the subject.

On occasions, however, the need to 'stimulate abroad an interest in our country and foster understanding between our peoples' took on more precise dimensions. After incidents at a soccer match between Northern Ireland and Italy, for example, it was thought necessary to have Ireland's chargé d'affaires in Rome explain the situation in the North, that is the Irish claim and the British presence, because 'of misunderstandings among the Italian public and Press'. Further, the Minister for External Affairs had to give undertakings to the Dáil that this had been adequately taken care of.[3] On another occasion Deputy Ryan had asked

the Minister for External Affairs whether he is aware that a large house-size neon sign in Piccadilly Circus in London displays a map of Ireland under the slogan 'Australia sends her best to Britain': and if he has made or will make representations to those responsible for the advertisement, pointing out that it is politically, economically, geographically and historically incorrect, and a cause of annoyance to the citizens of this sovereign state.

The Taoiseach (no less) replied that representations actually had been made to the Australian High Commissioner who said that the sign was to be replaced shortly since it had outlived its usefulness.[4]

There were the occasions when the government too appeared to be concerned with the manipulation of the symbols of national dignity or identity for short-term political gain. A considerable portion of the debate on the External Affairs estimate for 1964, for example, was given over to discussion of an alleged Fianna Fáil bias in the history section of an information handbook put out by the Department.[5] On occasions, this politicking went beyond the usual accusations and counter-accusations in the Dáil regarding the parts played by the leading figures of each party, or their respective fathers, in the civil war that had taken place over forty years previously, and was carried over into the external environment. In 1960, for example, an adjournment debate was forced over the conduct of the Minister for External Affairs in a ceremony in which the Great Mace and Sword of the City of Galway were returned by the Hearst corporation, into whose possession they had come, to representatives of that city in New York. The original intention had been that they would be presented to the mayor of Galway in time for a certain anniversary. The Minister for External Affairs, however, became involved with the presentation and, himself, brought the artefacts back to Ireland. The substance of the criticism was that the original arrangements had been changed after an election which produced a new mayor of Galway who was not of the government party.[6]

It might be supposed that such is the stuff of small state foreign policies of prestige, a sequence of lofty principles being articulated in the midst of episodes of low farce, with the significance of either being hard to determine. This, however, would be an incomplete picture of the government's effort to present Ireland as a coherent national actor with a distinctive identity, the 'good international citizen'. The latter was, in fact, a composite identity. For example, Irish governments variously presented Ireland as a mediator or 'bridge' between blocs, as a facilitator of international reform in accordance with the values of Western and Christian civilisation, and as a model for how other states should behave. As a consequence, they had to manage domestic debate regarding the relative importance of the different components of the identity and political pressures from both home and abroad regarding the foreign policy which was appropriate to each interpretation of the role. The willingness of the Fianna Fáil government to mobilise resources in support of its own definitions of these when they became controversial, indicates that, within clearly defined limits, their commitment to international role-playing went considerably beyond simply making declarations of general principle.

The most obvious problem in this regard was the difficulty of reconciling Cosgrave's second principle, stressing 'independence', with his third, which emphasised Ireland's place among, and obligations to, the nations of the 'free world'. As far as the Fine Gael members of the government in 1956 were concerned, any tension between these two principles was to be resolved in favour of the latter. In Cosgrave's speech, for example, the commitment to act independently was accompanied by the qualification that such actions should be in accord with Irish interests and values, and the third principle was introduced as an elaboration of the source of these. Further, while he began his speech by saying that he was elaborating principles which should inform all of Ireland's foreign policy, his conclusion suggested that supporting the 'free world' against 'the spread of Communist power' enjoyed a special status as 'a principle not simply of our policy at the United Nations but of our foreign policy as a whole'.[7]

The suggestion has been made, in fact, that the whole speech followed very closely a memorandum designed to place Ireland 'squarely into the NATO bloc...without ever mentioning NATO', composed by someone in the Department of External Affairs.[8] Certainly, in the same debate, Costello, the Taoiseach, referred to Irish neutrality as a 'somewhat threadbare topic', and made it very clear that as far as his government was concerned, Ireland was resisting pressure from its friends to join NATO simple because 'no Government in this country could contemplate any such alliance while Partition existed'.[9] 'Independence', as spokesmen for Fine Gael made very clear once they were in opposition, did not mean that Ireland should refrain from pursuing its own vital interests or giving 'active support' to the Western Powers. According to James Dillon, preserving Ireland's independence and enhancing its prosperity was best done by multiplying the number of Ireland's friends and consolidating the relationships with those which the government valued most. And according to Costello, the very fact that Ireland was 'not in a position to have military alliances, or other alliances' made it all the more necessary to 'have friends'.[10]

These comments were provoked primarily by the activities of Frank Aiken, the Fianna Fáil Minister for External Affairs, at the UN. Indeed, Aiken had signalled the future policy of Fianna Fáil in the 1956 debate by pointing out that the sins in international politics were not always committed by the Communist side. It was the misconduct of those who should know better which offered the greatest opportunities to the USSR, particularly on the issue of colonialism.[11] The new focus, then, was upon the second principle, stressing both Ireland's 'independence' from blocs and its 'evenhandedness' in judging international disputes. In response to Dillon's assertion above that the purpose of a foreign policy was to maximise and consolidate friendships, for example, Aiken had replied that the vital issues were not alliance politics, but the dangers facing the whole world.[12]

One consequence of this new emphasis was that the Irish delegation to the UN had helped to initiate a move to discuss the admission of the People's Republic of China to the organisation and it had continued to support this effort in the face of US opposition and, eventually, indirect pressure on the Irish mission to the UN. In response to the argument that the decision of the US government to elevate a procedural question on China to a trial of strength between East and West should have determined Irish policy on the issue, a spokesman for the government replied that the threat posed by 500 million Chinese made the question of their representation at the UN, rather than Ireland's supporting the United States, the crucial issue. The principal value of the UN, according to de Valera, was not that the members subscribed to its principles and were prepared to act on them, but that 'opposing groups' were ready to talk to each other there. According to Lemass, Ireland disapproved of many countries and their actions, but this disapproval could not be a reason for excluding them from the UN. As Aiken put it, Ireland should 'keep in contact with all the countries who have power over the fate of the world whether for good or for evil'.[13]

This 'independent' stance courted considerable political opposition, however. For example, in 1957, the Irish government revived the policy of making arms control proposals, first on European disengagement and secondly, with regard to halting the spread of nuclear weapons.[14] According to the spokesmen for Fine Gael, the proposals on disengagement were unfair in that, by asking both WTO and NATO forces to withdraw in equal numbers, they did not

48

reflect the lack of symmetry in the situation as it presently existed. They were also unwise in that the Western Powers had expressed hostility to such measures and they were immoral in that any sort of mutuality in the treatment of East and West failed to acknowledge who was actually to blame for the existing state of affairs.

As the period progressed and Ireland's involvement with the UN, notably in its peacekeeping operations, deepened, the criticisms sharpened and became increasingly focused on how Ireland's position on colonial issues stood in the way of its attempt to join the EEC. In an attack on Ireland's UN policy in 1961, for example, Dillon pursued his theme of Ireland's need for friends. Under the present government, he argued, Ireland's foreign policy was that of 'the Miller of Dee who used to say: "I care for nobody and nobody cares for me".' In their desire to become the 'acceptable spearhead of moderate opinion in Africa', as he put it, they had 'kicked France in the teeth...Belgium in the stomach...and stabbed America In the back'.[15] Earlier that year, in a debate which had moved from discussion of whether, in a recent visit, President Sukarno had asked Ireland to be represented at a forthcoming meeting of the Non-Aligned Movement in Belgrade to the question of EEC membership, he had noted that as a member of the Council of Europe and possibly the EEC, Ireland would have close ties with the Netherlands, a country which was then in dispute with Indonesia. How, Costello wanted to know, would the Irish deal with such a 'conflict of loyalties', could they both 'become good Europeans and remain an uncommitted neutralist state?'[16] He doubted it.

How then, did the Irish government deal with these problems of incompatibility, real or asserted, within the role which they had constructed for Ireland or between the various sets of foreign policy behaviour which were derived from it? Several commentators on Irish foreign policy have argued that these tensions did not really present any kind of problem at all because they existed mainly in the realm of declaratory policy with few implications of substance. There is also some indirect evidence to suggest that Ireland was so unimportant to other governments that it would escape notice virtually whatever it did. As far as Britain was concerned, for example, a former ambassador to Dublin spoke of the 'Isle of Wight syndrome', a tendency to forget that Ireland existed as an independent state apart from the 'yearly butter wrangle' which was characterised by bargaining, agreement and lunch, in that order.[17] It may also be remarked here that for politicians, problems of consistency and contradiction do not demand a logical solution as the precondition of further action. The important thing for them is to avoid situations in which these problems become exposed to public scrutiny, and if this fails, to deny that any problem of consistency exists.

Thus, on occasions when Irish foreign policy became a 'political football' in the Dáil, the government was frequently willing to make its stand on the grounds of political expedience rather than political principle. At Question Time, Aiken would simply deny that there was any contradiction, for example, between Ireland's position on South Africa at the UN and holding talks with commercial enterprises from that country about developing trade links with it.[18] In addition to refutations or denials, spokesmen for the government would also use a series of techniques arising out of parliamentary procedures or privileges to remove or deflect pressure from themselves. Any technical inaccuracy in a question put down would be used as a reason for refusing to answer the substance of it and Aiken became notorious for opening the annual debate on the External Affairs estimate with a very short speech restricted to details of expenditure and a brief survey of international developments, about half of which was delivered in Irish. In addition, spokesmen for the government often emphasised the procedural details of positions they adopted at the UN to blur their political significance and, hence, deflate criticism. Both their support for discussing the admission of China to the UN and their justification for not supporting the decision to allow Kasavubu, who was supported by the Americans, to take the Congo's seat at the UN in 1960 may be understood in these terms.[19]

Within a political culture where the suggestion that the government was soft on a country which tortured priests might sway a by-election and where pressure on the government could consist of reading out hostile articles from American newspapers or commenting on the preference of the Minister for External Affairs for remaining at the UN rather than attending the funeral of a pope, at Question Time in the Dáil, the willingness to resort to procedural measures is to ensure a quiet life is understandable.[20] Their use, however, should not be taken as evidence that Irish foreign policy was primarily a matter of domestic and rhetorical significance, for the purpose of the government was to protect an external exercise of considerable substance. It is to this, the support which the Irish government gave to UN peacekeeping operations and the peacekeeping 'idea' between 1960 and 1966, to which I now turn.

Peacekeeping, 'UN political control of a local conflict by politically impartial, essentially non-coercive methods', had its origins in the failure of the collective security procedures provided for in the Charter to come into operation. As a result of both this and the efforts of the Secretary General of the UN, Dag Hammarskjold and a few governmental allies, a substitute system known as 'preventive diplomacy' was established.[21] The latter was characterised both by its objective of keeping the superpowers out of local disputes around the world, thereby minimising the risk of global nuclear conflict arising out of such 'brushfire wars', and by its emphasis on *ad hoc* measures and the role of the Secretariat in them. When consensus at the UN permitted it, lightly-armed forces composed of troops from countries which were not, generally speaking, directly involved, could be sent to facilitate the resolution of particular disputes. In Patrick Keatinge's words, the extent of Ireland's contribution to this process 'does not suggest an attempt to gain international prestige on the cheap'. The Irish contribution to the UN force in the Congo consisted of at one time nearly 1,400 men and maintained an average strength of 700–800 between the start of the operation at the end of 1960 and its winding down in 1964. The Cyprus contingent maintained an average strength in excess of 1000 in 1964, the first year of its operation, and then was reduced to some 500 men for the rest of the period under examination.[22]

The scale of the Irish contribution of manpower to peacekeeping may be measured in a number of ways. For example, a total of eight infantry battalions, two infantry groups and two armoured units participated in ONUC at different times, and according to Larry Fabian, by 1967 the Irish army had provided ONUC and UNFICYP manning tables with well over 10,000 men. But the best idea of the scale of the contribution may be arrived at by setting the average contingent strengths detailed above against the size of the army as a whole, an establishment which, according to Fabian, was 'generally several thousand men below its authorised strength of 12,000'. Indeed, during one period in 1964, when both ONUC and UNFICYP were operating, about one-sixth of the Irish army was overseas on peacekeeping duty. The contributions consisted largely of lightly-armed infantry and armoured or scout car units for mobile patrols. In addition, however, Ireland provided a commander for the Congo force and staff officers for UNFICYP.[23]

To the general degree of support and effort embodied in the provision of these forces may be added more specific costs which arose in the course of these operations. Peacekeeping in the Congo, in particular, involved a series of combat operations at a fairly high level of violence in which Irish troops were involved and casualties sustained. Twenty-six soldiers died in the Congo, fourteen in combat and nine of these in a single ambush. The general consensus of commentators is that, despite the shock which these losses gave to the general public, both they and the government regarded this as an acceptable price to pay for such operations. Indeed, these casualties, it has been suggested by some, were regarded as the substantive component of a peacekeeping policy which itself was seen as a '"membership fee" paid by the country for its international identity'.[24] When the bodies of eight of the soldiers killed in the ambush were returned to Ireland they were buried in Dublin at a funeral attended by some 300,000 people, as well as members of the government.

Later, however, when a company of the Irish army (some 150 men) was forced to surrender in one operation and it was rumoured that they had been overrun and had sustained 57 casualties, the Irish commitment to the policy was badly, if temporarily, shaken.[25] Aiken flew out to the Congo to see for himself and O'Brien suggests that had the soldiers all been killed then the rest of the Irish contingent would have probably been withdrawn. It is beyond this point in time that one may trace a much more circumspect attitude on the part of the Irish government with regard to the mandates as well as the financing of peacekeeping operations.[26] Nevertheless, the difficulties experienced by the Irish in the field and the problems which beset UN peacekeeping in general provided the basis of a broader Irish policy at the UN. This emphasised Ireland as a model peacekeeper, both in its practice and its proposals for improve-

51

ments, and as a model for how the smaller members of the UN should endure existing arrangements. In both of these, the willingness to accept costs was a crucial part of the policy.

The innovative and *ad hoc* qualities of preventive diplomacy constituted both its strength and its weakness. Initially, this approach made considerable progress by exploiting the paralysis and the caution of the permanent members of the Security Council. The problem of force participation was apparently solved by the elaboration of the middle power concept and the problem of using UN forces for the coercion of misbehaving members seemed to be solved by the principles of self-defence, host-state consent and non-involvement in internal political affairs.[27] In fact, all that had happened was that an energetic Secretary General, working with a number of friendly governments, had exploited the ambiguities of the Charter and the hesitations of the major powers to achieve a series of *faits accomplis* and establish a number of, if not questionable, then certainly vulnerable, precedents regarding the role of the Secretariat. Once the novelty was over and the significance of peacekeeping operations and their part in the Secretary General's strategy of widening his own sphere of competence became clear, opposition to preventive diplomacy began to take shape and its achievements began to look very fragile.

The problems with UN peacekeeping were essentially political in nature. By definition it was both necessary and very difficult to get everyone to agree to an international force when the principal actors continued to see each other, rather than the anarchic character of the international system as a whole, as the major threat to their security, and saw themselves as the only trustworthy guarantors of their own interests. In the absence of a strong sense of international solidarity, it was all but inevitable that UN peacekeeping operations were regarded as the instruments of policy of certain states or, with more justification, as serving the interests of certain states, rather than the interests of the system as a whole. In practice, the USSR came to regard UN peacekeeping as both undermining its position in the UN and serving the interests of imperialism. The French shared the Soviet concern for the 'illegality' of preventive diplomacy and hence the erosion of their position on the Council and the position of the Council within the UN as a whole. The British supported peacekeeping in principle, despite instinctive hostility, but then based their actual policy on a case-by-case analysis of each potential peacekeeping force to see whether their interests were served. The Americans were generally satisfied with the way peacekeeping operated.[28]

As a consequence of these differences, the peacekeeping efforts of the UN were accompanied by continual disputes about whether such forces should exist at all, if so, when, under whose control they should operate and, in particular, at whose expense. These difficulties left the Irish government and others that supported peacekeeping with three problems: how might they attempt to improve procedures for international peacekeeping; how might they best help the Secretary-General to mount peacekeeping operations under current conditions; and, how might they best serve their conception of their own national interests with regard to peacekeeping policy?. The responses dictated by each of these questions were by no means necessarily consistent with one another, and it was in the absence of any easy consistency here that the importance of Ireland's international role came to the fore. It did not do so, however, in the sense of a simple and secure national identity indicating how the Irish government should respond to each of these problems. Rather, what occurred was a progressive elaboration of an international role which then had to be sustained. It was in support of this effort, and not in the pursuit of more substantive goals such as improving peacekeeping mechanisms *per se*, that the government was prepared to commit resources.

Because they had troops in the field, the first problem which confronted the Irish government directly was the question of who should control peacekeeping operations. If their present or future effectiveness was to be guaranteed (assuming that the members of the Security Council would remain divided), then the protection and strengthening of the leading role of the Secretariat was called for. A crucial aspect of the whole peacekeeping idea was that it avoided the political controversy which had frozen the collective security provisions of the Charter. From the perspective of more narrow considerations of national interest, however, the desirability of strengthening the Secretariat was by no means a foregone conclusion. This is not to suggest that the Irish government had narrow national interests of its own which were to be pursued by participating in the control of such operations (although some contributing states do appear to have pursued such ends). Having troops on the ground itself, however, generated national interests as a peacekeeping operation unfolded. For example, in the case of the Congo, the mandate of the force was extended on several occasions, it became involved in highly controversial military operations and the level of threat to which Irish troops were exposed fluctuated in accordance with these and other developments. Also, it might be argued that the long-term Irish national interest lay in the development of the effective control of peacekeeping operations by the General Assembly rather than by a clique of international civil servants.

Irish policy with regard to the question of political control stressed that this was the preserve of the UN, and by this they meant the Secretariat and the advisory committee of concerned parties which functioned with each operation (of which, of course, they were a member if they had troops participating). Initially, the question of political control does not seem to have been regarded as a major issue by the Irish government. On being asked, a few days before Irish troops left for the Congo in 1960, what kind of commitments the government was getting into, the Taoiseach, Lemass, replied that Ireland would be free to withdraw in the unlikely event that the UN force was used for political purposes. On being informed, after being vague about the duration of the operation, that the Swedes had only committed themselves for a month, he replied that it was a 'fair assumption' that should circumstances arise which would make the Swedes withdraw, then these would probably result in Ireland's withdrawal also.[29] What is important here is not the clarification of an 'escape clause', but rather the assumption that it was unlikely that a UN operation could be controversial in any sense which would worry Ireland.

The Congo operation did not remain uncontroversial for very long. As a result of the collapse of the country's government into a number of competing factions, each with its own source of external support, the UN was left with a difficult choice regarding with whom, if anyone, it should work. This situation was exacerbated by an armed secession of one of the richest provinces of the new country which was supported by European private interests enjoying the sympathy of the governments of their countries of origin. Nevertheless, the position of the Irish government on the question of political control did not change in its essentials despite domestic pressure. This pressure was centred on the assertion that the government had been taken by surprise by events and that the only way to prevent a repetition of this and to safeguard Irish interests was to appoint a political representative on the spot. In his reply to this, Lemass acknowledged that the government had not been sufficiently informed to make a 'proper appreciation' of the situation in the Congo but claimed that it was not the task of the Irish government to make such an appreciation. Irish troops were in the Congo and Irish blood had been shed there for the highest of motives and not from any self-interest. Thus, he rejected the suggestion of a political representative on the spot because this would have had the effect of getting Ireland 'involved in the internal political affairs of the Congo' and would hinder the effective functioning of the force by necessitating prior consultations. Lemass also pointed out that the representative of Ghana had been thrown out of the Congo for precisely this kind of alleged involvement. The Irish government obtained information on the Congo from the United Nations Advisory Committee, on which they were represented as a contributor of troops to ONUC. Any suggestions that they had about the Congo policy of the UN were, according to Lemass, made there.[30]

In the debate upon the amending of the Irish constitution to permit Irish soldiers to go abroad on active service, itself a measure of the commitment of the government to peacekeeping, however, the Taoiseach clarified the area of decision which the government retained for itself. While Irish policy on the Congo would be based on the assumption that what the UN decided to do was '*prima facie* right', the 'extent and duration' of Ireland's own contribution to 'any action' which the UN might embark upon was for Ireland, alone, to decide. More specifically, he said that the movement of a new battalion out to the Congo depended on whether, 'in the judgement of the Government', UN forces, or European participation in them, were still required and whether the original objectives of 'helping to keep peace and order' until the Congolese could do this for themselves remained the same.[31]

This policy, which was also maintained with regard to the Cyprus force, was defended, in part, on practical grounds, particularly when the opposition

54

inquired as to whether considerations of 'high policy' had influenced it. Lemass argued that conditions were put on Irish participation so that where even a 'clear, legal obligation' existed, the country would only have to accept commitments proportional to its resources.[32] According to the government, practical considerations also ruled out the appointment of a political representative at the headquarters of either force. To avoid an unnecessary duplication or complication of lines of communications, Aiken claimed, communications between contributing governments had to be conducted with the Secretary-General, and while contributing governments might have different views, according to Lemass, 'any discussion of a political kind' about UNFICYP ought to take place in New York. While there would be no difficulty in finding out what was going on in Cyprus because Irish officers were stationed at the headquarters of UNFICYP, a situation in which each contributing government gave orders to its own contingent of troops would be inconceivable.[33]

There were, of course, few political incentives for the Irish government to become involved in the control of peacekeeping operations or the disputes which necessitated them, or at least to be seen exerting such a measure of control. As Lemass pointed out, comments in the Dáil regarding political developments in the Congo might result in Irish troops being singled out for special treatment and the appointment of an Irish representative to the Congo would involve the exceedingly political question of to whom, out of several contending groups, he should present his credentials. It was better to adhere to the official UN line, and if that was deemed political by someone, then at least Ireland could not be singled out on the basis of its position.[34]

One thing which did emerge from the discussions of control of UN peacekeeping forces, however, was that the Irish government did have direct communication channels with its own troops. Replying to a question with regard to contact with the Irish contingent in the Congo, a government spokesman for defence said that communications between the Irish troops and their government should be restricted to 'matters of routine administration' and that all 'reports and communications' had to be in accord with the 'rules and procedures [of] the Supreme Commander acting for the Secretary General'. Nevertheless, he went on, 'the contingent is in constant touch...within the restricted sphere mentioned'.[35]

There is only slight evidence of one instance in which this link was used for more than routine matters and that was on the occasion, noted above, when Aiken flew out to the Congo. He went when a very direct Irish national interest in the operation materialised with the surrounding of an Irish company by mercenaries and Katangese gendarmerie at the small town of Jadotville. On the evening of the day he arrived, the garrison, confronted with the failure of a relief attempt and an apparent choice between dying of thirst or being massacred, on the one hand, or surrendering, on the other, opted for the latter. According to Raymond Smith, a journalist who covered the Congo operation for an Irish newspaper, in one of its last transmissions the garrison requested a decision from Aiken, presumably with regard to whether or not it should surrender.[36]

Set against this one possible, and understandable, involvement with directing the operations of UN troops, however, is a record in which cooperation with the UN command predominated and in which the Irish government were content to reserve the right to determine whether to participate, the scale of their contribution and the right to withdraw if they disagreed with subsequent developments. Indeed, it might be argued that there is one episode in which the UN line was followed even though this could be regarded as costly to the prestige and painful to the sensibilities of the Irish government. This was when Conor Cruise O'Brien, who had been seconded from the Irish foreign service to the UN, was dismissed for allegedly taking unauthorised military action in an attempt to end the Katangan secession.[37] O'Brien himself argues that he was the victim of pressures on the Secretariat from great powers threatened and angered by his energetic interpretation of ONUC's mandate. Others have suggested that his greatest sin was the failure of his attempt to seize the leaders of the secession. At no point has anyone, including O'Brien himself, suggested that he was following a particularly Irish interpretation of ONUC's mandate. The issue as it was presented by some elements of the opposition to the Irish government was one of sticking up for their own diplomat who had simply done as he was told, or caving in along with the UN Secretariat to the pressures being brought to bear by the Western Powers.[38]

The position of the government, according to Lemass, was that anything O'Brien did while working for the UN was not something on which they could pass comment, that his subsequent resignation from the Irish foreign service was his own decision and that anything he had said since then regarding alleged British, French or Belgian interference with ONUC's mandate did not represent the views of the government. Aiken, despite initial sympathy with O'Brien, argued that the latter's views when published were distorted by 'his decision to claim martyrdom'. Acccording to MacQueen, Aiken was particularly angry at his attacks on the Secretariat. Whatever the merits of the respective claims – and it is perhaps significant that the commander of the ONUC forces, General Mac Eoin, himself an Irishman, supported O'Brien in public and asked to be relieved of his post at the end of the year – the government shared the official UN view of the events. They did so either because they believed the Secretariat's version or because, believe it or no, they thought that their prior duty and interest lay in supporting and protecting its position.[39]

Ireland's support for the UN Secretariat's control of peacekeeping operations was primarily justified on pragmatic and political grounds, as the specific situation demanded. On occasions, however, spokesmen for the government situated the policy within a broader conception of Ireland's role in the world. Aiken, for example, discussing the problems confronting the UN, argued that the organisation would never be effective until countries were prepared to accept 'majority decisions' made there. While Ireland had its 'votes and voice' in the UN on peacekeeping and other policies, it would accept the decisions of, for example, the advisory council to the Secretary General, even if this moved policy in a direction other than that argued for by the Irish government. The UN could not operate without the adherence of its members to democratic principles and the Irish government considered itself to be bound by such principles. According to Aiken, one reason for the difficulties which the UN was experiencing in the Congo was that 'many governments acted otherwise'.[40]

However, Aiken's policy of projecting Irish behaviour and the principles which informed it as a model for others to follow was most in evidence, not on the question of the political control of peacekeeping operations, but rather on the methods of financing them. Here too, the issue affected the Irish directly in that they were supposed to be reimbursed for their efforts, and, here too, their particular problem was an instance of broader difficulties.

The financial problems of the UN were both simple and crucial. The question was whether members had to pay for activities undertaken by the UN of which they did not approve, and whether they had to continue paying for operations of which they no longer approved. The short answer was that they did not; they simply refused to, and stopped paying.[41] It was with the consequences of this, the progressive running into debt by the UN and the various measures taken to deal with it – threatened legal sanctions, proposed institutional reforms, the floating of loans, calls for voluntary contributions and creative accounting – that Irish policy was accordingly concerned. The smaller UN operations had been financed out of the regular budget,[42] but with the establishment of UNEF,[43] a special account had been set up to which members contributed on the basis of a scale assessments similar to that for the regular budget. A similar system had been established for the financing of ONUC, but as in the case of UNEF this had proved inadequate and bonds were sold and voluntary and advanced payments were requested to pay for the force. As ONUC's operations became more controversial and costly, its finances became an instrument of leverage in the exchanges between the permanent members of the Security Council regarding the mandate of the force. These problems had not been settled before the UN was requested to provide another force, this time for Cyprus. Indeed, the invocation of Article 19 by the United States denying voting rights to those who were in arrears in their contributions to the UN by a certain amount, reduced the UN to functioning in a limited way for a time on the basis of a number of procedural fictions.

Until the creation of UNFICYP, Irish policy on the question of UN finances consisted largely of attempts to mobilise opinion in the General Assembly against those who had fallen behind in their payments. Aiken argued that, like submitting to the will of the majority expressed through the organs of the UN, financial constancy was at the heart of the effectiveness of the UN 'as an instrument of collective international action'. While the small states could accept the veto possessed by the permanent members both as a reflection of the realities of power and the fact that it was provided for in the Charter, he argued that it was wrong to allow what was in effect 'a second veto, a financial veto' by which the permanent members could nullify decisions of the Security Council or General Assembly properly arrived at.[44]

He made proposals, which amounted to exhorting everyone to pay up promptly, increasing the regular budget to cope with present demands and letting the Secretary General borrow money to cover the Organisation's costs if problems were being experienced.[45] More substantially, he had asked the Dáil for a supplementary estimate the previous year, so that Ireland's UN assessment could be paid six months before it was due. He also asked for an additional $25,000 for the Congo fund. Aiken made it clear that, while every little bit helped (the Secretary General was looking for $100 million for ONUC), the payments constituted 'a concrete manifestation of our loyalty to the United Nations Charter and our determination to stand by it'. It was not that the UN would 'go broke' without the Irish contribution being made early, but with the UN under such 'very fierce attack', Ireland ought to make this 'gesture of confidence'.[46]

The method of financing UNFICYP, however, resulted in an attempt to adopt a much more prominent Irish position on the question of finances which emphasised both the government's conception of what a good peacekeeper should be and the price they were prepared to pay to sustain it. In order to avoid either a Soviet or a French veto on the establishment of this force and to avoid a deepening of the financial crisis and increase in the UN debt, it was agreed in the Security Council that UNFICYP should be funded by the contributors themselves and voluntary subscriptions. The Irish response was to refuse any financial support from the voluntary fund because this, according to Aiken, constituted an 'unwise departure' from the UN's principle of 'collective responsibility'. He went on to say that Ireland would pay the usual overseas allowances for its troops and 'accept no reimbursement from the United Nations unless it was levied on all the members...in the normal way'.[47]

Not only was this lapse of collective responsibility bad for the UN, however, but also, as the government pointed out, it was bad for Irish interests. According to Lemass, the government did not wish anyone to think that Ireland's provision of troops for the Cyprus operation was 'conditional in any way on this or that country making a voluntary contribution to the funds'.[48] And Aiken, speaking later in 1964 at the UN General Assembly, made this point clearer by saying that it was vital for a small country like Ireland that the status of its UN troops should be 'clear and unequivocal'. This meant that they should be financially dependent only on the Irish Exchequer and 'funds contributed under the regular assessment procedure' by all the members of the UN.[49]

Clearly, the Irish government was concerned about the safety of Irish troops being threatened by any question mark over the status of the force in which they were participating. They were also very sensitive about adopting measures which would contribute to the *de facto* acceptance of the emergency procedures by which the UN was being kept running. The major considerations of national interest, however, which led the government into accepting what Aiken called a 'heavy financial burden' were brought to the fore by the specific crisis in Cyprus rather than the ongoing one at the UN.

As has been remarked above, the Irish government was cautious about getting involved in the Cyprus problem and not just because of the difficulties they had experienced in the Congo. As a reflection of this caution, indeed, Aiken had spoken in April 1964 of 'conditions' which had been laid down for Irish participation in the force. The force should be used for maintaining the peace only, not mediating in or shaping a settlement. The governments of Britain, Greece and Turkey were to give assurances that they would not intervene and would not impose a settlement. The Greek and Turkish troops on the island should be put, if possible, under UN command, and if the operation lasted longer than three months, then other countries should be asked for soldiers and financial support and the Irish government should be free to withdraw its contingent.[50]

What was worrying the government were the risks of forceful external intervention and settlements imposed from outside Cyprus. The most likely imposed settlement would have been a partition of the island and the Irish government had made it clear that it wanted no part of that, should it occur. According to Lemass, there was little similarity between the Irish problem and the problem in Cyprus, but 'if anybody wants to solve an international problem anywhere by means of partition, he must not come to us for a recommendation for it'.[51] The other difficulty was that the Cyprus operation exhibited a marked tendency towards looking like a NATO affair. The original dispute had been fuelled by the tension between two NATO allies, Greece and Turkey. Another NATO country, Britain, was central to the peacekeeping operation, providing both troops and logistical support from its bases on the island. Indeed, a NATO peacekeeping force had originally been proposed for the island when the British had declared that they could no longer control the rival communities by themselves. On top of all this, the voluntary funding arrangements meant that UNFICYP was principally financed by the United States, West Germany and Britain.

As constraints upon the foreign policy of a small state, one might have expected that these considerations would have resulted in the Irish government either refusing to participate in the Cyprus force, or accepting the funding policy and pleading that necessity ruled over principle as a defence against domestic opposition. A refusal to participate might have been justifiable. Irish troops were, after all, still in the Congo. The circumstances of the Cyprus problem, however, made it very difficult to formulate a response based upon expediency with regard to participation. The appeal for UN troops had come

59

from the government of a small, European state proclaiming its non-alignment and struggling to assert its independence in the face of external threats, the possibility of partition and the very concrete presence of the former colonial power manifested in the sovereign bases. The actual and potential similarities with the Irish situation were too obvious to ignore.

Further, peacekeeping itself was in danger of failing. Aiken argued in the General Assembly that if small states relinquished the power to mount peacekeeping operations when the Security Council failed to act, then this would

> be regarded as sure proof that we did not deserve to have it and that we failed in our duty to the peoples of the smaller States, and indeed the common people of the great states as well.[52]

This being so, it would have been very difficult for Ireland to refuse to join the peacekeeping force. Having decided to participate, the next question facing the government was what policy to adopt with regard to the funding of the force. Taking the money and keeping quiet risked a domestic attack upon the credibility of the government's position. Prior to the announcement of the policy, one Deputy had warned the government to beware American and British generosity in financial support, but this line of attack was not developed as a consequence of subsequent policy. Indeed, other speakers from the left who might have been expected to echo this criticism and to applaud the government on the policy it decided to adopt, suggested that they should not be too proud to take money from any source.[53]

An orthodox view of the way in which the governments of small states respond to the demands of the external environment and attempt to reconcile their own goals and values with these external demands and domestic constraints, might suggest that the Irish would have participated in the force and accepted the method of funding. Common wisdom would indicate, and subsequent events were to show, that as the government of a small, relatively poor state, they would find it easier to justify taking 'dirty money' for good deeds rather than taking no money at all. The policy priority would be in taking up the chance to do something concrete and smoothing over the obstacles to taking that opportunity. It would not be in locating that concrete action in the context of a broad, directed external strategy called 'Irish foreign policy'. Indeed, a 'passive' consistency could have been used to justify Ireland's participation in UNFICYP, in that in so acting, the government more or less remained consistent to their principles, helped a small country, pleased the Western Powers, contributed to international peace and security and offended no one in particular.

The decision to participate in the force and, more importantly, to adopt the funding policy which they did, suggest that the Irish government did not see themselves as being in an essentially passive position. The Cyprus policy was

60

not a classic small state compromise between a series of competing demands, but rather an attempt to commit domestic policy resources to assertive action with conditions, consistent with and supportive of Ireland's international role as the government saw it. As such, it demonstrated the extent to which the Irish government were prepared to go in support of their foreign policy. The refusal to accept reimbursement from the voluntary fund, Aiken argued in 1965, entailed that the UN owed Ireland £500,000. Fabian estimates the total cost of the policy to Ireland as being around $2 million.[54]

The funding policy was a central component of what became a distinctively Irish approach to the problems of UN peacekeeping. This approach was characterised by a refusal to acquiesce in accepting temporary measures to keep UN forces operating which, it was considered, either eroded their integrity as truly impartial international forces or deflected the efforts of the members of the UN away from addressing the fundamental problems in the peacekeeping process. On these grounds, the Irish government rejected the efforts taken by some supporters of peacekeeping to improve readiness among themselves, outside the UN. 'Preparedness', Aiken argued, in terms of earmarking units as standby forces for the UN, was too expensive, and given the size of the Irish army, the whole force would have had to be so designated if it were to make logistical sense.[55] Fabian argues that, *de facto*, this was already the case, and the Irish government apparently had no desire to formalise this state of affairs. As the Minister for Defence argued, the use of international police forces might be becoming more popular, but this was not a reason for Ireland to maintain forces at its own expense 'for no other purpose than to maintain peace all over the world', particularly if this might be construed as acquiescence in the existing UN *ad hocery*.[56]

While the funding policy serves as an example of the extent to which the Irish government was prepared to go in support of its foreign policy, however, its fate indicates both the internal and external limitations which constrain such a policy. Ireland's refusal to accept voluntary contributions had been announced in April 1964. By June 1965, the policy had been abandoned and in the following October the Taoiseach announced to the Dáil that the Secretary General had agreed to reimburse Ireland from the voluntary fund.[57]

There are a number of reasons for this change in policy. First, it was during the period of self-denial that the peak of the financial crisis at the UN was reached and passed. It could be argued by the Irish government that now the members of the UN were taking steps to solve the problems of the institution, there was no longer any need to maintain their refusal to accept financing from the voluntary contributions. The problem with this argument, however, was that the kind of solution achieved at the UN was not consistent with the Irish policy of insisting on firm adherence to the obligations taken under the Charter by all members and strict enforcement of the provisions of the Charter against all those who did not comply. Rather, the members of the UN, and in particular the superpowers, had agreed to postpone their disagreements and maintain the *ad hoc* approach to problem-solving which had emerged, while a special committee on peacekeeping examined the international security functions of the UN in a calmer atmosphere and, as it turned out, at great length.

It was clear, however, that the Irish funding policy was serving no useful purpose other than that of internal consistency. No other country contributing soldiers to UNFICYP, including the neutrals, followed the Irish line. They preferred, rather, to emphasise the importance of getting UN troops into the field over everything except the safety of their own men and the certainty of financial support, from no matter where, for their efforts. Indeed, it may be argued that in the context of both the drama of the Cyprus crisis and the general drift towards pragmatic rather than political-legal solutions to the financial crisis of the UN, it is doubtful whether the funding policy made much of any impact on anybody at all.

The priority of maintaining the internal consistency of Irish foreign policy might have enabled this stance to be persevered with despite external indifference, however, except for the intrusion of considerations from outside the realm of foreign policy conceived in political terms only. The problem was that while the policy may have met with only indifference abroad, there was a hostile reaction to it at home, particularly from sources within the government.[58] In the absence of achievements of substance, it was hard to argue against the assertion that scarce resources were being expended for little more than a point of principle. It was this kind of argument that was put forward by the then Minister of Finance, Jack Lynch. In an interview for this book, he suggested that much of Irish foreign policy could be characterised by the efforts of governments to play a part – the part of 'good boys' – at the risk of offending other governments and in circumstances 'where it did not always serve them well'. While generally approving of this willingness, he indicated that he had argued at the time that the funding policy, which he associated with the Foreign Minister, was taking things a little too far.

Such opposition, in that one would expect the representative of the Department of Finance in the cabinet routinely to voice caution and hostility with regard to points of principle which cost money, was hardly significant. Indeed, the Finance Minister had also voiced reservations concerning certain aspects of participation in the Congo force. (It may be noted here that he had also had experience of the principled aspects of Irish foreign policy when he was Ireland's representative to the International Labour Organisation.[59] It became significant, however, in the context of the increasing difficulties confronting the Irish government in other aspects of its external relations.

Ireland's role as an 'international good citizen' was the product of the efforts of the government during 1957–66 period. Nevertheless, the performance of the role was dependent upon the international system, in the sense that the latter provided both opportunities and a favourable climate for middle power activism. By the mid-1960s, the system was developing in a direction which reduced the opportunities for such activity. Most of the problems associated with the decolonisation and disintegration of formal empires had been resolved. The United States and the Soviet Union were beginning to manage their own conflict and competition directly and the limited potential of 'preventive diplomacy' as practised by the UN Secretariat and its middle power allies had been clearly exposed. The international organisation principle of functionalism, even on an *ad hoc* basis, had only a very limited application in the resolution of international disputes and as the efforts of the UN in this regard became politicised, as they usually did, then their attractiveness to the governments of small states as a relatively safe way of obtaining political prestige declined.

This is not to say, however, that the opportunities for pursuing an 'independence' policy in the international system declined. Rather, the choices which confronted the Irish government came more sharply into focus and, therefore, more risky. For example, another definition of the 'independent' role, that of the 'Non-Aligned' or Afro-Asian bloc, was becoming more important and it embodied an attitude to East–West conflict which was both too neutral and too militant for the Irish government.[60] Not only did the governments of these states see both East and West as more or less equally responsible for the threat to peace in the international system, but they were also critical of the UN itself, suggesting that at times it served as an instrument of US foreign policy. Indeed, several of those states whose forces were serving in the Congo had threatened to withdraw in protest at what they saw as the failure of the UN both to support the government of Lumumba and to ensure his personal safety, and some had actually done so.

More embarrassingly for the Irish government, the major threat to international peace by the mid-1960s was clearly the war in Vietnam, but on this, as O'Brien put it, 'the silence was deafening'.[61] The government justified its inaction on Vietnam in the same way that it had on several other cases, for example, Rhodesia and the British intervention in Kuwait. They would act only if there was a prospect of some success. The role of Ireland's mission at the UN, according to Aiken, was not to exhaust its energies denouncing every injustice but 'to make constructive contributions to the search for true peace'. Speaking about Rhodesia, he had argued that Ireland quite simply was not in a position 'to ensure round the world that every man will have a vote and that the votes will be of equal value'. In the case of Vietnam, therefore, because there was no agreement in the Security Council or the General Assembly, all that the Irish and other small countries could do was to 'hope that all the states involved will be wise enough to negotiate a settlement'.[62]

Not only was the international system providing fewer opportunities for international role-playing, however, but also, the attention of the government was being drawn to other external matters, the potential consequences of which were far more important and immediate. As a result of the failure of the British application to join the EEC, Irish trading policy and economic policy and planning had been formulated on the government's own admission in conditions of increasing uncertainty. In particular, the Irish economy had been shaken by the British decision not to exempt Ireland from a temporary 15 per cent surcharge levied on all imports in the autumn of 1964. By November of the following year, the government was presenting a picture of an economy confronted by an increasing balance of payments deficit, trade imbalances and inflation. In such an environment, the criticisms offered by the Department of Finance became much more compelling. From this point until 1969, Ireland's UN policy was increasingly restricted to the elaboration of complex schemes by which the political control and financial support of peacekeeping operations might be put on a firmer footing, addressed to the General Assembly as a whole and the Peacekeeping Committee in particular.[63] At the same time, the attention of the government was drawn away from the political foreign policy of international activism towards managing problems in Ireland's external, economic relations. Their efforts in this regard will be examined in the next chapter.

Notes

1. The public figures interviewed for this book were Conor Cruise O'Brien, Brian Lenihan, Liam Cosgrave and Jack Lynch.
2. For examples, see 191, 481-2; 208, 849; and 214, 197.
3. Aiken, 167, 26-7 (15 April 1958).
4. 184, 1017 (16 November 1960).
5. 208, 849.
6. See 184, 992-6 for details of this issue.
7. 159, 144.
8. O'Brien, in a private interview.
9. 159, 622.
10. For Dillon, see 164, 1196 and 1202. James Dillon was a prominent spokesman for Fine Gael and later lead the party in opposition. He was the only member of the Dáil openly to oppose Irish neutrality during the Second World War. For Costello, see 164, 1226. (All these comments are from a debate on a motion to disapprove the foreign policy of the government in November, 1957.)
11. 159, 148.
12. 164, 1202.
13. See 164, 1256 for de Valera; 176, 663-4 for Lemass; and 176, 715 for Aiken on the value of the UN.
14. See for an account of US pressure on Ireland's delegation to the UN, Conor Cruise O'Brien, *To Katanga and Back*, Hutchinson, London, 1962, p.17. See 164, 1168-78 for Aiken's disengagement proposals and opposition thereto.
15. 194, 1387 and 208, 1109. The 'kicking' and 'stabbing' section is taken from Aiken quoting Dillon.
16. 191, 565 (11 July 1961).
17. See Norman J. D. MacQueen, 'Irish Neutrality: The United Nations and the Peacekeeping Experience, 1945–69', unpublished doctoral thesis, New University of Ulster, 1981, pp. 136 and 212–15 for this view of the Aiken/Cosgrave differences, also shared by O'Brien in an interview. See John Peck, *Dublin From Downing Street*, Gill and Macmillan, Dublin, 1978, for the 'Isle of Wight syndrome'.

18. 190, 1097.
19. See 182, 800 for Aiken's justification of his approach; and 163, 597, for Costello's view of Aiken's style. See 185, 174, for details of the Congo vote.
20. See 164, 1232 for the reference to the treatment of priests in China; see 164, 1190 for the selections from American newspapers; and see 176, 703 for comments on Aiken's absence from the funeral of Pope Pius.
21. See Larry Fabian, *Soldiers Without Enemies,* Brookings Institution, 1971, p. 16 for the definition of peacekeeping. See Brian Urquhart's *Hammarskjold,* The Bodley Head, London, 1973, for a discussion of the Secretary-General's approach to preventive diplomacy.
22. Keatinge (1978), op. cit., pp. 158-9; and Raymond Smith, *Under the Blue Flag,* Aherlow Publishers, Dublin, 1980, pp. 233-4. UN forces are commonly known by their acronyms, ONUC for the Congo force and UNFICYP for the one in Cyprus.
23. See Fabian, op. cit., 1971, p.158, for these details. See Smith, ibid., pp. 12-13 for details on UN command and staff positions held by the Irish army.
24. MacQueen, op. cit., p. 7. See also 185, 987 for Lemass's claim that Ireland's acceptance of these casualties without calls for the withdrawal of the contingent was a sign of the nation's 'maturity'.
25. Smith, ibid., pp. 80–2, 125.
26. See Keatinge (1978), op. cit., p. 161.
27. Hammarskjold's four principles for the successful operation of peacekeeping forces were as follows: host state consent to the force; non-controversial troops only to participate; no involvement in the political affairs of the host state; and, the use of force only in self-defence. For a brief account of these, see James A. Stengenga, *The United Nations Force in Cyprus,* Ohio State UP,1968, pp. 10-11. See also Hammarskjold's *Summary Study of the Experience Derived from the Establishment and Operation of the Force,* UN Doc. A/3943, 9 October 1958.
28. Alan James, *The Politics of Peacekeeping,* Praeger, London, 1969, remains a useful analysis of the peacekeeping experience.
29. 183, 1901-2 (20 July 1960).
30. 185, 170-2 (23 November 1960).
31. See 185, 982 for the general formulation, and 185, 780 for the more specific one.
32. Dillon made the inquiry, 185, 786. For the reply see 185, 982.
33. See 208, 1060-96 (7 April 1964) for these points.
34. See185, 982 for Lemass's argument about avoiding remarks n the Dáil which would single the Irish troops in the Congo out for special treatment. See 195, 984 for his statement of the credentials problem. Lemass also used this argument to oppose the idea of sending a parliamentary delegation to the Congo.
35. See 185, 1345.
36. Smith, op. cit., p.141.
37. For details of this episode from a variety of points of view, see O'Brien (1962), op. cit.; Urquhart, op. cit.; and MacQueen, op. cit.
38. See, for example, 192, 1242 and 1322-27 (6 December 1961).
39. See 192, 1245 for Lemass's view. See MacQueen, op. cit., p. 259, for the attitudes of Aiken and Mac Eoin to the episode.
40. See 186, 908-9.
41. For an account of the financial difficulties of the UN see Fabian, op. cit., pp. 140-1, 190-2. At the start of the crisis in 1964, the USSR and ten other countries were in arrears on 'peacekeeping dues'.
42. See details in James M. Boyd, *United Nations Peacekeeping Operations: A Military and Political Appraisal,* Praeger, NY, pp. 161-85.
43. The United Nations Emergency Force was established in 1956 to facilitate the withdrawal

of British, French and Israeli troops from Egypt and to clear the Suez Canal. See Indar Jit Rikhye, Michael Harbottle and Bjorn Egge, *The Thin Blue Line: International Peacekeeping and its Future*, Yale UP, New Haven, 1974, for case studies of peacekeeping operations.

44. Aiken in Open Debate, 1142 plenary meeting of the General Assembly (17th session) 4 October 1962, cited in Aiken, op. cit., p. 8.
45. Aiken, ibid., p. 13.
46. 186, 846 and 902 (23 February 1961).
47. 208, 1063 (7 April 1964).
48. 208, 1093.
49. Aiken, 1295 plenary G.A. (19th session), 8 December 1964, cited in *Ireland at the UN: Speeches by Frank Aiken,* Dublin, p. 10.
50. 208, 1061, (7 April 1964).
51. Lemass, 208 1098-9 (7 April 1964).
52. Aiken (1964), op. cit., p. 7.
53. See, for examples, 208, 896-7 and 1083.
54. 214, 201; and Fabian, op. cit., p.161.
55. For details of UN 'preparedness' measures, see Fabian, ibid. For an account of the measures to be taken by contributing states, see Alistair Taylor, David Cox and Jack Granatstein (eds), *Peacekeeping: the International Challenge and the Canadian Response*, Canadian Institute of International Affairs, Toronto, 1968. For Aiken's argument about the expense, see 208, 1116.
56. Bartley, 214, 159 (9 March 1965).
57. 218, 14.
58. See Keatinge (1978), op. cit., p. 160 for this.
59. Lynch recalled in the interview that he had voiced the doubts of his own department with regard to Ireland's participation in peacekeeping. See also B. Farrell, *Chairman or Chief? The Role of the Taoiseach in Irish Government,* Gill and MacMillan, Dublin, 1971, p. 72, for a reference to Lemass's handling of doubts within the cabinet regarding Ireland's participation in the Congo force.
60. An indication of the Irish attitude to the Non-Aligned position on the Congo may be obtained from Aiken's response to questions in the Dáil regarding a march by Afro-Asian students on the Belgian embassy in Dublin and the ensuing scuffles with the police; 186, 710 (15 February 1961).
61. See 'O'Brien' in Edwards, op. cit., pp. 131-3 for this point; and MacQueen, op. cit., p. 326, for some comments on it.
62. See 176, 693 for the role of the UN mission, 196, 1460 for the Rhodesian policy; 191, 961–2 for Lemass justifying silence on Britain's intervention in Kuwait, and 216, 479 for Aiken speaking on Vietnam in 1965.
63. See MacQueen, op. cit., pp. 301-27.

5 'Political' foreign policy and 'economic' external affairs: Ireland, Europe and Britain, 1956–66

To this point, I have argued that, between 1956 and 1966, Irish governments created and pursued a foreign policy involving the performance of a role as an 'international good citizen'. This role was derived from the components of an asserted Irish national identity as a small and (hence) law-abiding, independent, Christian, Catholic, Western country. It was manifested in a number of international servicing functions carried out under UN auspices and concerned with the reduction of tensions and conflict between and within states. These actions were given coherence by the development of a certain kind of foreign policy style which presented Ireland as a model of dedicated, principled, selfless and indeed self-denying, international behaviour which others might do well to emulate.

The purpose of the policy taken as a whole was to procure prestige for Ireland and, on the basis of that, diplomatic influence. Much of it was necessarily declaratory in nature but, as I argued in the previous chapter, the Irish government was prepared to absorb considerable domestic criticism and commit substantial resources in support of the policy. However, while the policy was comprehensive in that, through it, the government sought to present

67

Ireland as a coherent and distinctive actor on the international stage, it was by no means so comprehensive in terms of the issues and interests to which it was directed. In particular, the thrust of foreign policy in the direction of the UN virtually excluded all aspects of relations with Britain and the rest of Europe and, hence, matters pertaining to the economy, foreign trade or, in a direct sense, Partition.

It was not that these aspects of Ireland's external affairs were considered unimportant. Indeed, the instrumentalist formulation of the policy of prestige, implied that there were such interests, in support of which the Irish government wished to accumulate usable influence. They were dealt with separately, however, primarily because the Irish government accepted the distinction (made in Chapter 2) between the 'high' political concerns of foreign policy and the 'low' economic preoccupations of the rest of their external affairs. This was so because most of the political elite had been participants in, or were the products of, a struggle for national independence that had not resulted in a revolutionary transformation of social or economic relations either within Ireland or between it and Britain. Further, they represented the triumph of that section of the nationalist movement which had regarded political independence as sufficient to their purpose. As a consequence, Irish economic policy since independence had come to be characterised by two assumptions. The first was that problems of economic development, whether internal or external in their origin, could be 'solved' by using political independence to create a favourable environment in which the Irish economy might prosper. In the policy of fostering domestic industries behind tariff barriers, for example, the role of the government had been to enforce a separation between sectors of economic life in Ireland and the world outside. The second assumption was that Irish economic policy ought to be about discreetly managing the established links with the British economy to Ireland's best advantage. Indeed, the one extended attempt to mobilise economic instruments of policy in the pursuit of 'external' objectives during the 'tariff wars' had been both costly and unsuccessful.

In contrast to the government's approach to Ireland's political foreign policy, therefore, which was assertive, reformist, strategic and global in its scope, their approach to its external economic affairs was essentially reactive, conservative, piecemeal and localised. As such, this approach was satisfactory from the government's point of view so long as they remained happy with their existing trading relationships ('happy' in this case meaning that while they could imagine being worse off, the government could not conceive of a realisable situation in which Ireland would be better off), and so long as these relationships remained stable. The problem for the government during this period was that Ireland's established trading relationships became very unstable, largely as a result of efforts to set up a European trading bloc, or blocs, which were being undertaken at the time. The economic question with which this confronted the Irish government was that given probable British participation in whatever arrangements finally emerged, how were they to preserve Ireland's preferential access to the British market while at the same time avoiding, or at least slowing down, the process of granting reciprocal rights of access to Britain, and more importantly to other countries which might be in the same trading group as Britain and Ireland.

Their difficulties were compounded, however, by the fact that the moves towards some conception of European unity did not conform to the government's own distinction between political and economic policy. These efforts were pursued not so much by discreet negotiations as by international conferences and public speculation on 'grand designs' embracing all of Western Europe and, failing that, the formation of trading groups characterised by reciprocal benefits offered by the members of each group to one another. In this process, it often seemed as though the high political problems of Anglo-French rivalry, and a broader concern for peace and security within Western Europe, took precedence over the issues of economic integration and eventually political cooperation. As a result, the lack of Irish influence in this process and the irrelevance of their foreign policy to it were clearly demonstrated.

It was in the consequences of this 'politicising' of European economic cooperation, rather than in the more narrowly diplomatic risks courted by the 'independent' stance, that the real external costs of international role-playing were incurred. Some of the diplomatic problems have been mentioned already. On issues of decolonisation, the government's sympathy towards the position of newly-emerging nations made disagreements with the former imperial powers highly likely. On issues of East–West relations, the Irish government did, on occasion, incur the displeasure of the United States.[1] These policies did not really entail precise external costs in the sense that those who were offended retaliated in any concrete manner. One reason for this is that it would be rather difficult to take such measures against a government whose efforts to be a 'good UNer' rather than pursuit of more narrow national interests, had given cause to offend. Another, more likely reason was that the Irish effort was in itself not important enough to be singled out since it was always part of some broader UN effort which was regarded as troublesome.[2]

The diplomatic costs to the Irish government, therefore, were not in terms of concrete acts of retaliation but in the bringing to bear of more intangible 'diplomatic pressure', often through indirect channels like editorials in authoritative newspapers or comments from authoritative public figures abroad. The effect of this process was neither to punish nor to modify Irish behaviour, but rather to emphasise the limits within which it was undertaken. Often, the external loss implied by such diplomatic pressure was compensated for by the domestic support for the government which it might engender, for example, when foreign sources criticised the conduct of Irish soldiers in peacekeeping operations.

The political nature of European cooperation, in contrast, created major problems for Irish foreign policy-makers. On the one hand, the objective of this policy had been to create and sustain an international role for Ireland as an active independent, drawing on its colonial past and its revisionist objectives, as well as its Western and Christian orientation, to substantiate this claim. On the other, the developments in Europe created another image of Ireland, that of a small, poor country, the government of which was finally giving up the struggle for autarkic development behind protective tariffs and surrendering to the realities of its external, economic circumstances. Their response was given respectability by the announcement of a long-term strategy by which Ireland would pay for its imports by developing a competitive, export-oriented economy, a change which became known as the 'Whitaker Revolution'. In the short-term, however, it amounted to a search for safety by joining whatever was available in terms of economic arrangements, on the best terms possible, and because Britain at first rejected, and then was refused, entry to the EEC, the extent to which the Irish government depended upon what its British counterpart decided to do was demonstrated at length.

External economic affairs did not spring into existence as a policy issue for Ireland with the British decision to apply for EEC membership. Even the great debate of 1956 on Ireland's admission to the UN went beyond trying to decide which of Cosgrave's three principles should be emphasised. There was a clear consensus existing across party lines that the government ought to pursue an active foreign policy there. Nearly everyone was willing to discuss it in terms of the broad issues of international peace and security, the concerns of high politics as I have defined the latter. Nevertheless, one can also detect a sense of uncertainty as to whether such terms of reference were actually appropriate to the policy of a small country like Ireland. These two sentiments were not expressed by two distinct groups of people espousing the particular emphases. Rather, both themes re-occurred in the speeches of particular individuals.

For example, Sean MacBride, who himself had been Minister of External Affairs in the inter-party government just after the Second World War, began by emphasising the economic aspects of foreign policy. There were, he said, very few of the 'old type of diplomat left in any foreign service', as the important concerns were now with economics, trade, tourism and acquiring 'democratic good will in other countries'. Foreign policy, he argued by way of example, was about getting the French to accept Irish periwinkles and he suggested a scheme of cash bonuses for Irish representatives who increased Ireland's trade with the countries or areas to which they were accredited. It was not that power politics were unimportant, however, but that Ireland lacked the economic, technical and scientific resources to contribute on what he called 'the material plane'. Hence, he argued, Ireland's contribution was to be made on the moral plane, a moral counter to a materialist world (the need for a contribution of some sort was assumed), and a speech which began by emphasising periwinkles soon moved to discussing Irish foreign policy in terms of a strategic choice between the UN or the Council of Europe. He preferred the latter as it had a parliamentary, as well as governmental, dimension which would tend to dampen down the role of power politics in favour of democratic values.[3]

Similarly, de Valera argued that while it was hard to put a cash value on the returns of having a foreign service, the government and the service itself should pursue the country's interests 'in any respect, not merely in culture but in trade'. Further, because Ireland could not afford to have representation everywhere, his own government had operated on the principle of committing significant resources to a few chosen countries. His list of priorities for overseas representation, however, consisted of the Vatican (and none dared gainsay him), the United States, the United Kingdom and 'perhaps' France, the 'door' to Europe. He too talked of the strategic choice between membership in the UN or the Council of Europe (he favoured the former).[4]

Even those backbenchers who throughout the period managed to keep up a sustained barrage of criticism regarding the pretentious tendencies of Irish foreign policy were rarely able to remain consistent with the implications of their own criticism. Deputies Browne and McQuillan, in particular, frequently attacked both the foreign policy of the government and the foreign policy establishment itself as extravagances which Ireland could not afford, while at the same time arguing that the government was not prepared to pursue its independent policy with sufficient vigour. In the 1956 debate, McQuillan asserted that Ireland had

> greater pretensions to grandeur than the British Empire itself...[and that]...a little bit of the Spartan outlook would be no harm at all when it comes to the question of alleged prestige.

The Department of External Affairs, he argued, should give value for the money spent on embassies and parties by promoting foreign trade, and the government should cease in its pronouncements on the situation in the Soviet Union or events in the Middle East. What was needed was a more 'realistic' foreign policy designed to earn the respect of small nations by offering 'our criticisms equally of all nations'![5]

The real problem for both of these deputies was not really that the whole idea of pursuing a foreign policy was a pretension that the Irish could not afford. Rather, it was that the government was not pursuing the particular policy which they wanted; namely, one which emphasised the problem of Partition and adopted a position much closer to that of the members of the Non-Aligned Movement. In this sense their activities serve as a typical (although the best developed) example of the way in which uneasiness about having a foreign policy as such was exploited to oppose particular policies. Each instance was, no doubt, a product of tactical considerations, in the sense that an accusation of wasting money would be regarded as a broader standard for rallying opposition than an articulation of particular preferences. The effect, however, was to maintain throughout the period some doubt about the necessity of pursuing a political foreign policy at all.

There were good reasons why this existed. While the government worked throughout the period to establish and sustain Ireland's international role and called this foreign policy, much of the day-to-day business was far less dramatic. The more trivial or absurd aspects of the concern with prestige have already been remarked upon in the previous chapter. It may be noted here that such considerations occasionally played a part in Ireland's external affairs more broadly conceived. For example, Ireland's reputation as a law-abiding nation was cited by a government spokesman as a reason for refusing to pursue a policy similar to Luxembourg's regarding the transmission of radio broadcasts, and the Taoiseach could get into trouble for allegedly demeaning the reputation of Irish meats abroad by including low-grade beef which Ireland exported to the United States for use in sausages, salamis and other processed meat products in the statistics on Ireland's beef exports.[6] But this, as much as peacekeeping in the Congo or working on proposals to avert nuclear proliferation, was the stuff of Irish external affairs. While Aiken could be in the thick of things in the committees of the General Assembly, he still had to return home to field questions on such matters as the need for a consulate at Lourdes and what exactly he intended to do about the inability of British Railways to run a punctual service between Holyhead and Liverpool.[7] In the 'great debate' of 1956, once the front benches had had their say, the discussion soon shifted around to the hardy perennials of fish, the government's responsibility for the material, and failing that, moral welfare of Irish youth in Britain, and what steps the Irish government was taking to put pressure on the British to return the body of Roger Casement to Ireland.[8]

The government, however, developed a general division of labour during the period in which the Department of External Affairs looked after the 'international milieu', largely UN matters, while the Taoiseach and his department dealt with matters pertaining to Northern Ireland, and the Taoiseach and the 'economic departments', largely Finance, Industry and Commerce, but also Agriculture and Fisheries, were concerned with British and European relations.[9] This division was manifested in a number of ways, for example, by the number, distribution and destination of trips abroad taken by leading figures in the government. From data presented to the Dáil regarding the number of foreign trips undertaken by senior ministers between 1957 and 1961, it may be seen that from a total of 115 trips lasting 856 days, the Minister for External Affairs made 27 visits for a total of 396 days. He was closely followed by the Ministers for Industry and Commerce during the period who logged a total of 26 trips, but lasting only 107 days. From these figures alone, it may be seen that Aiken had no monopoly of the external contacts undertaken at ministerial level by the government.

From a breakdown of similar figures given for the shorter period 1957–60, however, it may be seen that of a total of 18 trips abroad taken by the Minister for External Affairs, four were made to Britain, one to the United States accompanying the Irish president on a state visit, nine to either the Council of Europe or OEEC meetings and four to the UN. It should be remarked, however, that the four trips to the UN lasted a total of four and a half months and that the Minister took no trips to European capitals other than London (two of these being for cultural purposes). The Ministers for Industry and Commerce managed 19 trips between them, five to Britain to discuss economic matters and trade, ten to European capitals again for economic discussions, three to the US inaugurating airline services and one to an OEEC meeting. Of a total of 26 ministerial trips to Britain, the Minister for External Affairs was responsible for only four. Of a total of 18 trips to European capitals (as distinct from Council of Europe or OEEC meetings) he was responsible for none.[10]

While some of these foreign visits may be regarded as having little political significance, for example, it was regarded as 'form' for an Irish representative of ministerial status to be present at major Irish and Catholic events in Britain, with others this was clearly not the case. The trips to Europe, for example, were undertaken at a time of important negotiations regarding the entry of Britain and Ireland into the EEC, and the Minister for External Affairs did not become involved in these until the need for salvaging operations in 1963,[11] nor was he involved in the final negotiations of the Anglo-Irish free trade area in 1965. In his report to the Dáil on these meetings, Lemass made it clear that it was the Ministers for Finance, Industry and Commerce, and Agriculture who had accompanied him to Britain.[12]

This division of labour was also reflected in the procedure of the Dáil. Routinely, European matters were dealt with in the estimates for the Department of the Taoiseach or Industry and Commerce, and questions on these matters would be fielded by spokesmen for these departments or by the Taoiseach himself. On one occasion during the period, Lemass asked a deputy to refrain from asking a question on Ireland's participation in GATT negotiations until the Minister of Finance made a statement which would include a 'general survey' of Ireland's external trade relations. On at least two occasions, the chairman of the Dáil cautioned deputies speaking to the External Affairs estimate that in touching on problems concerning foreign trade, loans and export stimulation, they were not addressing matters which fell within the estimate.[13] Perhaps the most striking evidence of this division was in the way the Minister for External Affairs presented his estimate to the Dáil, beginning with a review of the year. For example, in 1961 he managed to speak of Europe only in connection with a UN conference in Switzerland, contributing to a cultural fund for Romanesque art in Spain and the Irish drafting of a successful resolution on the Austro-Italian dispute over South Tyrol. This was the day after a major debate following a statement by the Taoiseach on the questions of EEC membership and the formation of the OECD, in which the future of Ireland and the whole meaning of the struggle for independence had been discussed in very painful terms.[14] Similarly, he spoke to the 1963 estimate, dealing with Ireland's membership of the Security Council and the financial difficulties of the UN but not mentioning Europe, less than three months after de Gaulle's veto had brought about the failure of Ireland's application to join the EEC.[15]

A number of explanations have been offered for this division of labour by other students of Irish foreign policy. MacQueen, for example, sees it largely as a 'rationalisation of personal interests'.[16] The people interviewed certainly confirmed the impression of Aiken being a committed internationalist. He was, according to one of them, very serious about the threat of nuclear catastrophe, to the extent that he apparently had nightmares about the subject (although the same source also suggested that he enjoyed 'cutting a fairly significant figure...at the United Nations'). His presentations to the Dáil suggest that Aiken was uninterested in European matters except in so far as they fitted into his conception of Irish role-playing. Keatinge states that personal preferences were also a factor in determining the area of policy reserved for himself by Lemass. Before becoming Taoiseach he had been the Minister for Industry and Commerce and had 'chaired the cabinet committee...which finally accepted the change from protection to free trade'.[17]

Personal preferences, however, important though they may be in a small policy process such as that of Ireland, are derived from perceptions of the nature and the importance of the issues being dealt with. De Valera had attempted to retain offices of both Taoiseach and Minister of External Affairs for himself for as long as possible, because he considered them to be the two most important positions in the government.[18] According to Keatinge, the preference of Lemass for retaining control of his area of policy when he became Taoiseach coincided with the taking root of the notion that 'the economy was there to be directed' and that the 'era of "big government" had arrived'[19] External relations, or their economic aspects at least, were now, presumably, too important to be left to the diplomats.

A final perspective on the idea of perceived importance of issues is offered by O'Brien. He suggests that Ireland's external economic policy (largely concerned with 'Europe' at the time), like all policy as far as an elected government is concerned, was handled in accordance with its perceived electoral significance. Thus the EEC was important as a 'Common Market', not 'Community', issue, because it was in these terms that it became electorally significant and significant in the press.[20] Both Keatinge's and O'Brien's interpretations suggest an emergent or established primacy of economic considerations in government policy-making. The former offers a picture of 'big government' managing the affairs of the national society as a whole, or an era, at least, in which such ideas, if not the facts suggested by them, achieved considerable
prominence. The latter focuses on a democratic 'last instance' in which the preoccupation of the electorate with bread-and-butter issues is the major determinant of how policy is handled.

For the general argument that I wish to make, it is O'Brien's interpretation which is of more interest. It is not so for any theory of electoral democracy which may lie behind it, but for its emphasis on government calculations with regard to how to present an issue. While, for O'Brien, Ireland's European policy was formulated, or at least presented, in accordance with the economic priorities of the electorate, it may be seen that on occasions, questions of sovereignty, political independence and a distinctive, if costly, foreign policy, as well as bread-and-butter issues, had significance for the electorate. The point here is that external economic issues and 'Europe' offered little opportunity for such domestic political gains. Indeed, they offered a picture of Ireland which contradicted the image of Ireland's place in the world elaborated by the government through its foreign policy, and demonstrated the failure of the attempt to purchase influence in external affairs as a whole, through a policy of prestige derived from international role-playing.

It is certainly true that personal preferences, the government's desire to extend their role in the making of major decisions with regard to the operation of the economy, and electoral considerations all played their part in the shaping of this division of labour. But the major cause was the government's decision to find a place for Ireland in the political and economic rearrangements taking place in the rest of Europe and the international economy. Participation in this process gave high salience to the contradiction between the image of a politically independent Ireland going its own way in the world and the actual extent to which external economic relationships characterised by dependence entailed that the major decisions regarding Ireland's future were made beyond its boundaries. The government's response to this was to pursue their political-economic interests abroad as well they might while attempting to maintain a distinction between political independence and economic dependence, between foreign policy and external affairs, in both the making and the presentation of policy.

This procedural and organisational division of labour was reflected in an ideological separation of political foreign policy and economic external affairs. This distinction became more apparent during the period as 'Europe' and Ireland's trading relationships became more salient issues. Prior to their emergence, 'Europe' was dealt with as both a foreign policy and an external affairs issue. Relations with Britain were largely an external affairs matter, although those concerning Northern Ireland were regarded as raising constitutional questions and were, hence, the preserve of the Taoiseach and his office.[21] It will be recalled that during the 1956 debate some speakers appeared to regard the Irish government as having to make some kind of strategic choice between the Council of Europe, and the UN. As an issue of high policy, 'Europe' was seen by some to present itself as a potentially dangerous arena in which the interests of small states might be overlooked. De Valera pointed to the dangers of a future 'United States of Europe' in this respect and there had been the experience of the failure of raising the issue of Partition in the Council

75

in the years following the Second World War. As an arena for low policy, the Council of Europe was regarded favourably as one of the few opportunities for external activities, particularly for Dáil deputies as well as the government, prior to membership of the UN.[22]

As far as the government was concerned, however, only Aiken in his rare pronouncements on European policy continued, throughout the period, to deal with the issue in high political terms. He followed de Valera's lead with regard to his hostility to the emergence of strong European political and economic arrangements and the question of Irish participation. He opposed, for example, British 'grand designs' for a fusion of the Council of Europe and the OEEC and seemed to see it as his task to explain the significance of European developments for Irish problems. Thus, in the 1957 estimate when others were addressing the question of European unity, Aiken could argue that the 'one new development' in Europe, significant both for world peace and Partition, was the demand that had been placed on the USSR to hold a reunification plebiscite in Germany. He hoped that this election would be held and that 'the same principle would be applied to Ireland'.[23] Even in answering the charge, in the aftermath of the failure of the first application to join the EEC, that he had neglected European affairs, Aiken was at pains to express his support for the European 'idea' in terms of its consistency with the aims of Irish foreign policy. Membership of the EEC he argued, was a constitutional matter and, hence, the concern of the Taoiseach. Nevertheless, he had always been a strong supporter of the EEC as 'example to the rest of the world of how neighbours could live in peace and cooperate to develop their resources...'. To this end, in support of the 'Coal and Steel Pact' he had been prepared, as he put it, 'to pay a little bit more in order to see the French and German people getting together and using their steel for peaceful purposes rather than for weapons of war to hurl at each other'.[24] He remained, however, cautious of the extent to which a small state could participate in such developments without putting its own interests at risk, and he tended to emphasise, in a way which was unusual for a government spokesman, that an effective EEC would involve a loss of sovereignty. In such an entity, he argued on one occasion, Ireland would occupy a place similar to that presently occupied by Galway and Cork in Ireland.[25] The only other examples of European policy being treated as high policy (as distinct from the high political implications of EEC membership becoming an issue in domestic political debate) were a couple of pronouncements by spokesmen for the opposition on different occasions to the effect that they would leave European policy alone so that it would not become a domestic 'political football'.[26] Naturally, both declarations of intent were subsequently hugely ignored by all concerned.

The initial response of the government to the movements to create some kind of new European trading system consisted of support in principle tempered by caution over the details. Speaking in 1957 on behalf of the Taoiseach, his parliamentary secretary stated that the important point was that a country should be able to enter the organisation 'without fear of serious damage to its economic fabric'.[27] When the opposition proposed the establishment of a joint select committee to examine the consequences of Ireland's joining or not joining the EEC or a European Free Trade Area, Lemass (as Minister for Industry and Commerce) made it clear that Ireland could not join the Community 'in circumstances in which our nearest neighbour and largest customer remained outside it'.[28]

With the failure of British diplomacy to broaden and dilute the EEC and the consequent decision to establish EFTA in 1959, it became clear that Irish policy was based upon doing anything that would preserve or improve their trading arrangements negotiated with Britain in 1938. These gave Ireland preferential access to British markets and any new arrangements, it was considered, would involve the granting of reciprocal access for others besides Britain to Irish markets. In reply to the argument made by the opposition that Ireland was in danger of being left out of the two emerging trading blocs (and with a very unflattering status at that), Lemass (now Taoiseach) explained that the government had approached both the EEC and the European Free Trade Association (EFTA) with a view to obtaining tariff reductions that the members enjoyed with a temporary suspension of the reciprocal obligations on Ireland's part. They had been unsuccessful in this but, according to Lemass, it was not of critical importance since 'It [was] clear...that in any circumstances our main interest lies in trading with Britain and nothing could conceivably happen in Europe which could alter that situation in any way'.[29] Hence, by 1960, it was established Irish policy that they would not join any economic grouping '...of which Britain, our principal customer in Europe, was not also a member'. Nor, according to Lemass, would they join EFTA, because '...the disadvantages of membership seriously outweighed the advantages so long as we had...tariff-free entry for our products to the British market...'.[30] Quite simply, as Lynch pointed out in retrospect, the EFTA agreement did not take into account agricultural products and would not have improved Ireland's access to the British market while opening up their own to the other members of EFTA.[31] Indeed, EFTA constituted a distinct loss for Ireland in that it would erode their preferential access to the British market *vis-à-vis* other EFTA members, but this loss was blunted, according to the Taoiseach, by the fact that the ten-year transitional period for removing tariffs constituted a period of grace during which Irish industry might adjust to competing on more favourable terms.[32]

While in April 1960, Lemass stated that the maintenance of the arrangements with Britain was the most important consideration, he also argued that the 'best situation' would be one in which both Britain and Ireland became members of the EEC and a satisfactory account was taken of Ireland's circumstances. In the discussion of the transformation and expansion of the OEEC into the OECD in July of 1961 this positioned hardened when the Taoiseach announced that, conditional on the British doing likewise, Ireland wished to become a full member of the EEC (while still hoping for concessions in the process of the negotiations for entry). It would support wholeheartedly the objectives of the Community, participate in Community policy-making and seek to enjoy to the fullest extent the benefits of membership.[33] On 1 August, the day following the British announcement of their intention to apply, the Taoiseach made a similar announcement regarding Ireland.[34]

In doing this, the government acknowleged that membership of the EEC raised, if not problems, then a number of questions for Ireland. In addition to the economic problems of adjustment, there was also the general question of the supranational aspects of the Community and Irish sovereignty, and the particularly Irish problem of how membership of the EEC could be consistent with Ireland's proclaimed stance as an independent neutral. The latter question was raised principally by the political opposition, both in terms of whether Ireland could be a member of anything other than the UN and in terms of whether, once in, Ireland could keep out of the high political exchanges which might be expected to characterise any organisation of which the British and French were both members. In response to such points being made, Lemass argued that the issues raised by joining the EEC were 'primarily of an economic nature'. While there were certain 'political implications', in his opinion these did not make Irish membership of the EEC 'undesirable'.[35]

Whether this was true or not, the immediate objective of Lemass was to deal with the domestic criticisms which suggested that EEC membership involved Ireland in contradictory foreign policy roles. From the left came the voice of conscience suggesting that by such an act the Irish government was either reneging on its active, independent role, or exposing it for the hollow sham it had been all along. For Fine Gael, the point was to demonstrate that the government was at long last returning to its senses or waking up to the realities of Ireland's external circumstances for the first time. In this view, Aiken's 'independence' policy had been a mistake and now constituted an obstacle to the pursuit of Ireland's real interests.[36]

The government's response to the suggestion of a tension between the 'independence' policy and applying for membership of the EEC was to make a bland assertion of their perfect consistency. On being asked the implications of the application for Ireland's UN policy, the Taoiseach replied that it might 'be affected in some degree' but that Ireland's 'general support' for the UN and its 'attitude' on the main issues there would not, 'of course, be changed'.[37]

Indeed, Ireland's particular brand of independence and neutrality were presented as definite assets for the Irish application. Unlike Britain, the Taoiseach had suggested earlier, Ireland presented the members of the Community with no problems regarding ties of sentiment or politico-military commitments in the wider world. Nor did Ireland constitute a threat to the established position of any existing member. More interestingly, if less clearly, he asserted that Ireland did not have

obligations under international agreements or arising out of traditional national policies, such as appear to arise in the case of Switzerland, Austria and Sweden which need cause us to hesitate in accepting the authority of the institutions of the European Economic Community.[38]

With regard to the question of supranationalism, Lemass's position was that it was early days to be worrying over much about a loss of Irish independence, simply because the issue had not been settled in the EEC as yet. Echoing Aiken, he accepted that small countries which entered a union with large countries would have to closely examine the power which was given to the institutions 'to manage the union'. During the discussions which established EFTA, the Irish had argued for a 'unanimity rule', but in a good or fair international organisation, he argued, '...strengthening of the institutions would serve our interests'.[39] Evidently, he regarded the EEC as such an organisation, for about a month later, the day after announcing Ireland's intention to apply for membership, Lemass claimed that a loss of sovereignty was a problem only for major powers. No similar difficulties existed for small states like Ireland, because the establishment of a situation in which interaction was governed by rules rather than bargaining would constitute 'an extension of our freedom rather than the reverse'.[40]

The only exception to this perfect compatibility between Ireland's established foreign policy and the application to join the EEC allowed by the government seemed to be on the question of European defence in the future. On being asked again about the implications of EEC membership for Irish neutrality in October 1962, two days after the Soviet Union had agreed to withdraw its missiles from Cuba, Lemass made a reply which stressed both anti-Communism and Christianity as basic characteristics of Ireland. He argued that the country had always supported the bringing together of the people of Europe; it had been a member of the OEEC and the Council of Europe to that end, and that, while Ireland had not joined NATO, it had 'always agreed with the aim of that Treaty'. Indeed, by December of that year, he was arguing that Ireland's neutrality consisted only of the absence of a 'contractual obligation' to become involved in a war. If such a war were to occur between 'the Western democracies and the Communist powers', then Ireland would be 'clearly on the democratic side', and everybody, West and East, knew this to be the case. Finally, he added that policy declarations made by him or his predecessors should not be treated as 'straitjackets' or commandments 'carved in stone which must guide our policy for all time'. Certain 'immutable principles' directed Irish policy, but the policy itself had to change with circumstances.[41]

Membership of the EEC was presented by the government as an economic, external affairs matter. In so far as it became a foreign policy issue, it did so on the initiative of the political opposition who attempted to suggest that joining the EEC was inconsistent with the existing foreign policy of the government. The heavy hinting about the possibility of change in the future excepted, the government was content to respond to these arguments by reiterating their economic emphasis and reasserting that joining the EEC posed no problems for any aspect of Irish foreign policy.

What was conspicuously absent in the government's presentation of its policy towards 'Europe' was the whole vocabulary and framework of assumptions of international role-playing which had characterised and continued to characterise Ireland's UN policy. The domestic factors which might, in part, account for this have already been noted. It was an era in which even the issue of Partition was approached by a 'depoliticised' functionalism which attempted to disown the utility of the political symbols and assumptions of the past in favour of a new 'rationality' of economic growth and development. Further, it might be expected that the reasons why the government of a peripheral state with an underdeveloped economy and less than three million people did not enter the EEC, EFTA and OECD talks proclaiming an Irish role as leader/mediator/model in the process are self-evident. Possibly, but they are equally self-evident for why such a government should not try to play a similar part in the UN. The reasons why the Irish government did not take its characteristic foreign policy approach towards European issues became clearer when that policy got into difficulties. With the initial British rejection of the Community, followed by the Community's more important rejection of Britain, an extended period of uncertainty followed during which the limitations of Irish political independence were clearly exposed, as were the limitations of the government's efforts to portray the political and economic realms as separate.

Three problems in particular proved difficult for the Irish government in this respect. The first was ongoing and consisted of the balance of payments problems engendered by a modernisation strategy in which the value of imports persisted in growing at a faster rate than the value of the exports which were intended to pay for them. The others were crises generated as a by-product of British responses to their own difficulties with movements to reorganise the European economic and political systems, first, the establishment of EFTA, and second, the imposition of a 15 per cent levy on all industrial imports by the Wilson government.

The Irish government responded to these problems in a manner that was radically different from the way in which they addressed political foreign policy issues. First, they emphasised their own incapacity to influence the external events which were regarded as the source of these problems. Secondly, they stressed the importance of ties with Britain, positively, as the precondition of Ireland's economic survival and future growth, and negatively, as a constraint upon the pursuit of alternative paths to these ends. Finally, as the external options of the country began to narrow, the government started to claim that only through their own efforts to become a more effective exporter and less prolific importer could the Irish solve their problems and achieve independence in a fuller sense of the word than had been previously suggested.

The willingness of Irish governments to emphasise the limits of their capacity to influence external events where they thought this to be necessary has been noted above. Indeed, it was in economic matters that the government was prepared to accept, albeit reluctantly, an unflattering international status to obtain concessions in external arrangements, for example, in the OEEC negotiations and with regard to the composition of Ireland's contribution to the World Bank.[42] Despite a measure of domestic difficulty caused by the willingness of the government to accept this kind of status, protestations of helplessness at the highest level of generality in the Dáil were usually accepted with few objections. For example, a month or so prior to the final British, and hence Irish, decision to apply for membership of the EEC, the Minister for Industry and Commerce, Jack Lynch, could claim that Ireland should enjoy a longer period for dismantling its tariffs should it join the EEC because it had not been able to match the performance of the 'more advanced industrial countries of Europe', but at the same time acknowledge that Ireland could have 'no effective control' over many changes in future economic conditions.[43]

The global process of tariff reductions and European developments were both presented as possibly unpalatable for Ireland in some respects, but certainly inevitable. Speaking in 1965 with regard to the process of tariff reductions, Lynch stressed how Ireland really had little choice in the matter. At that time, Ireland was one of the few countries which had not acceded to the GATT process because of its obligations under its existing arrangements with Britain. Whatever benefits obtained from the latter, however, according to Lynch, the Irish had to be 'realistic'. Free trade, at least within the EEC and EFTA groups, would be a reality within the year and Ireland could not isolate itself as an 'economic island' if its position in the world was to be maintained. To do this, he said, the process of 'voluntarily and unilaterally reducing our tariffs' had to begin.[44]

While the Taoiseach might speak philosophically about participating in the movement towards European integration as the best option in a world which the Irish government could not fashion to its liking,[45] the specific consequences of this helplessness and the response of the government to them was not so easily managed. At the abstract level, Ireland's problems were those of a small, penetrated, developing national economy, the managers of which were committed to the process of liberalising international trade and bringing their own country into that process at a controlled rate which safeguarded its ability to prevent a 'fair' share of that trade from being swept away by the sudden access of stronger actors to its markets. In the concrete, however, they revolved around the nature and extent of the relationship with Britain. It was this which prevented the government from taking Ireland into the EEC, the first practical step in the country's participation in world trade liberalisation, prevented it from achieving alternative arrangements with the Community, the so-called Greek and Austrian options,[46] and isolated it even from the British-organised alternative to the EEC, EFTA. Worse, the failure of the Irish attempt to join the

EEC was seen, in part, as a consequence of what were termed 'high political' differences between the British and the French in which Ireland had no interest and to which Irish, as well as British, prosperity was being sacrificed.[47]

The government's response to these difficulties focused on an effort to preserve, and indeed extend, the trading regime which existed between Ireland and Britain. The first threat to this regime came with the establishment of EFTA in 1959. As noted above, the commitment by its members to remove tariffs on each other's industrial products over a ten-year period called into question Ireland's preferential access into the British market, which the Irish wished to preserve without opening themselves up to the other members of EFTA. According to Lemass, in a series of negotiations in which the Taoiseach himself participated, the 'special trading relationship' had been reconfirmed and a new formal consultation procedure had been established. The Irish had also proposed a closer coordination of agriculture in both countries. What they had wanted was the application of the British farm price-support system to Irish livestock and dairy produce. To obtain it, they had offered to the British an extended preferential system, a bilateral free trade agreement and/or Irish participation in EFTA, but the British had refused the offer. Nevertheless, according to Lemass, the government was satisfied with the 'Supplementary Trade Agreement' because it had preserved their access to the British market when the latter had seemed threatened. Further, the creation of the consultative process had strengthened this arrangement which, he emphasised, the British were under no contractual obligation to maintain. It was because they chose to continue treating Ireland as a Commonwealth country, for these purposes, that its preferential access to their market was maintained.[48]

The second crisis occurred in 1964 when the new Labour government in Britain imposed a 15 per cent temporary levy on industrial imports in an attempt to ameliorate their own balance of payment problems. The Irish were neither exempted, nor were they consulted prior to the move. Again, Lemass travelled to London and argued that the Irish should be exempted from this policy because it hurt them disproportionately. He pointed out in the Dáil that 21 per cent of Irish industrial exports went to Britain compared to an average of 5 per cent from other European countries and 2.5 per cent from Commonwealth countries. Further, he stated that trade with Ireland, the pound of which was kept in parity with sterling, had no bearing on Britain's efforts to protect its dollar holdings or gold reserves. The British were apparently apologetic, emphasised the temporary nature of the levy, but otherwise said that they could do nothing.[49]

In response to this, Lemass announced to the Dáil that the Irish government was virtually powerless in the situation. Retaliation would hurt Ireland more than Britain. The trouble with bilateral trading arrangements was that they would hold only so long as they were mutually advantageous. However, they were the only way of doing business for the time being. In the long run, only 'world-wide or regional' trading systems could put international trade on a firmer and more equitable footing, and for once, the Irish 'internationalist' formulation was applied to the international economy by Lemass.

> For a country of our size, whose bargaining power in bilateral negotiations can never be very great, the prospect of operating under the impartial and permanent rules of an international community has many attractions and particularly the attraction of immunity from abrupt and unilateral action to our detriment by another country in economic difficulty or embarking on a change of policy.[50]

Indeed, he said that when the British had announced their measures, the Irish government had considered 'immediately reactivating' their application to join the EEC because they regarded this as 'the means of escaping from excessive dependence on the British market...'. Unfortunately, while there was no 'policy of dependence' on the British market, the bulk of Irish exports going there because it was where they could be sold to 'best advantage', there could be no change in the short run, according to Lemass. This was because the British market still provided the best return since most alternatives involved tariffs 'even higher than the temporary British surcharges'.[51]

Despite these protestations of helplessness, however, between November of 1964 and October of 1965 thirteen meetings were held with British representatives, two in which the Taoiseach headed the Irish delegation, to establish a new trading agreement. In the course these meetings, according to Lemass, the possibility of negotiating a free trade agreement emerged. The Anglo-Irish trading agreement (AIFTA) was signed in December 1965. According to the terms of the agreement, the British would remove nearly all restrictions on Irish imports by July 1966, and Ireland was to remove its restrictions on British imports over a period of ten years. Particularly important to Ireland was the raising of the British quota on Irish bacon and butter, in return for which the Irish were to dismantle special terms granted to foreign investors and management. The details of the agreement could be adjusted only by mutual consent.[52]

There was certainly an attempt on the part of the government to present its external trade policy as a coherent strategy aimed at preparing Ireland for effective competition in a world trading system characterised by declining trade barriers. The government had made a series of unilateral, 10 per cent tariff cuts, one each in 1963 and 1964 and one scheduled for 1965, and as has been mentioned above, they constantly situated the policy in its presentation to the Dáil in the context of the emergence of European trading blocs to which Ireland had to adjust whether it liked it or not. The trading policy towards Britain, especially in the 1965 agreement, was expressed in the same terms. With regard to this agreement, the Taoiseach announced that the goverment intended to let it regulate trade with Britain until it was 'absorbed' by arrangements arising out of Ireland joining EFTA, the EEC or 'perhaps, a combination of both'. In the same session, he also informed the Dáil that he had accepted an invitation to address the Assembly of the Council of Europe because it would provide an opportunity to explain how the agreement with Britain fitted into Ireland's 'wider European objectives', further Western European economic integration and an enlarged Community.[53]

Ireland's trade policy was presented as part of an economic grand strategy. Relations with Britain would be a model for how they would soon be with the rest of Europe and how they ought to be in the world as a whole. On occasions, it was even presented as one aspect of Ireland's quest for a more just and orderly international system. In practice, however, it consisted of high-level, low profile negotiations with Britain designed to patch up or strengthen their existing trading regime; all other objectives took second place to the preservation and strengthening of Irish access to the British market. Membership of EFTA was considered and ruled out on the basis that it did nothing to improve this position, and Ireland could maintain the position without joining EFTA. Trade diversification, while lauded both in principle and in the long run of EEC membership, could not be attempted at the cost of damaging the Anglo-Irish regime.

The thinking behind this approach, which had the support of the two major political parties, was summed up by Cosgrave in the debate on the OECD Convention, when he stated that

> Since the establishment of the State it has been our traditional policy to develop and exploit the trade potential between Ireland and Britain while at the same time asserting and defending our political rights.[54]

Such a distinction was sustainable as long as the Anglo-Irish trading arrangement remained stable. It was so to the extent that in discussing Ireland's application to the EEC in 1961, the Taoiseach could emphasise 'the critical importance for us of whatever decision the British Government may take' in the following terms. If Britain did not join the EEC then Ireland would not join the EEC since joining would entail the loss of preferential access to the British market. If Britain did join, then Ireland would have to join, since not joining would entail the same consequences. As he put it, the same argument would keep Ireland in or out, depending on what the British did.[55]

Change and uncertainty, however, emphasised the political as well as the economic price which Ireland paid for such a regime. Peck's characterisation of Anglo-Irish relations in terms of the annual, routinised 'butter wrangle' could not apply to the Irish efforts to patch up the regime in the face of British measures to solve their problems at the expense of both the regime and Ireland.[56] Then, the limits to Irish independence were given salience by the government's own protestations of its powerlessness to act, the negotiations and proposals initiated by the Irish to preserve and deepen a relationship at odds with their long-term objectives, and the admission that delays in negotiations were at times caused by the difficulty of getting the attention of the British government, for example, when elections were pending.[57]

84

Lemass conceded in the debate on his own EEC statement and the OECD convention, that the Irish had long realised that the establishment of their own 'free political institutions' did not change the 'economic realities' which kept the arrangements with Britain central to Ireland's trade policy.[58] But the fusion between the political and economic realms in their implications for independence were put more starkly by Deputy Browne speaking to the same issue when he claimed that the Irish had 'no power of decision on this matter, good, bad or indifferent'. Nor was this something one could shrug off as the way of the world, as he went on to argue, because it threw into question the whole meaning of Ireland's struggle for independence and subsequent difficult history.

> You cannot blame my generation for asking what all this 1916 and 1922 was about. What were you fighting about? What were you fighting for? Why did you kill one another? Why did you imprison one another? What was the objective of this whole movement when, 40 years later, you are sitting here waiting for a despatch from Whitehall before you will guide the country's footsteps in one direction or another?[59]

In addition, according to his colleague, McQuillan, Ireland's foreign policy had done nothing to address Irish problems or further Irish interests; rather, it had served as a distraction from the pursuit of those interests.

> We were engaged in settling the affairs of the world. We were threatening the Russians one day and the Chinese the next. We were settling the dispute in the Congo. In fact, it now appears that we have some of the most brilliant men in the world today in this country, and without their assistance, it would be impossible to settle several major world problems. The terrible tragedy is that it would appear that their assistance is of such tremendous importance abroad, while at home we do not seem to have the ability, the courage or the initiative to settle the problems in our own backyard. We can look after everyone's business except our own. When the conditions that obtain in this country are exposed, the answer is 'Look at the glorious work we are doing abroad'.[60]

There was little the government could do in response to these criticisms or the assertions of the opposition that Ireland's role in the world was that of 'cattle ranch' or larder to Great Britain, or that Ireland was looked at by Europeans as 'an integral part of Britain, a shire of England, a nonentity not to be recognised'.[61] Lemass stressed the formal attributes of independence, that as elected representatives of the Irish people, his government had 'sat as equals' with the British and worked out a new trade arrangement.[62] Beyond that, all he could do was re-state Ireland's fundamental circumstances. As he had said in 1962 during the first round of EEC negotiations, the country, more than any other in Western Europe, depended on exports for its prosperity and, as he put it, 'no other nation cares one hoot whether Ireland goes ahead or goes back'.[63] Therefore, Ireland was on its own; its salvation had to come through the efforts of its own people.

He maintained this line that internal change must proceed in the face of the first failure to enter the EEC and the imposition of the British import levy. With regard to the latter and the balance of payments problems to which it was contributing, the government imposed its own levy and asked Irish importers not to purchase non-essential items covered by the levy during the period of its existence.[64] As a consequence, it is around this time that one notices a number of political exchanges and Dáil debates, in the context of a 'Buy Irish' campaign, concerned with such matters as the use of imported bathtubs in a housing project, the importation of Romanian matches and the appearance of three slices of hardboard marked 'foreign' in a batch of 50 used by a state-sponsored body.[65]

These difficulties clearly exposed the limited ability of the government to act as they wished in the conduct of their economic external affairs. As the period progressed, however, Lemass began to articulate the implications of his economic priorities for the conduct of Ireland's 'independent' foreign policy. In 1963, for example, instead of offering the usual formula wherein the latter was derived from national attributes and values, he suggested that Ireland's 'freedom to act' was 'proportionate' to its ability to become a 'stronger and more independent economic entity'.[66] Three years later, he claimed that there was no real independence in a country which could not sell its exports without having to haggle for preferential treatment'. Indeed, he claimed that

> The people of this country fought for their freedom through the years not merely because of patriotic impulses, nor merely to give Ireland her proper status among the nations of the earth, but so they could organise themselves to develop their agriculture and industry and improve their standard of living by the application of their own policies.

The aim of the government, he went on to say, was to make Ireland a significant producer and exporter of industrial goods like other smaller European countries such as Belgium, the Netherlands and Denmark for 'Ireland's independence will always be as real as our economic development makes it'.[67]

These last remarks, made by Lemass in 1966, should not be taken as the conclusion of a story about how an initially over-optimistic and naive country received a ten-year lesson, from the UN to AIFTA, in the harsh realities of international politics. Still less is it an account of changes in the general character of international relations and foreign policy. Irish foreign policy did not become Irish external relations, in the terms I have defined both of these, during the period. Most of the controversy associated with the 'independence' foreign policy was over and done with before European developments and trade issues began to influence Irish policy-making directly, but the more stable and established components of the independence policy were being pursued at the same time as the difficulties of internal development and external trading policy were being experienced.

The Irish government did not respond to demands from the external environment of the country with a single, if evolving, strategy. Rather, they acted as if that environment constituted two different realms of international activity, the political-strategic on the one hand, and the economic-pragmatic on the other, and they worked to keep these apart. Regarding these two realms, the government had very different perspectives about how to operate in each of them and their room for manoeuvre and prospects for success in each of them. It may be seen that this distinction resulted from the experience of the political elite as nationalist revolutionaries, from their perception of the international system and the actual demands upon them emanating from that system. The political-strategic realm was, in effect, viewed as an arena of opportunity for Ireland to behave as an independent nation-state and to be seen to be doing so. On the basis of these assumptions, the Irish government put into practice their policy of international role-playing. This was generally successful in its immediate objectives and very successful in its overarching objective of establishing Ireland's reputation as a distinctive, independent participant in international life.

One may point to a number of reasons for this success. First of all, in terms of national attributes, it would seem that the Irish government was fundamentally correct (in the sense that other governments accepted it), in their estimation and proclamation of Ireland's suitability for a middle power role. Secondly, the government was prepared to devote reasonably scarce resources, money, manpower and skilled personnel, to the pursuit of an active-independent foreign policy, and they enjoyed popular support or acquiescence in this policy. The Irish success in respect to this policy was, however, also contingent on external factors. First, the middle power role itself had been defined by other governments and it depended upon both situational and institutional opportunities which themselves rested on a limited and fragile international consensus regarding the nature of international stability and the role of preventive diplomacy in safeguarding it. Secondly, issues of war and peace, or their international management, at least, were dealt with by processes which emphasised the participation of states as notional entities, both as problem-causers and problem-solvers. Thirdly, in so far as problems of war and peace directly affected Ireland, they did so as a systemic problem rather than as a state or sub-state-based threat during the period.

The external economic environment was never regarded with the same enthusiasm and sense of opportunity by Irish policy-makers. Generally speaking, they did not articulate an Irish role as a system-maintainer, system reformer or small state role-model. Least of all did they attempt to use this policy area in an attempt to establish or manifest an Irish identity, quite the contrary. They were candid about their reasons for this. Economic matters had a profundity and permanence which were apparently lacking in the more fluid world of diplomatic manoeuvre. In refuting the suggestion that Ireland had been 'told' to join the EEC by the British and the Germans, Aiken provided a very good example

87

of this attitude. To say that Ireland was thinking about joining the EEC because it wished to 'ape' the British was as silly as saying that Ireland was aping the Russians because the earth followed the Russian satellite around the sun. Whatever the vagaries of this parallel, Aiken's point was that there were 'natural forces operating' in Europe and the world which were beyond Ireland's control. The trend in Europe was towards economic and political unity and Ireland had to fit itself this.[68]

The international economy, like gravity, was simply there, and there was very little one could do about it. But stating that gravity is inevitable in no way minimises the fact that it does have a profound effect upon the way one behaves, and Aiken's answer, for example, did not actually refute the, admittedly unlikely, possibility that the demands of inevitability were being communicated through the services of a visiting German minister. What Aiken was really addressing was the question of what it was reasonable to ask any Irish government to deal with and what it must be expected to leave alone. This position was acceptable so long as Ireland's trading relationships remained stable and 'satisfactory' to the government and domestic sources of pressure upon it. Then, so long as moderate growth was sustained, or, at least, any real decline was averted, the government could be left to tinker with and manage the inevitable in the economic realm while accruing prestige and making itself useful in the international system through its active foreign policy of role-playing.

When these external relationships were upset, however, the government's margin for manoeuvre decreased and, at the same time, domestic demand for it to act effectively increased. Under this kind of pressure, the 'reasonableness' of the government's definition of what an independent Ireland could or could not be expected to do evaporated along with the distinction between political and economic independence. The government's problems in these circumstances were compounded by the nature of the practical actions they thought they must take to address immediate problems, preserving or strengthening the link with Britain, and by the fact that their independence policy was addressed to other issues and, hence, irrelevant as far as these crises were concerned.

It was here, perhaps, that one might identify the greatest single shortcoming of Irish foreign policy during the period. While it was successful in its own terms, establishing an Irish identity and serving as an expression of Irish national and international values, there is little evidence to suggest that the international prestige achieved by the policy had any convertibility into influence in policy areas other than the one in which it was accumulated. It certainly had no impact upon relations with Britain, either on questions of trade or the issue of Partition. While the success of Ireland's foreign policy sufficiently compensated for these shortcomings, in the sense that it was not abandoned because of the latter, it could be argued that this success itself was damaging in that it established a definition of Irish independence which had little relevance to pressing Irish problems.

It is with this in mind that the shifting emphasis in the government's, and particularly Lemass's, definitions of foreign policy is best understood. It was not the product of a learning process with regard to the nature of international relations in an interdependent and modernising world, but rather a response to fluctuations in the prominence of differing sets of issues. It is these, in the form of pressures generated by external economic uncertainty and adjustments, which brought the government to focus on the pragmatic and piecemeal management of external relations. Ireland's political foreign policy, in the meantime, was not abandoned. Rather, during the years immediately following the period examined here, it became, for the time being, an increasingly detached and remote effort to improve the operating and funding procedures of the UN in general, and peacekeeping in particular.

Notes

1. See for examples, the arguments and evidence put forward by Fine Gael spokesmen in their motion of no confidence in the government's foreign policy in 1957, 164, 1168-204 especially.
2. For an example of this view see 'Lemass', in Schou and Brundtland, op. cit., p. 115. He refers to the UN as 'a shield behind which some initiatives might be undertaken without undue risk of undesirable conflict with other nations'.
3. See 159, 591-600.
4. 159, 432–40.
5. N. Browne – Minister for Health in the Inter-Party Government, 1948-51 and J. McQuillan were, during this period, the two representatives of the National Progressive Democrats in the Dáil, providing usually articulate, if ineffective, criticism of the government from a radical socialist perspective. See 159, 430 and 219 for their comments.
6. See 181, 1657 for the radio episode, and 181, 70-3 for the beef affair.
7. 167, 267 for Lourdes, and 181, 1031 for Irish policy on British Railways.
8. 159, 641-2. Sir Roger Casement was executed by the British for his part in trying to secure German help for the Easter Rising in 1916. For many years a campaign was waged to secure the return of his body from England to Ireland.
9. For a very good account of this see Keatinge (1978), op. cit., p. 209.
10. See: 101, 2232; 179, 37-44; and 221, 587. Of 355 days which Aiken spent abroad between 1961 and 1966, 272 were spent at the UN.
11. 219, 1152.
12. 219, 1154-5 (4 January 1966).
13. 167, 266 and 294.
14. 191, 479-94 for Aiken's speech and 191, 204, 338, for the EEC/OECD debate.
15. 201, 930-8.
16. Op. cit., p. 69.
17. Op. cit. (1978), p. 209.
18. Keatinge (1973), op. cit., pp. 56-7.
19. Op. cit. (1978), p. 209.
20. Interview.
21. See for evidence of this allocation, Aiken, 201, 1075.
22. See 159, 440 for references to European matters in the 1956 debate. The source of the comments on the Council of Europe is interviews with members of the Irish foreign service.

23. 163, 618-9 (3 July 1957).
24. 201, 1076.
25. 194, 1418.
26. See, for examples, Costello 163, 667-8 and Corish (head of the Labour Party), 141, 2605.
27. 161, 279.
28. 163, 644 (3 July 1957).
29. 176, 1573-4.
30. 181, 35.
31. 218, 1400, Lynch speaking in 1965.
32. 179, 685 and 182, 714.
33. 191, 270-2.
34. 191, 2246.
35. Lemass, in response to a question from Costello, 198, 79.
36. For criticism from the left, see 193, 22;and from the right, see 194, 1387.
37. 193, 22 (14 February1962).
38. 191, 268, (5 July 1961).
39. 191, 282.
40. 191, 2573.
41. 198, 1480.
42. For the respective examples, see 176, 900 and 184, 391.
43. 190, 1252 (29 June 1961).
44. 218, 1402–3
45. 196, 3372
46. See 219, 1150-2, 1153 and 1517 for details of these.
47. Lemass, 199, 925; and Cosgrave, 199, 1188.
48. 181, 37-45 (26 April 1960).
49. 212, 660-1.
52. 663-7.
51. 212, 666-7.
52. See 217, 5-10, for discussion of the negotiations. See Lyons, op. cit., p. 632, for the Irish concessions; and 219, 1140 for the adjustment mechanism.
53. 219, 1140-8.
54. 191, 242 (5 July 1961).
55. 191, 204.
56. Peck, op. cit., p. 24.
57. 219, 1142-3.
58. 19l, 284.
59. 191, 290.
60. 191, 637.
61. 219, 1197, 1224 and 1245.
62. 219, 1160.
63. 194, 1792 (11 April 1962).
64. See 218, 1334 for details of the difficulties, see 218, 808 for the counter-levy.
65. 218, 382 (matches), 1625 (bathtubs) and, 219, 4 (hardboard).
66. 199, 939 (30 January 1963).
67. 219, 1160, 1949, 1951 and 1953.
68. 19l, 664 (11 July 1961)

6 Irish policy in the intervening period

Irish foreign policy between 1956 and 1966 was the policy of a small, weak state. During that period Irish governments sought to exploit the opportunities with which UN membership provided them for broadening their scope for independent action. Their efforts in this regard were largely devoted to constructing and performing an international role as a peace-loving, independently-minded, active member of the international system, an international good citizen.

This policy was pursued for a number of reasons. Its long-range purpose was to contribute to the development of a more orderly and rule-governed international system, one which would favour those states which possessed few of the traditional elements of national power, in particular. It was also regarded as a projection of Ireland's distinctive and independent national identity and values into the wider world. In this sense, it fitted into the nationalist tradition of conferring a significance upon the struggle for Irish independence which went beyond the affairs of the Irish people alone to the world as a whole. Ireland had not struggled for independence merely for its own good. Following from this, it may also be seen that international role-playing, the fulfilment of Irish destiny on the world stage, served as a substitute for the failure to fulfil a more immediate Republican objective, the unity of the island. Spokesmen for the government rarely articulated such a rationale, but several members of the foreign service suggested that some of their political masters regarded interna-

91

tional activism as a welcome substitute for a more direct approach to Irish unity. Finally, and whatever the grander visions into which Ireland's activism could be made to fit, the immediate purpose of the policy was to accrue prestige and thereby, it was hoped, diplomatic influence.

Clearly, the Irish government was aware of changes which were taking place in the international system and they argued that if Ireland was to be both prosperous and secure, then it would have to become increasingly involved with this system. Their view of this process of change, however, did not accord with the picture of international transformation suggested by theorists of interdependence. For the former, Ireland was not some ancient nation, the identity and internal organisation of which had been established in previous times of sparse international interaction and relative isolation, experiencing and adjusting to the demands on, and decline of, its autonomy in an increasingly interdependent world. It was already a 'penetrated state' *par excellence* as a consequence of its former colonial status and continuing links with Britain. Not only that, the sense of nationhood of its people was as much a product of the need to differentiate and separate themselves from the foreign, exploitative presence with which they were closely involved as of the Celtic past which had to be virtually disinterred. This being so, what was important to the government was that by dint of Ireland's own efforts and as a consequence of changes in the international system, the autonomy of the country had been increased to the point of achieving formal sovereignty. Further, engagement with the international system, it was hoped, would give more substance to Irish independence.

The government saw independence and membership of the UN as providing Ireland with new opportunities for effective action, but these were not really the opportunities suggested by interdependence theorists. The latter argue that mutual need, new issue priorities and the consequent establishment of regimes of rule-governed behaviour tend to make the traditional instruments of state power less important in determining the outcome of interactions between states. The nearest the Irish government came to this was in their claim that an international system based on the rule of law and the principles of justice would be fairer on small states, and any progress in this direction had to be an improvement. The work remained to be done, however, by exploiting opportunities for moral persuasion and setting an example. In so far as the world had already changed, it had done so in terms of the emergence of the possibility of nuclear catastrophe, the deadlock between the superpowers, the decline of colonialism and, as a by-product of all these, the opportunity for Ireland to have a foreign policy. Shifts in the distribution of power in the international system, not changes in its rules, had both made the world a more dangerous place and presented the Irish with their opportunity.

That the changes which were taking place in the international system did not accord with the predictions of interdependence theorists is borne out by the high political character of the Irish response to them. The latter was primarily addressed to the traditional issues of war and peace and emphasised coherence and consistency in that it was directed at establishing the idea of Ireland as an international personality. The nature of this response may, in part, have been determined by the fact that the UN was still preoccupied with the type of issue which had originally given rise to it. But the government's intention was to make the most of these 'peace and security' opportunities to enhance Irish status and influence as a whole, on the assumption that gains in influence and standing in one area were convertible into influence and standing in another area of policy.

This assumption proved wrong. Ireland's international role-playing policy was very successful, both in the sense that Ireland made worthwhile contributions to the effort to resolve the specific international problems to which its policy was addressed, and in the sense that it became known for doing this. The influence purchased by the achievement of this status, however, proved useful only in the same areas of policy, that is, in the establishment and operation of international military forces, certain areas of arms control policy and, to a lesser extent, in the politics of international organisations as a whole. It did not extend into other areas of interest of Irish foreign policy. This became very clear as the changes in the regional trading systems of which Ireland was a part began to work themselves out. The establishment of these trading regimes constituted changes which were of the order of the ones to which interdependence theorists refer. Even so, the significance of these changes lay neither in the new orders which they heralded nor in whether their net effect was to enlarge or reduce the capacity of the government to undertake independent action. Rather, it was the process of change itself, and its associated uncertainty which demonstrated the inability of the government to safeguard their definition of Irish interests. Thus change and uncertainty exposed a contradiction between the image which the government sought to create of Ireland as a 'go-ahead', 'progressive' little republic, wielding international influence disproportionate to its size and respected for it, and the fact that the Irish were forced to wait on the deliberations and policies of others to find out what their position would be once the dust had settled.

This discrepancy is no great discovery; indeed Irish politicians did little to conceal the gap between what they would have regarded as their aspirations for the future of the country and its present circumstances. Of more interest is the tension which was revealed as existing between the avowed objectives of Irish foreign policy and the external conditions necessary for its effective practice. Ireland was defined by its government as one of the disadvantaged states of the international system, both in general terms, it was a small state and the international anarchy is not fair to small states, and in particular terms, it was partitioned and its development was constrained by Britain. Ireland's foreign policy, therefore, was essentially reformist in its intent, directed at mitigating the effects of anarchy in the international system in the short term and removing its causes in the long term. The independent foreign policy looked its best, however, when the international system was more rather than less stable. Stability allowed the Irish government to assert Ireland's independent identity in certain policy areas with a fair degree of credibility. There was a range of international problems which Irish governments addressed in a distinctive manner, different certainly from the way the British, for example, addressed them. System changes, however, merely underlined the extent to which the Irish were not masters of their own fate and exposed the irrelevance of their foreign policy to the management of the difficulties which these changes presented.

In such circumstances, it was the practice of the government to try to insulate their independent foreign policy both from the exposure of their helplessness in the broader sphere of their external relations, and from domestic pressures to follow through the implications of their independent postures to the point of risking significant external costs. It is, perhaps, this paradox of requiring stable external conditions in which to practice a revisionist foreign policy, that best underlines the extent to which Irish foreign policy as a coherent strategy was designed for participation in the existing international system rather than for changing it, as its component parts may have suggested.

As I shall show by examining Irish foreign policy in the second period between 1977 and 1983, the ability of the government to insulate 'political' foreign policy from 'economic' external affairs was severely curtailed by membership of the EEC. This change is consistent with the predictions of interdependence theorists regarding the breakdown of the distinctions between economic and political issues, and between foreign and domestic policy. As I shall also show, the political and statist character of the Irish response to these changes is not. Before passing to an examination of the second period and the impact of conditions of complex interdependence in the form of membership of the EEC upon Irish foreign policy, however, I shall offer a brief review of two major developments in the intervening ten years. The first is the re-emergence of Northern Ireland as a major policy problem and the second is the process by which Ireland finally became a member of the EEC.[1]

The origins of the problem of Irish unity have been recounted at length elsewhere and so only a brief account will be offered here.[2] As a result of the demands of the Irish Unionists and the reluctance of powerful elements within British society to foresake anyone who wished to remain within the Union, Ireland was partitioned by the agreement which established the Irish Free State in 1922. Twenty-six counties became the Free State and six of the counties of the old province of Ulster became Northern Ireland, still under British jurisdiction although with more local autonomy than Scotland or Wales.

In dividing the island, the British government operated on the principle of retaining the largest number of counties possible in which an overall Unionist, and broadly Protestant, majority could be maintained in the face of a Nationalist, and broadly Catholic, minority. This division was objected to by the Irish nationalists both on the grounds that it thwarted the basic objectives of the movement – independence for the whole of Ireland – and that it meant that Britain retained the economically most developed part of the island. They were, however, presented with a choice by the British government between accepting the independence of the twenty-six counties or the status quo, and presumably a resumption of the hostilities which had been temporarily suspended. By accepting the British offer of independence for the majority of the island, the Irish negotiators split the Nationalist movement and a civil war was fought between those who supported the Treaty and those who wished to fight on for a republic of the whole island. The pro-treaty forces, with the advantages of controlling such state apparatus as there was, considerable military assistance from the British and probably the support of most of the population, won the civil war.

In accepting the Anglo-Irish treaty, the 'Free Staters', as they were known, argued that the formal ties with Britain embodied by the place of the monarch in the Irish constitution, were not crucial obstacles to the Irish running their own internal affairs. They could probably be removed at a later date should this be regarded as necessary. They also argued that the British had suggested, and that the 'imperatives' of economics and geography dictated, that Partition would only be a temporary phenomenon. Subsequent events proved them to be correct with regard to the constitutional links with Britain, but Partition proved to be no temporary matter. The Boundary Commission of 1925, on which the Free State government had based its hopes of creating a momentum leading to the unification of the island, recommended only minor adjustments to the border in both directions. These were not acted upon. Since then, all Irish governments have been left with the problem of what to do about the 'North'.

This problem has had certain enduring constants for all Irish governments to date. The first is that they lack the power to force Irish unity upon the North so long as the British are prepared to support the wishes of the Protestant-Unionist majority. It is even doubtful whether they could force a military solution in the absence of this guarantee. This is not only a fairly obvious conclusion to be drawn from any estimate of the balance of forces in the area. It is also a product of the fact that Irish governments have envisaged unity in terms of the Six Counties joining the Republic as it is presently established, with relatively minor social and constitutional adjustments at most. Any armed struggle initiated by Ireland, while it might be successful in the long run, would almost certainly see the demise of the Republic in its present form, reduced by the security burden of the North to O'Brien's 'shabby military dictatorship',[3] transformed by the revolutionary processes of a 'people's war' or both. Class interests, liberal values and the balance of forces have combined, therefore, to make Irish governments reject the military option not only as an unlikely way of obtaining unity but as a likely way of destroying what they, themselves, represent.

The second constant is that Irish governments cannot, and do not want to, renounce the principle of Irish unity, however this might be achieved and whatever form it might take. At the heart of both the republican and nationalist traditions from which the state derives its legitimacy is the claim that Ireland consists of the territory and people of the whole island and that the independence struggle is incomplete until all of the territory and all of the people are free. All Irish governments, therefore, have been committed to taking measures short of force which will bring about Irish unity, and to claiming that until this is achieved, a national and international problem exists.

The third constant is that all Irish governments have needed, and most of them have wanted, good relations with Britain. Again, this has been the case for both fairly obvious geopolitical reasons, and because of the close economic relationship between the two. Thus, even when, as in the case of de Valera's governments between 1932 and 1948, policies of confrontation and non-cooperation have been pursued, this has been done, except for short periods, within fairly well-defined limits.

If these three constants may be said to constitute the structural elements of the problem as far as Irish governments are concerned, then within these structures three basic sets of issues have constantly re-surfaced demanding a response from them. The first has been the plight of the Nationalist minority, or that section of the Nationalist majority which has been artificially displaced in the North. Irish governments have claimed an interest in the welfare of this group and have seen it as their duty to take a stand on or publicise the system of injustices by which the Unionists strengthened their ascendency in the North, at least when the Nationalists were reacting to these injustices. Secondly, and to varying degrees, they have also regarded it as their responsibility to create the conditions, real or atmospheric, which might persuade the Unionists that the maintenance of Partition was no longer necessary. Finally, all policy towards the North is formulated in the context of political opposition ranging from party political rivals interested, usually, in making party political points, to the various republican groups who claim to be, and are generally recognised as, the heirs to a competing version of the republican tradition. Although its upholders were defeated in the civil war, this may still be regarded as occupying a potentially powerful place in Irish politics. No Irish government can suffer lightly the charge of 'not doing enough' on the North, if it is seen to be failing in that respect and not delivering significant other benefits, namely the fruits of sustained economic growth.

One may chart a series of approaches to the Partition problem taken by Irish governments, all failures if they are to be judged in terms of the achievement of Irish unity. The Free State government of Cumann na nGaedheal pursued a conciliatory policy of 'neighbourly comradeship'. Fianna Fáil, under de Valera, practised a policy of limited confrontation with Britain combined with a series of interventions in the politics of Northern Ireland and a maximalist strategy of claims to 'the whole island of Ireland' embodied in the constitution of 1937. The Inter-Party government of 1948–51 attempted to internationalise the question by publicising it in the Council of Europe.[4]

The first period under examination here saw the complete failure of the IRA campaign between 1956 and 1962 and the emergence of a policy of cooperation with Northern Ireland undertaken by the Lemass government. This policy and the government perceptions that appeared to go with it fit the characterisation of change offered by the interdependence and modernisation theses very well. Coinciding with economic development and increasing prosperity, there appeared to occur a decline in old Nationalist and religious concerns, even on the part of the Nationalist community in the North. In contrast to the occasionally heroic, often farcical, and utterly unsuccessful campaign waged by the IRA, the government offered face-to-face negotiations with their Northern Ireland counterparts, and as a consequence of these meetings, a series of exercises in economic and functional cooperation. The Irish would be brought together, in some vague and unspecified sense, by facing the future challenges of achieving growth and prosperity, a shared problem, by a shared effort, not by trying to resolve the differences of the past.

Laudable though functional cooperation might be in itself, however, the policy was neither entirely clear nor honest about its methods and objectives. With regard to the former, it was not the imperatives of modernisation and functional cooperation which brought Lemass and O'Neill together, but a political decision to give a high profile to this kind of cooperation. As opposition backbenchers were swift to point out in the Dáil, cooperation in the field of transport (coordinating bus timetables) and other mundane cross-border efforts had gone on for years. With regard to the objectives of this kind of cooperation, there was no clear statement of how it would bring about unity, if that was its purpose, or whether unity, in this 'old-fashioned' sense, indeed, remained an objective.

Whatever its real purposes, the policy was overtaken by events in the North in 1969. The campaign organised by the Northern Ireland Civil Rights Association to improve the circumstances of the minority within the six counties was interpreted by those who controlled and constituted the security apparatus of the province as a new variant of the old Nationalist threat. The repressive nature of their response to peaceful marches provoked rioting in Derry and Belfast. This, in its turn, precipitated a breakdown in the discipline of the local security and police forces which were seen to be leading the attacks on the Nationalists and Catholics in some areas. As a consequence, units of the British army were sent in to restore and maintain order and the IRA was reactivated, initially in its role of protecting the minority, but eventually to wage a guerrilla campaign against the British presence in Northern Ireland, with a view to forcing it to leave.

These events took the Irish government by surprise. It is, for example, hard to find any references to the North as a looming problem in the literature on Ireland in the late 1960s prior to August 1969. They also created problems with

97

the image of the modern, influential Republic by emphasising how little circumstances in the North had changed and how little influence the Irish government had on the shaping of events there. The crisis in the North initially produced a wide range of foreign policy responses on the part of the Irish government. They suggested directly to the British that a UN peacekeeping force or a joint Anglo-Irish force should be deployed. When the British declined both suggestions they asked for the matter to be discussed by the Security Council of the United Nations, citing Article 35 of the Charter concerning the peaceful resolution of disputes.[5]

This episode provides a useful illustration of the kind of prestige Ireland enjoyed at the UN, the kind of influence this prestige procured and, indeed, the levels of expectation with which the Irish government, or some of its members, at least, pursued their foreign policy. According to Cremin's account, the Minister for External Affairs, Patrick Hillery, travelled to New York to address the Security Council. The British representative, Lord Caradon, argued that the Northern Ireland agenda should not be accepted on the basis of Article 2, which states that the UN should not intervene in matters of domestic jurisdiction, and on the basis of assurances by his government that the disturbances were now under control and the necessary reforms were to be implemented. The Finnish representative suggested that Hillery might speak in order to clarify the nature of the problem – an unusual procedure in that the representative of a country calling for a meeting of the Security Council is usually not permitted to speak until the agenda is adopted. Hillery did indeed speak, arguing that the Council's past discussions of apartheid and the Cyprus problem established the fact that the Council did discuss internal matters which had an external dimension. The representative of the USSR supported the Irish position, the British continued to object and the Zambian representative proposed an adjournment which was agreed upon. Northern Ireland was not discussed by the Security Council again.

A month later, in September 1969, Hillery again received an opportunity to speak, this time before the General Committee of the General Assembly in its discussion of the provisional agenda for the forthcoming session. Discussion followed much the same lines as in the Security Council, with the representative of the USSR supporting Ireland and the others suggesting that Ireland should consider the British response. Finally, later that month, Hillery spoke in the General Debate of the Assembly citing Ireland's record of support for the UN and its previous reluctance to inflict its own national problem on that organisation. It had done so now because the lives of so many people were at stake and Anglo-Irish friendship was also endangered. The British representative reiterated the commitment of both his and the Northern Ireland government to the implementation of reforms which would eliminate the cause of the problem. He also emphasised the importance of the UN not becoming involved in an internal dispute, particularly in view of the fact that there had been some suggestion that the 'good offices' of the Secretary General, involving either himself or a representative, should be offered to the parties in dispute.[6]

Of interest here is the contrast between the criteria applied to diplomatic activity and actual, substantive issues in attempting to evaluate the success or failure of the policy. In substantive terms, the Irish government was furious about the state of affairs in the North, critical of the British approach to handling them, and endeavouring to exert an influence on events there and obtain British recognition of the right to exert such influence. Field hospitals had been established on the border to aid refugees from Nationalist-Catholic enclaves in Unionist-Protestant areas of the province. Reserves had been mobilised and armed intervention had been briefly contemplated, giving way to covert logistical assistance by a significant section of the government to those willing to fight in the North. In these terms, those of having a direct impact on events in the North, the UN initiative had yielded nothing (neither had the 'concrete' measures they had taken, of course).

As a diplomatic exercise, however, it was regarded as a considerable success, both by representatives of the Irish government and commentators on the politics of the UN.[7] Because of its status in the UN, Ireland had been allowed to 'make its point', in spite of procedural difficulties, and to make its point against a senior club member of good standing. Britain had been forced to give an account of itself and its policies in Northern Ireland to the international community, if not quite in the formal sessions, then in the UN corridors and the mass media. Further, it was a point that had been well made in that exchanges had been confined to the matter in hand and solutions to the problem. The UN had not been used by either party as a weapon of foreign policy, in the sense of a device for discomforting its opponent even at the risk of exacerbating the conflict.[8] In short, the exercise served as a model for how these things should be done and contributed to and reinforced Ireland's identity as a good, conscientious, and this time restrained international citizen.

The details of the Irish government's attempts to deal with the problem of Northern Ireland and its impact on Anglo-Irish relations up to 1977 do not concern us here. Irish policy on the North, combining as it did, constitutional initiatives, responses to incidents and outrages in the province and the effort to sustain cooperation with Britain over day-to-day security problems, became, in effect, *sui generis* and not integrated into Irish foreign policy.[9] In so far as it continued to play any part in Ireland's international role-playing it did so in terms of its component elements rather than the national question as a whole. For example, the Irish government brought Britain before the European Court of Human Rights with regard to its techniques of interrogating IRA suspects.[10] They devoted considerable effort, particularly in the United States, to attempting to counter the unfavourable image that events in Northern Ireland gave to the whole of Ireland, and to distancing the Republic from the strategy of the IRA. And each year, their representative to the UN would take the opportunity of the General Debate to give his government's appreciation of the situation in the North and call for political initiatives there.

In assessing the importance of the Northern Ireland problem at the beginning of the second period under examination, two things need to be noted. First, although the North was a major problem to which considerable and expanded policy resources were devoted,[11] it cannot be said that Ireland had developed a single-issue foreign policy in which all resources and all contacts were mobilised to obtain Irish objectives in the North or even to put pressure on Britain to weaken its guarantee to the Unionists. Secondly, however, Northern Ireland became and remained a very salient threat, if not to the survival of the Republic directly, then to both its image as a modernising, developing member of the EEC and to the idea that Ireland's best interests were served by a foreign policy of international role-playing and good citizenship. The responses of the Irish government to the periodic flaring up of tensions in the North could generally be characterised as exercises in damage control. When these tensions coincided with mounting economic difficulties at home and disappointment with the evolution of the EEC, however, it became less easy for them to 'sacrifice' the North to other Irish interests. As I shall show below, Irish governments became increasingly tempted, in the short term at least, to put external interests at risk in order to work for progress on the North, or, at least, to defend their own Republican reputation.

The second major development during the intervening period was that Ireland became a full member of the EEC, along with Britain and Denmark. Irish governments had been committed to achieving EEC membership for Ireland since the early 1960s, but it was the Hague summit of 1969, removing as it did the blockage constituted by de Gaulle's objections to enlargement, and the pace of the British application process which were largely responsible for Irish membership being achieved when it was.

Like the British, the Irish were interested in membership 'on the right terms', and again like the British, it was the degree of willingness to join which determined the severity or otherwise of the terms, and not the reverse. The Irish government wanted a transitional period in which certain 'sensitive' industries could continue to be protected and during which the government retained its 'right' to attract foreign investments and aid export industries by a variety of methods.[12] They also wanted the Anglo-Irish trading regime to be preserved and the EEC to recognise formally that Ireland was a 'special case' – by the standards of the Community a lesser developed country. They obtained transitional periods of varying lengths for different sections of the economy, a cash grant of £30 million to substitute for Irish subsidies, and recognition in Protocol 30 of the Treaty of Accession that Ireland indeed constituted a region of the Community deserving special assistance.

Joining the EEC was a popular move. Both Fine Gael and Fianna Fail, the two major political parties, supported it, as did five-sixths of those who voted in a national referendum on the issue.[13] As a domestic political issue, it was presented by the supporters of membership as very much a 'bread and butter' or 'Common Market' affair. This may be explained both by the need to present the issue to the electorate in terms immediately relevant to them and by the fact that the political aspects of membership, touching as they did on questions of sovereignty, independence and neutrality, promised at best only future and ambiguous pay-offs.

The case for membership focused on the beneficial effects to Ireland of participation in the Community's Common Agricultural Policy (CAP). This would immediately result in higher prices for Ireland's agricultural produce and, it was argued, stimulate a growth in both agriculture and related servicing and processing industries. In addition, Ireland's industrial sector would receive the stimulus of both favourable access to EEC markets and increased foreign investments attracted by its new opportunities. Finally, membership of the EEC would result in cash transfers to Ireland under the Community's regional and social policies and would allow Ireland to participate in its policy-making bodies.

Those opposed to membership argued that the dynamic consequences of EEC membership were at best uncertain. For example, they pointed out that the only certain thing to flow from participation in CAP was not expanded Irish output but a higher food bill for the Irish people. Further, they argued that it was futile to suppose that Irish industries could ever compete effectively with those of the European core and at the same time both make up for the losses sustained as a consequence of new foreign access to Ireland and provide jobs for the fastest growing population in the EEC. The static benefits of membership, cash transfers, were miniscule when set against these dubious effects and, indeed, CAP promised its own distortions by favouring the established producer in the agricultural sector. Finally, membership of the EEC would further diminish what little influence the government retained over the outflow of Irish labour and capital and involve Ireland in close association with old colonial powers in such a way as to compromise its traditional foreign policy.[14]

The merits of either side in this debate are not a central concern here. To judge by subsequent events, the opponents of membership offered a more accurate assessment of its consequences for Ireland than did those in favour of it. The weakness of the opposition's case, however, was not to be found in the debate which focused upon the effects of EEC membership. Rather, it lay in the fact that Ireland, unlike Britain, was not confronted by a choice between joining and the *status quo*.[15] Unless Britain stayed out, it was very difficult to make a case for Ireland remaining outside the EEC that did not entail a major transformation of its economy or, at least, immediate costs and disruptions, neither of which would have been conducive to electoral success for the government of the day.

By the start of our second period of examination (1977), it is possible to chart three main sets of consequences arising out of Ireland's membership of the EEC. First, at the 'bread and butter' or 'Common Market' level, Ireland was receiving considerable cash transfers from the Community. Between 1970 and 1978, farm incomes increased by 75 per cent in real terms and agricultural prices trebled.[16] In addition, Ireland was the 'principal beneficiary' of the EEC's regional and social policies, transfers from these sources accounting for about 2 per cent of government spending in the first years after Ireland joined. However, agricultural output did not increase significantly and the spin-off developments in related industries did not clearly materialise. Rather, industries geared to the export market expanded with the help of increased foreign investments and government borrowing.

Secondly, and in conformity with the interdependence thesis, the pace of Ireland's increasing involvement with the international system, or part of it, was accelerated by EEC membership. The value of both imports and exports taken as a proportion of GDP increased from 26 and 40 per cent respectively in 1968, to 33.3 and 43.6 per cent in 1973, and 48.4 and 66.6 per cent in 1980.[17] Similarly, the value of foreign investments as a proportion of GNP increased from 15 per cent in the 1950s through 20 per cent in the 1960s to 30 per cent in the late 1970s.[18] By 1977-8, the Irish economy was recording the fastest growth rate of all OECD nations. This growth was largely financed by government borrowing from abroad which increased from an amount equivalent to 6.3 per cent of GNP per annum in the period 1967–73 to an average of just under 12 per cent by 1978.[19]

Thirdly, and again in conformity with the interdependence thesis, Ireland's deepening involvement with the international system was reflected by its increased participation in the procedures by which relations were managed in the system of which it had become a part. It might be argued that Ireland's increasing economic involvement with the international system was a trend which was merely accelerated by membership of the EEC, that is, that it had already developed. Ireland's increasing participation in the systems of rules and laws and the processes of decision-making and policy coordination designed to manage this deepening involvement, however, was almost entirely a consequence of joining the EEC. By doing this, the Irish government involved itself in new external relationships with the Commission and the governments or representatives of the other members of the EEC in the Council of Ministers.

By most criteria, therefore, Ireland's external relations had, as a result of joining the EEC, increased. Ireland was involved in a greater number of cross-boundary transactions with a greater number of other actors. Its relations had also become more complex, both in the sense that more transactions with more actors involves more complexity in itself, and because more policy issues acquired new international ramifications. Finally, its external relations had taken on a more interdependent character in the sense that, in so far as those relations were more regime-regulated, both Ireland and the other members of the EEC had an increased input into each other's internal and foreign affairs. In short, by 1977, Ireland had been participating for four years in a system and its associated processes which involved an increase in the conditions and relations of what Nye and Keohane have termed 'complex interdependence'.

Notes

1. While both of these are critical issues for any student of Irish politics and history, detailed attention will not be given to them here. There are several accounts of the campaign fought over membership of the EEC to which references will be made below. My primary concern has been to examine how two different but relatively stable external environments have shaped Irish foreign policy. Northern Ireland, *per se*, I do not regard as a foreign policy issue, although the effects of its existence clearly permeate the entire activity and in so far as they do, I refer to them. A chapter devoted to it could not do it justice; it would require a book, and this is not a book about Northern Ireland.
2. See Chapter 1. There are a large number of studies of the origins of Partition. For general introductions see: Lyons, op. cit., pp. 141-315 and 695-780; Kee, op. cit., passim; and Insight, op. cit., passim.
3. O'Brien, interview.
4. See Keatinge (1978), op. cit., pp. 105-113, for the details of these approaches. See Lyons, op. cit., p. 591 for the 'sore thumb' characterisation of the latter policy.
5. See Con Cremin, 'Northern Ireland at the United Nations: August/September 1969', in *Irish Studies In International Affairs*, Vol. 1, No. 2, pp. 67–8. The following narrative of events rests heavily on this article.
6. 'Cremin', in ISSA, ibid., p.73.
7. See ibid., for example, p. 73 and, in particular, its reference to Andrew Boyd, *Fifteen Men on a Powder Keg: A History of the UN Security Council*, Stein and Day, NY, 1971, pp. 318–29.
8. For an account of the operations of the UN from this perspective, see Abraham Yeselon and Anthony Gaglione, 'The Uses of the United Nations in World Politics', in *Intellect Magazine*, April 1975.
9. For an account of these matters which stresses the extent to which 'Northern Ireland' is a process which runs to its own logic see 'Keatinge', in Desmond Rea, op. cit., p. 307.
10. See Keatinge (1978), op. cit., p. 187.
11. See ibid., pp. 211-12 for details of the expansion of the policy machinery and the creation of the Anglo-Irish and Information Division of the Department of Foreign Affairs.
12. For details see Trevor C. Salmom, 'Ireland', in Carol and Kenneth Twichett (eds), *Building Europe: Britain's Partners in the EEC*, Europa Publications, London,1981, pp. 195-6; and N. J. Baxter Moore, 'The Impact of European Community membership on the Republic of Ireland', in N. Orvik and C. Pentland (eds), *The European Community at the Crossroads*, Centre for International Relations, Queen's University, Kingston, 1983, pp. 45-6.
13. Keatinge (1978), op.cit., p. 144; and Anthony Coughlan, 'Ireland' in Dudley Seers and Constantine Vaistos (eds), *Integration and Unequal Development*, St Martin's Press, NY, 1980, p. 123.
14. See 'Coughlan', op. cit., in Seers and Vaistos, p. 125, for most of these arguments.
15. See 'McAleese', in Gibson and Spencer, op. cit., p. 142.
16. See 'Baxter Moore' in Orvik and Pentland, op. cit., p. 57, and 'Coughlan', in Seers and Vaistos, op. cit., pp. 125-30, for the following statistics.
17. James Meenan, *The Irish Economy*, Liverpool UP, Liverpool 1970; and 'Baxter Moore', in Orvik and Pentland, op. cit., pp. 60-1.
18. 'Coughlan', in Seers and Vaistos, op. cit., pp. 123; 129.
19. Ibid., p. 130; and the OECD report on Ireland in 1982 estimated the Irish public borrowing requirement at 21.5 per cent of GNP that year.

7 Images of the EEC and Ireland's role within it

The development of Ireland's economic involvement with the outside world was a gradual process which pre-dates EEC membership and continues to this day. In the act of joining, however, Irish policy-makers transformed the external environment of the country into a situation where the relations of complex interdependence might be expected to come into play. This being so, one would expect the international role-playing which was a prominent feature of Irish foreign policy for ten years after 1956 to at best retain the marginalised and insulated status to which it had been relegated by the late 1960s or to disappear completely. According to complex interdependence theory, Irish governments should have found more attractive opportunities within regime politics to which to commit their scarce policy resources.

Far from disappearing, however, international role-playing was retained and new forms of it became central to the Irish effort to obtain what they wanted from the EEC. Within the Community, Irish governments pursued a version of their UN strategy, seeking influence and favours by creating a reputation for the country as a strong supporter of the 'European' idea. In addition to this *communautaire* role, they also developed a technique of threatening to obstruct Community processes when the latter posed problems for Irish interests. Presenting themselves as a *demandeur*, that is one who wanted a *quid pro quo* in return for cooperation, involved exploiting some of the rules of the EEC regimes but it was built upon a specific identity which they claimed for Ireland. Finally, as a result of disappointments with the way the EEC operated, role-playing within the Community was undertaken as an end in itself and the use of Ireland's membership of the EEC as a component of the role they continued to play in the wider world became more important.

Like joining the UN back in 1956, EEC membership was presented by the government as a great opportunity for Ireland. This time, however, the benefit was defined in more substantial terms than the recognition by other states of Ireland's rightful place in the community of nations. The EEC was presented as a means by which Ireland might diversify and change the character of its external and foreign policy relationships. It was argued that by such diversification, dependence upon Britain, viewed either in terms of a relationship of exploitation or as a relationship in which Ireland was 'held back' by the sluggish performance of the British economy, would be reduced.[1] Certainly, Ireland's entry into the EEC was accompanied by, and probably hastened, the relative decline in the importance of Britain as a target for Irish exports, although Britain remained Ireland's most important single trading partner.[2]

In the context of daily economic policy-making, however, the EEC's most immediate significance was as a source of money. The net benefit to Ireland from financial transfers through the Community budget increased from £30.5 million in 1973 to £455.3 million in 1979.[3] In 1974, net transfers accounted for 4.6 per cent of government expenditure or 2 per cent of total GNP. By 1980, these two figures had risen to 10 per cent and 5.5 per cent, respectively.[4] Important though the transfers were, however, according to the government they were still insufficient given the scale of the economic problems which Ireland confronted. Since the country had become a member of the EEC, its standard of living had declined in comparison to the Community average.[5] Throughout the period, therefore, a major objective of Irish policy was to increase the amount of money which they received to help pay for both the provision of a system of social services and benefits comparable to that which existed in the other members of the EEC and the development of a modern economic infrastructure.

How Irish governments pursued these objectives was dependent on the terms in which they understood the new external environment in which they were operating. No single vision of the EEC predominated, but it is possible to identify three broad images of it which were presented by spokesmen for the government, each with its own implications for international role-playing. The first was very similar to de Gaulle's conception of *l'Europe des patries*. The EEC was regarded as collection of sovereign states with each of which Ireland was more closely related and, hence, to each of which its government had to pay more attention in formulating and pursuing their own interests. It might be expected, therefore, that the old freewheeling policy of the 'active independent' speaking out 'without fear or favour' at the UN would be considerably constrained by this new environment.

Retired policy-makers, ex-diplomats and commentators on Irish foreign policy disagreed with this and minimised the sense of constraint suggested by such a view. They did so, however, for contradictory reasons. One former Taoiseach, even though he had employed a very activist foreign minister, suggested that since there was barely anything one might call world or European opinion, there was very little opportunity for Ireland to pursue a foreign policy of great significance, either at the EEC or the UN. To suggest, therefore, that it could get into trouble with its European colleagues over matters of high policy was to imply an inflated or 'pretentious' view of what the Irish could hope to achieve. A commentator on Irish political affairs with ministerial and diplomatic experience suggested that Ireland came under 'absolutely no pressure' from its European colleagues to behave itself. As he put it, any international difficulties into which Ireland got were 'entirely of our own creation'. At the same time, however, he suggested that Ireland did little because it was 'more tightly involved' in the international system than ever before. The point which was common to these remarks was that one did not need to find evidence of other governments constraining Irish foreign policy to explain the limited scope of the latter. The fact that Ireland was a small country, deeply involved in the international system constituted an explanation which was both simpler and sufficient.[6]

Those who were currently in office or who had been more closely involved with Irish foreign policy since joining the EEC were, naturally enough, less inclined to suggest that Ireland attempted little of significance to its European partners and, hence, were more likely to elaborate their sense of the constraints offered by these countries. For example, speaking in 1977 when he was Foreign Minister in the coalition government, Garret FitzGerald argued that over contentious matters in the EEC, the defence of national interests remained very important to all participants. Indeed, he claimed that a 'balanced policy covering the interests of all' would only emerge if each country involved fought its own corner. Up to a point, however, the pursuit of self-interest by members was constrained by the laws and conventions of the Community. There was not 'complete equality', but everyone was constrained by the need to make the system work and the 'disastrous effects' on all of them if it broke down.[7]

Such language is very suggestive of the complex interdependence characterisation of regime politics. However, FitzGerald offered an important modification on the idea of a general distribution of constraint. The pursuit of a national interest 'beyond a certain point of unreason', he argued, was constrained by the risk of evoking hostility from others. If one provoked a 'large and important' country on a specifc issue, for example, it was likely to oppose you on others. Clearly, however, not all the members were equally constrained, for as FitzGerald went on to say, it was easier for large countries than small ones to get away with the pursuit of national interests in the face of general opposition.[8] Speaking in the Dáil a year later, he suggested why this was so. The EEC in its present form preserved a place for a degree and type of national sovereignty which helped 'the big countries boss small ones' but which did not 'give small ones any great power to stop themselves being bossed'.[9]

This view of the EEC as a series of national constraints upon Irish policy was typical of neither FitzGerald nor his Fianna Fáil successors. As I shall show below, it is not to be found when specific Irish goals were being thwarted, but rather when joint efforts to develop the Community as a policy-making entity in itself ran into nationally-based opposition. It was in their efforts to contribute to a restructuring of these relationships, or as they would have put it, to get certain members to live up to the more dynamic aspects of commitments into which they had entered when they accepted membership of the EEC, that Irish governments expressed the most frustration at the way in which specific governments could obstruct policy. The only other circumstance in which Irish governments would address the proposition that EEC membership entailed that other governments could circumscribe Irish policy was on the issue of neutrality, and they would do this only to reject the suggestion out of hand. According to the serving members of the government and diplomats who were interviewed for this section, national constraints on Irish policy in the EEC were not those associated with high political manoeuvring. While foreign policy in the EEC was practised in what one serving minister called a 'more nuanced and sensitive situation', it was so in the sense that it involved 'a lot of phoning around' to one's opposite numbers at ministerial or administrative levels to make sure that something which one proposed to do was agreeable to everyone else and did not contradict previous decisions which had been jointly made.

Far more common was the idea that EEC membership somehow enhanced Irish capabilities and, hence, should be regarded as an instrument of Irish foreign policy. According to Jack Lynch, speaking as Taoiseach in 1977, the Community constituted the greatest trading bloc and the second largest economic power in the world and, hence, had to be listened to when it spoke with a collective voice. Ireland, he went on to say, had a 'place and a voice in these counsels' and EEC membership gave it a 'weight and influence' which it could never have acting in isolation.[10] This formulation suggests that Ireland's enhanced capabilities came from being subsumed into a greater, if compatible, European position. Other spokesmen for the government, however, argued that it was Irish influence *per se* which was strengthened by membership of the EEC. Speaking of the European Political Cooperation process by which the governments of the EEC attempted to adopt joint positions on international issues of common concern, Michael O'Kennedy claimed in 1978, that it had underlined 'the greatly expanded role' which Ireland was now playing in international affairs. Any balance sheet of influence lost and gained as a result of EEC membership would clearly indicate that the Irish had gained more in the 'relevance and effectiveness' of what they

107

could achieve than they had lost in 'the freedom to take up whichever position we please'. Indeed, he argued that retaining the ability to pursue established objectives of Irish foreign policy had been a precondition of membership. Having struggled so long to 'assert our own identity and independence', he maintained, the Irish government committed Ireland to the EEC only when they were sure that through membership these 'aims and hopes' could be realised 'to greater effect'.[11]

These formulations regarding Ireland's 'more significant role' and 'greater weight and effectiveness'[12] were generally made with regard to foreign policy matters outside the Community. Ireland, speaking as one of the Nine on a position agreed to by all of them, for example, at the UN or the Conference on Security and Cooperation in Europe (CSCE), would now do so with the weight of the Nine behind it. Occasionally, however, it was suggested that membership of the EEC also strengthened Ireland in its relations with the other members and that this strength did not only exist when common positions were established. Speaking on EPC in 1981, for example, FitzGerald suggested that it not only allowed the Irish to make a contribution to policy-making 'in disproportion to our size', it also allowed them to put forward views which were not held by the majority and, indeed, might not have been adhered to by 'more than one or two other countries'.[13] Spokesmen for the government saw EEC membership and the new close relations which it entailed with the other members of the Community as enhancing, rather than constraining, their ability to pursue Irish foreign policy goals. Nevertheless, they also presented an image of the EEC as an external environment which corresponds closely to the characterisation of regime politics offered by theorists of complex interdependence. For example, they displayed little of the customary reticence of governments when asked if membership of the organisation compromised the sovereignty of the state. As O'Kennedy pointed out in 1977, speaking on the establishment of a joint committee to review the impact of EEC legislation upon Ireland, by joining they had adopted a new legal order which took 'precedence' over the 'national system of law-making in areas covered by the Treaties'.[14] Similarly, speaking to the Dáil in 1981, the Taoiseach, Charles Haughey, made it clear that, in joining the EEC, the Irish government had conferred certain powers on the institutions of the Community which 'in consequence, they themselves cannot exercise'.[15]

Further, members of the government noted an increase in both the range and the complexity of the issues with which Irish foreign policy had to deal. In a private interview, the Minister for Agriculture at that time stressed that it was increasingly a negotiating job concerned with 'all sorts of arrangements, price reviews and quotas, highly technical issues, trade and economic and financial issues'. Speaking in 1977, Lynch acknowledged what he called the 'merging of matters of home and foreign policy'. This, he maintained, was 'what the Community is all about'[16] and O'Kennedy, speaking the following year to the Foreign Affairs estimate, argued that

Ireland like every country, large or small, merely by existing as an independent State in a world of other States, is involved in a network of relations within the international community. It is clear to everyone from many recent developments, and especially since we became involved in the EEC, that these relations are important and that we are deeply affected by events outside our own shores.[17]

Not only did Irish policy-makers at times characterise the EEC as a policy environment in the general terms and sometimes the precise language of complex interdependence, they also made much of the organisational burden of responding to the challenges which it presented to them. This was reflected in changes in the foreign policy process and their own involvement with external affairs. With regard to the latter, for example, in the first fifteen months of the Fianna Fáil government elected in 1977, the Taoiseach and thirteen of his ministers made a total of 154 trips abroad, some two-thirds of them on EEC-related business and less than twenty of them involving visits to Britain. Of these, the Foreign Minister, O'Kennedy still made the greatest single number of visits (29 plus 17 by his minister of state). It should be noted, however, that he was closely followed by the Ministers for Agriculture (23) and Fisheries and Forests (17). In addition, ten parliamentary secretary positions, five of which had formal, external responsibilities, were reclassified with the new rank of Minister of State in recognition of their increasing importance.[18]

The Department of Foreign Affairs itself had been expanded after Ireland joined the EEC and the change in the Department's name from External to Foreign Affairs was itself indicative of a perceived change in both its character and status. While the commercial and economic roles of the Department, for example, in advising and employing the officers of other departments and undertaking negotiations with state-trading nations were emphasised, however, expansion took place within the Anglo-Irish and Political sections of the Department as well as the Economic Division.[19] This was because the response of Irish policy-makers to this perceived complexity and the actual expansion of Ireland's international relations was articulated not in terms of the ongoing management of complexity, but rather, the need for a single, national strategy integrating both domestic and foreign policy into a coherent whole. O'Kennedy argued, for example, that to act effectively in such an environment, Ireland could not pursue policies which were 'worked out in isolation' on what he called a 'freewheeling basis'. What was needed was a 'coherent overall policy...in the internal as well as the external field'.[20]

There was, therefore, no decline in the standing or status of the Department of Foreign Affairs or its Minister of the kind suggested by Maurice East.[21] According to O'Kennedy, speaking in 1978, the Department remained 'primarily, though not solely responsible for Ireland's external affairs', since for a member of the EEC, '...the work of most Departments of State... will have certain international aspects'. Nevertheless, it was up to the government to set

109

'a general direction for our foreign relations as a state' and within the government it was the responsibility of the Minister for Foreign Affairs 'to coordinate and give overall direction to our foreign relations and to give expression to an Irish foreign policy'.[22] Speaking for the previous government in 1977 on Irish fisheries policy, Kelly had clarified the division of labour that should exist between the Department of Foreign Affairs and, in his example, the department responsible for Fisheries. The task of the former was largely a negotiating one, whereas that of the latter was largely 'technical and economic' in its nature. According to Brian Lenihan, when he was Minister for Agriculture, Foreign Affairs and ex-Foreign Affairs people dominated the permanent Irish positions in the EEC and would work closely with ministers from other departments, such as himself at that time, if they had to go to Brussels to conduct negotiations.

The importance and extent of this coordinating role is difficult to assess. Keatinge has suggested that the Departments of Finance and Agriculture still tended to do their own coordinating, although Foreign Affairs' particular skills do give it a 'foot in the door'.[23] According to one junior official, a member of the department would often chair inter-departmental meetings in Dublin, for example for shaping Irish policy on the question of the Community's milk super-levy. On the other hand, a foreign delegation on a 'functional' issue could be comprised of personnel from the relevant domestic department. For example, the International Civil Aviation Conference convened in Montreal to discuss the issues raised by the shooting down of a Korean airliner by an aircraft of the USSR was attended by people from the Department of Transport. In such circumstances, the role of the Department of Foreign Affairs was restricted to briefings regarding the issue, policy positions and their implications for Ireland's broader policy and interests.

Nevertheless, it is not a question of the decline of the department, but rather the extent of its emergence as a powerful coordinating organ which is at issue. It is clear that a considerable debate took place within the government during the late 1960s and early 1970s regarding the future role of the Department of External Affairs, as it then was, in the conduct of Ireland's European policy. According to one senior official with UN experience but based in London when interviewed, External Affairs had been regarded as a 'UN department' and as EEC membership was seen very much as an economic issue, the Departments of Finance and Agriculture tended to dominate. Once Ireland had joined, however, he suggested that it was the weakness of External Affairs which helped it assume its new position. The 'powerful barons' of the other departments could agree to its coordination of European policy where they could not agree to the domination of their domestic rivals. Further, he suggested (in contrast to East's predictions)[24] that the generalist skills of the department were regarded as an asset for EEC politics. From this, he claimed, had emerged a department which not only sought to keep its domestic counterparts' 'various interests in balance' by pointing out the interrelatedness

110

of issues and actions, but also attempted to locate them within a broader conception of Ireland's foreign policy. As he put it, the role of Foreign Affairs was 'to take an overview...less narrow than that of someone directly concerned about the super-levy...and to try to recall that we have a larger perspective into which it must fit'.[25]

The Irish government worked with no settled view of the EEC although on occasions their spokesmen employed an imagery which corresponded to the characterisations of regime politics offered by theorists of complex interdependence. Their organisational response, if not the diplomat's explanation of it offered above, also conformed in part to the predictions of the theory. However, the principal strategy adopted by the Irish government for securing what they wanted from the EEC owed more to their international role-playing at the UN than to any innovation engendered by the international organisation politics of complex interdependence. The problem for the Irish was that the benefits of EEC membership, expressed in whatever terms one wished, cash transfers, participation in powerful institutions, or the enhancement of a distinctively Irish foreign policy, flowed neither from an unlimited disposition towards generosity on the part of the other members of the Community nor, more importantly, from an Irish capacity to extract them in the face of external opposition.

As a weak beneficiary, the Irish were in a potentially vulnerable situation. According to FitzGerald, they simply could not adopt a 'poor mouth attitude' saying to people who provided sums 'equivalent to ten per cent of our budget' that they were 'behaving badly by not providing much more'.[26] In the absence of significant means of leverage over other members of the Community, therefore, the Irish response to the problem of securing the benefits of membership was directed at creating a favourable disposition on the part of other governments towards Irish objectives. This was attempted by projecting an image of Ireland as a principled, effective and useful supporter of the principles upon which the EEC was based and the future evolution of its institutions. By projecting this *communautaire* identity, it was argued, the Irish would acquire goodwill and tolerance from their partners and, hence, a measure of influence over them.

Both the political and economic evolution of the Community were, of course, regarded as desirable developments for Ireland in the sense that any strengthening of international order would help the weak. The adoption of this stance in itself, however, was also claimed to be beneficial. FitzGerald, for example, argued that, while the Irish had obtained 'very substantial benefits' from membership, the high standing they enjoyed among the other countries was remarkable. Their success in this regard was due to the fact that other countries accepted them as 'a constructive member of the Community'. Hence they did not resent the scale of transfers accruing to Ireland. According to him, that was 'what diplomacy is all about; it is to achieve that result'.[27] Later, in discussing the 'immense advantages' which he claimed that the coalition government had obtained for Ireland, he argued that they had been secured by 'a mixture of skilled diplomacy' and 'goodwill' created by the 'positive character' of the Irish contribution to the Community in many areas 'where no vital Irish interest was involved'.[28]

It may be seen from subsequent elaborations by FitzGerald and others that they were not primarily referring to Irish diplomatic successes either in terms of mobilising allies or furthering specific objectives. Rather, they were discussing a broader effort to establish Ireland's standing with its EEC partners by impressing them on the principled and useful nature of Irish foreign policy. According to FitzGerald, Ireland's standing in the EEC resulted from its work for 'a more effective Community' and willingness to uphold 'the European view' in the face of opposition from countries 'pursuing nationalist interests'.[29] O'Kennedy maintained that Ireland's EEC standing derived from its 'whole-hearted participation' in the institutions of the Community and its 'constant support' for the Treaty of Rome.[30] The extent to which Ireland's European policy was designed to impress all or most of the other members, rather than simply to obtain the support of like-minded governments was underlined by FitzGerald's claim that even those who were hostile to 'European union' and disagreed with the Irish treated them with 'a certain sympathy and respect' and regarded them 'in a curious way as being the better Europeans for holding to this position'.[31]

In addition to the principled nature of Irish foreign policy, the manner in which it was pursued was also claimed as a virtue which impressed other governments. O'Kennedy, in particular, argued that it was not the good intentions of a policy alone which mattered, but also the extent to which it was pursued with consistency and determination. Powerful nations, he claimed, clearly related their foreign policies to their domestic needs and national priorities, not just the better to achieve their objectives but also to communicate clearly their intentions, objectives and resolve to other governments. States like Ireland, which were small in terms of 'resources ...international contact and connection', needed to be big in terms of 'consistency, persuasion and determination' if they were to work through international organisations for 'greater world stability and peace'. They would be judged by others in these terms, and since so many new opportunities for action now existed, it was important that Ireland pursue a 'consistent line' in each new area. Opinions and moral judgements delivered in 'an abstract sense', while personally satisfying, were neither effective nor did they constitute a foreign policy. Ireland's status in the EEC was derived from the consistent position which it adopted on regional, social, monetary and economic policy. According to O'Kennedy, an outside observer could see a 'clear and consistent pattern by which they could identify almost any issue on which Ireland is likely to stand'.[32]

The emphasis in both these conceptions was upon the qualities which Ireland offered rather than the spirit in which they were received by other governments. However, Lenihan, speaking in 1980 in the context of major budget

112

problems being experienced by the Community, provided the clearest statement of the use of small states, not just Ireland, to their larger counterparts. It was in the interests of the latter to have the support of small states for political and strategic reasons even if they did regard them primarily as recipients of 'largesse'. Without such support, the larger states would find themselves 'in a very naked position strategically and politically'.[33] A small state such as Ireland, therefore, could be useful to the other members of the Community in a number of ways. First, there was the minimalist sense in which Ireland constituted another vote and another small state whose adherence to a position might confer a measure of respectability upon the latter. Secondly, there was the extent to which Irish governments were prepared to pursue an active, principled and effective *communautaire* policy within the EEC. Finally, it was claimed that Ireland had a usefulness to other members of the Community which was derived from specific and unique attributes of its previously elaborated international personality.

In particular, it was frequently observed that Ireland was the only member of the EEC which was not also a member of NATO and had no imperial past. The significance of this, according to O'Kennedy, was that Ireland shared the historical experiences of many of the Third World countries with which it and the rest of the EEC were cooperating. As such its government had both 'an opportunity and an obligation' to reach out and establish the 'common ground' which existed between the African, Asian and European regional 'blocs'.[34] This was a particularly important function when one remembered that the developing countries did not regard some of the other members of the EEC with 'the same degree of admiration they have for our country'.[35] The value of these unique attributes, however, was not entirely in the way they might enable an Irish government to play bridging roles or undertake a dissolution of the blocs into which the world was divided. More mundanely, but more accurately, a serving minister in private interview stated that the EEC 'found it useful' to have a member country which was small and independent, particularly in its UN policy. This provided openings for the development of relationships between Third World countries and other members of the Community and it gave the EEC a presence in any peacekeeping operations which were likely to be mounted. Further, the larger European countries, he claimed, valued the fact that Ireland was a small country lacking in 'large vested interests' which could 'speak the truth or what approximates to it' in public on occasions.[36]

A central assumption of the *communautaire* strategy, like the 'good citizen' approach to UN policy which it mirrored, was the idea that other governments were in some way sensitive to moral pressure and example. Whether this was so in the sense that under such pressure governments would begin to behave like the source of morality, Ireland, or at least in a way which the Irish desired, or whether it was simply a way of enabling Ireland to be left alone as some strange, charmed member of the international community, is not altogether clear. When asked about this, those who were interviewed emphasised the sense of a moral imperative that Irish governments regarded themselves as being under to try, at least, to influence others in this manner. They regarded Ireland's successful struggle for independence as proof that by decent people trying to do decent things the world could be improved, and that while this might be a naive belief, it was, as one diplomat put it, 'intentional naiveté'. Were it not true, then there was very little else Irish governments could do to improve Ireland's position.

Certainly, in FitzGerald's articulation of European policy, the idea of Europe existing as a simple community of states bound, up to a point, by a common scale of values was very prominent. In it, their governments appeared almost as a conclave of sinners of various magnitudes, none, with the possible exception of that old reprobate Britain, sufficiently beyond salvation as to be impervious to the influence of good arguments and good example. They were all, if not vulnerable exactly, then sensitive at least, to Irish appeals on the basis of the European 'idea'. For O'Kennedy, on the other hand, the pursuit of status and reputation seemed much less a question of either policy content or the moral sensibilities of one's targets. The basic virtue of Irish foreign policy was not at issue, and O'Kennedy's arguments to the effect that intermittent displays of virtue were not enough, suggest that catching the conscience of other governments was not regarded as crucial by him either. What was important was the question of credibility, the need for Ireland to be seen to be performing at all times like a real state, a unitary actor with a coherent and consistently pursued set of interests and objectives. To get what it wanted from an external environment which had an increasing and profound impact upon life in Ireland, the Irish government had to orchestrate a national response and had to be seen to be so doing. At all costs, the appearance of dabbling in international affairs on an intermittent and detached basis had to be avoided. If they were to be impressed by anything, then the governments of other states would be impressed by the extent to which the Irish could behave like one of them while remaining true to their own values.

Common to both these conceptions of influence, and indeed, to Lenihan's more *realpolitik* formulation which focused on large state needs rather than small state qualities, was the concern with how Ireland as a state actor appeared to the governments of other countries. As with the UN, the government assumed that success in creating the right image might provide Ireland with either the tolerance of its needs by other governments or a measure of influence over them derived from Irish status and prestige.

The assumption that the EEC was like the UN only better was, in a general sense, true. The real question was whether this suited Irish interests as the government defined them. Like the UN, the EEC is an organisation whose members are formally committed to interacting with one another on the basis of agreed rules. In addition, the member governments have surrendered a measure of their authority to central organs, the Commission, the Council of

Ministers, the Court of Justice, the Parliamentary Assembly and the Economic and Social Committee, which are variously charged with initiating, administering, interpreting and enforcing legislation on matters which fall within their defined spheres of competence. Also like the UN, the EEC has been troubled throughout its history by 'statist rebellions'. On occasion, dissenting major powers have not only prevented the adoption of specific common policies to which they have been opposed, but have also stalled the political processes of the EEC by using what has been in effect a veto.[37]

Unlike the UN, however, the EEC and its associated processes have remained central to the relations of its members among themselves. There are several reasons for this. First, in comparison to the UN, the EEC is comprised of a few, similar and closely related members. The major cleavages between East and West or North and South which beset the UN do not have counterparts to anything like the same extent in the EEC. Secondly, no single member of the EEC is sufficiently powerful enough to dominate the organisation or even a significant sub-grouping within it, or to ignore it by conducting the greater part of their foreign policy without reference to that body. Thirdly, the government of each member country seems to accept that it cannot pursue its own particular economic goals without a measure of regularised collaboration with the other members.

As a consequence, therefore, the members of the EEC have enjoyed considerable success in making themselves into a single trading system distinguished from outsiders by a common tariff barrier and by the development of common policies for the organisation of their production, labour, finance, transportation and trade. This has been regarded by some member governments as an end in itself and by others as the precursor to the coordination of social and political policies in a future European state. In the latter perspective, the EEC institutions listed above have been regarded as the components of a future European government in embryo. How accurate this view is, and indeed the merits of the various schools of thought on 'whither Europe?', do not directly concern us here. What is important is that the EEC, as an international (regional) organisation in which Ireland participates, has both a history of successful integration and institution-building when compared to the UN, and provides an ideological paradigm of commitment to the further development of the Community, or at least to some kind of integrative momentum, within which relations of either conflict or cooperation between members take place.

It is in this sense that the EEC has been regarded by Irish governments as like the UN only better, and it is upon the assumption that a strong Community would mitigate the dangers and unfairness of an international anarchy for weak states that the *communautaire* policy was based. This policy has involved a number of things. First of all, there was a strongly articulated commitment on the part of Irish governments to conduct themselves according to the existing rules of the Community and to abide by the decisions of its institutions.

115

Secondly, in the debates about the extent to which power and authority did or should reside with each of the member governments over its own affairs or with varying forms of the collective expression of the will of the Community members, Irish governments have usually argued for their residing with the latter. Thirdly, Irish governments have emphasised the view of the EEC as an evolving community or international organisation, and to this end have stressed the importance of maintaining momentum in the strengthening of Community institutions and the expansion of areas of common policy.

According to FitzGerald speaking in 1977, 'strengthening the institutions of the Community' had been a 'consistent Irish position' respected even by those who disagreed with it, and it had been based upon calculations 'compounded of interest and idealism'. What Ireland needed to do, he continued, was to work to preserve an institutional structure within which the country remained 'capable of operating effectively' because it was such structures which protected small states and their interests.[38]   This enlightened self-interest articulation of the policy was, for example, in evidence in the Department of Foreign Affairs bulletin on Irish–Luxembourg relations released at the time of a visit by the Grand Duke and Duchess. It claimed that Ireland had benefited from the way in which Luxembourg pursued an 'active, positive and creative role' in developing the EEC. As the two smallest countries in the EEC, both realised the importance of 'preserving the fundamental principles of the Communities, of respecting their institutions and of developing their policies'.[39]

The *communautaire* policy found its strongest expression in support for the institutions of the EEC and, in particular, the Commission. The EEC Commission is, in the words of Dennis Swann, 'in effect the civil service of the Community'.[40] It was during this period comprised of fourteen commissioners each with responsibility for one or more portfolios and supported by a team of civil servants, his or her 'cabinet'. While composed on the basis of national quotas, the Commission was intended to define and promote 'European' interests in contrast to the national interests of the member states, expressed either individually or collectively by their governments. Article 157 of the Rome Treaty requires that the Commissioners 'shall neither seek nor take instruction from any Government or from any other body'.[41] In addition to its formal status of independence, the Commission was also given the 'sole right of initiative' by the Rome Treaty. This allows it to present the Council of Ministers with policy proposals. While the Council is under no obligation to accept these proposals, during the early years of the Community, when there was a consensus among the member governments regarding measures for integrating their economies, the Commission established a reputation for both leading and pushing members into adopting the measures required in the twelve-year transition period envisaged by the original treaty.

In practice, the scope and success of the Commission's initiating role has been dependent upon the degree of consensus existing among member governments with regard to what it has wanted them to do or accept. The Commission, nevertheless, has retained its status or reputation as the rallying point for those who wish to see the EEC function as a truly integrated body rather than one characterised simply by inter-governmental cooperation, and those who are frustrated when particular member governments prevent the adoption of joint policies. In a private interview, one serving minister expressed Irish policy towards the Commission in the following terms.

> We are very 'pro' the Commission in economic and social matters. We believe that the Community has a number of economic and social problems that need to be resolved and that the Commission is the agency through which these matters should be implemented, and a greater union in the economic and social sense and a greater regional fund, greater transfer of resources, strengthening of Community institutions, Common Agricultural Policy, all this area, the economic and social area, in all this we are for the Commission.

For a small state like Ireland, the Commission was regarded as a powerful ally which, through its right of initiative and commitment to the development of the Community, could serve Irish interests, although these were proclaimed as virtually identical with Community interests by Irish governments. If the Commission was seen as an Irish ally, then Ireland too was proclaimed an ally or prompter of the Commission. According to O'Kennedy, speaking to the Dáil as Foreign Minister in 1977, Irish policy in the future would seek to 'strengthen the Commission and give it the iron will' to pursue policies consistent with the Rome Treaty and Ireland's Treaty of Accession.[42]

The most powerful institution of the EEC has been the Council of Ministers. This is because Community regulations and directives become law only after the Council has agreed to them. It operates as a series of meetings attended by government ministers responsible for national policy on the issue being discussed. The Ministers of Foreign Affairs and Agriculture are those which are most frequently in attendance. The Council considers proposals emanating from the Commission or from its own members, which are presented to it with recommendations through the Council's own Committee of Permanent Representatives (Coreper), which works on proposals between its meetings. In spite of its importance, the Council of Ministers has not featured prominently in articulations of their *communautaire* position by Irish governments. The reasons for this are quite straightforward. If the Commission serves as the focus for sentiment favouring the emergence of 'Europe' as a single political entity, then the Council is proof of the extent to which it remains an organisation dependent upon inter-governmental cooperation. From a *communautaire* perspective, the Council serves as an arena in which support for the Commission and achievement of common policies should be offered and proclaimed by oneself and demanded of others. It is an institution to be used rather than defended. Only, as I shall show below, in the discussion of decision-making procedures within the Council have problems of a supranational significance arisen within that body, most notably over the nature of the majority required to have decisions adopted. These problems have presented Irish governments with some very difficult choices.

The European Parliament has been an institution which is more compatible with the *communautaire* perspective. It is comprised of deputies from the member countries, each country having a quota, previously selected by its own procedures, but now elected by the public. Originally, the parliament was 'consultative rather than legislative'[43] its only real power (threatened, although never used) being its right to dismiss the Commission through a vote of censure. Throughout the second period under study, however, the significance of the Parliament increased, both because of the establishment of direct elections to it and because of the extension of its right of approval over the Community budget from its 'free part' (the 5 per cent arising from operating the institutions of the Community) to the non-obligatory component.

One might expect the proponents of a *communautaire* approach to be supportive of a European institution whose members' views were not coordinated with those of their national governments. The Irish approach, however, has been cautious. R. K. Carty, for example, has claimed that a measure of disagreement has existed along party lines. According to him, Fianna Fáil has taken a nationalist perspective which tends to be suspicious of surrendering power to an institution in which Ireland has only had 3.5 per cent of the members.[44] In contrast to this, Kelly, speaking for the coalition government on the European Communities (Amendment Bill 1977) claimed that Ireland supported anything which helped the European Parliament gain control over the Community budget. This and the establishment of a European Court of Auditors, he argued, would contribute to the development of 'a more democratic and efficient Community'.[45] And Carty's remarks above notwithstanding, O'Kennedy, speaking to the Dáil as Minister for Foreign Affairs for the Fianna Fail government elected later that same year, claimed that direct elections would strengthen Ireland's position in the Community by providing a 'direct democratic link' between Irish citizens and 'decision-making in the Community'.[46] This was because, as both Kelly and O'Kennedy had earlier agreed, a European parliament with stronger budgetary powers would enforce a greater regard for the periphery of the Community.[47]

The *communautaire* policy, therefore, involved support for those institutions and procedures of the EEC which emphasised the extent to which it was a single entity rather than a means of inter-governmental collaboration. In this view, the member governments were committed to participating in the making of joint decisions and abiding by and implementing Community decisions properly arrived at even when, in their individual judgement, some of the consequences of these decisions were not held to be in their national interest. Further, the member governments were also committed to enlarging this process and extending the areas of common policy rather than simply cooperating when they regarded it as being in their own national interest, rather than in the interest of the Community as a whole to do so. As such, the strategy presented Irish governments with a number of problems. First, and most obviously, implicit in its logic was the idea that the sovereignty and autonomy of all governments, Ireland's included, should be diminished. What was advocated was not a change in the distribution of capabilities among the members of the EEC, but a transformation of the political character of the Community from a system of horizontal collaboration to one organised in terms of an hierarchical authority. Now the logical implications of a principle espoused do not necessarily have implications for subsequent political practice. The *communautaire* position was, after all, not a new one for Irish governments but rather an extension of the position they had adopted in the UN, and this had had few consequences for Irish sovereignty. What was novel, however, was that in the EEC, it was a position which was likely to have important consequences for the Irish government.

They were aware of the problem. One response, as has been noted earlier, was the glib formulation that those with nothing had nothing to lose. According to FitzGerald, a strong Commission with the right of initiative might hurt Ireland 'from time to time', but on the balance, Ireland still did better from its existence.[48] Further, on occasions, the Irish government justified the abandonment of particular policy positions on the basis of placing a higher value on the maintenance of Community solidarity. In the negotiations for a trade agreement between the EEC and Yugoslavia in 1980, for example, the Irish had found themselves isolated with regard to technicalities on the question of the importation of 'baby beef'. Lenihan justified what he called an Irish 'climb down' on the issue in terms of first, high politics, and then, *communautaire* principles. 'First of all' he had argued, the agreement with Yugoslavia had to be understood in terms of 'stability in Europe'. It had been primarily made for 'very important strategic and political reasons'. Secondly, however, Ireland had conceded on the 'baby beef aspect' because it was opposed by all the other eight governments. Thus, he continued,

> in the context of the overall situation we reluctantly agreed, primarily because in the Community one cannot act in isolation at all times. If there are strong compelling reasons pushed by eight of the nine one cannot hold one's position indefinitely.[49]

The future loss of sovereignty implicit in the *communautaire* strategy was not in itself a major problem. The evolution of the Community in accordance with its original supranational objectives was not expected to occur in the immediate future, but the Irish government claimed that they would welcome it. The real problem was whether, in the meantime, the projection and performance of the component parts of the *communautaire* role within the EEC could secure cash transfers, Community reforms, a place in European decision-making and a clearly Irish identity in the international system. Irish internationalism was predicated on the general assumption that the international system consisted of an anarchy characterised by disorder in which the less powerful were at a disadvantage. Hence, 'international order' *per se*, was a thing to be valued, and in the absence of its attainability in its fullest sense, any particular mitigation of anarchy or any general promulgation of orderly values as a hostile ideological environment with which to hinder the activities of the strong was much to be desired and worth working for. The emphasis, however, was on order *per se* and not particular orders. In this, Irish governments accepted the choice presented by traditional thought on international relations between order and stability on the one hand and warfare, and latterly, global destruction on the other.

Membership of the EEC confronted Irish governments with the problems of a particular international order in a way in which the UN never really had. Some of the problems were familiar, for example, office-holding and voting rights within Community institutions were allocated on a quota basis determined very roughly on the principle that a country's number of places or votes should reflect its size. Thus, Ireland had one Commissioner out of thirteen,[50] three votes out of 58 on the Council of Ministers and 15 seats out of 410 in the European Parliament, all in a regional organisation of sovereign states in which Ireland constituted one member out of nine and, latterly, ten. The rights and wrongs of this distribution are not at issue here. The point is that the mathematics suggested that Irish interests might be maximised by strategies other than the *communautaire* stress on anything which tended to erode the emphasis on sovereign states as the important actors.

Less familiar was the character of inter-state relations within the EEC. As the Irish became more unhappy with the way in which the EEC failed to develop or solve some of its problems during this period, they increasingly found themselves in the position of having to haggle for cash benefits by way of compensation for, or to secure their acquiescence in, developments in Community policy which they could welcome neither in fact nor in principle. In such circumstances, both the utility and the credibility of the *communautaire* approach were considerably reduced.

The external significance of these problems is necessarily diminished by the fact that the particular choice of policy towards the EEC made by Irish governments was not the prime determinant of the benefits they accrued from it, except perhaps with regard to active participation viewed as an end in itself. Of more importance was the set of domestic problems associated with the attempt to pursue an international role-playing foreign policy which emphasised national distinctiveness and independence, when one was in the process of becoming more deeply involved in the international system, or a part of it.

I have argued that Ireland's UN policy of international role-playing enjoyed a certain measure of success. Ireland obtained prestige from its activist strategy and, indeed, a measure of international influence although this was restricted to the issue-areas in which the prestige was achieved. This was a satisfactory state of affairs so long as the ideological or working distinction between politics and economics could be maintained. The former was the realm of prestige and principle in which even the costs of the policy themselves demonstrated the reality and the value of Irish independence. The latter was the realm of quiet management in which the government worked for the best deal possible. Independence might have been severely circumscribed, or enjoyed on a sectoral basis, but it was a form of independence that, except in times of external changes such as those in the trading regime with Britain, was not continually being called into question. For domestic purposes in particular, Ireland's foreign policy gave the government something both real and satisfying to point to as proof of Ireland's independence. Externally, it let them do some very worthwhile and laudable things.

Extending role-playing into the EEC, treating the latter in effect as a second UN, entailed a number of consequences, however. First, in an external environment in which Ireland was much more closely involved and in which politics and economics were closely intertwined, the claim that certain aspects of its national identity – for example, neutrality and the colonial past – were useful to other governments was much more likely to be tested in a costly manner. Secondly, this claim generated a debate in Ireland regarding the questionable contemporary 'utility' of what were once secure ends in themselves. Neutrality and international activism, for example, became recast by some as instruments for securing more concrete and immediate objectives, and by others as bargaining chips to be traded off for more substantial things.

It may be argued that this is not neccessarily a bad thing in the sense that a government does well to trade the jaded symbols of the past for concrete material gains when it is in a position to do so. There exists a considerable body of informed opinion in Ireland to the effect that this long overdue trade has implicitly taken place, with only the vestigial remnants of the 'independence' policy remaining to appease a more slowly adjusting public opinion and be exploited by unscrupulous politicians. There are, however, two difficulties with this. First, it has been very hard for any Irish government to disown the principles of the past. The legitimacy of the Irish state and its government rests in great part on the claim that 'independence' *per se* was worth having, even if this entailed a measure of relative material deprivation. While Ireland may have lagged behind Britain in terms of its economic performance and standard of living, this was presented as less important than the fact that its people were free to run their own affairs, restore their national culture and go their own way in the world. In this sense, to discuss the latter in terms of its being an obstacle to economic growth and material well-being could be seen as calling into question the whole meaning of and necessity for Irish independence.

More importantly, it may be seen that the Irish government was not actually confronted with a choice between defending obsolete political values and participating wholeheartedly in the essentially benign and apolitical administration of things which the EEC might be regarded as in this conception. At most, it was a 'choice' between holding to traditional political values and participating in an increasingly difficult economic and political environment. By extending international role-playing into its European policy, however, the Irish government attempted to deny the need to make such a choice and attempted to do both things at once.

This brings us to the second problem. By trying to do both things at once, by claiming that not only was Ireland's independent role useful to the EEC and, hence, Ireland's position in it, but also that membership of the EEC enhanced Ireland's own independent role in the wider world, the Irish government revealed a measure of ambiguity in their foreign policy. The original sense of this claim was to the effect that with the weight of the EEC behind them, the Irish could pursue their own cherished objectives, for example, in the UN, far more effectively. There was, however, another sense in which Ireland's independent role might be enhanced by membership of the EEC, and that was by using the latter as a forum within which Ireland could adopt distinctive positions when the opportunity arose. What the deepening international involvement implied by EEC membership entailed was that there was no longer an easy symmetry between, on the one hand, the effective pursuit of the immediate goals of the policies undertaken as components of Ireland's international role-playing, and the overarching objective of the policy, national prestige, distinctiveness and influence. An Irish effort, for example, to mobilise the rest of the EEC for an initiative in the search for peace in the Middle East, did not necessarily redound to the credit of Ireland as it would have in the 1950s. An Irish effort to 'go it alone' with regard to such a initiative, however, would not be the most effective contribution to the resolution of the specific problem which the Irish government was in a position to make.

Neither these two conceptions of the Community nor their respective implications for Irish foreign policy could be reconciled easily. The first involved the idea of working with Community partners to build consensus positions and, where the opportunity arose, leading them or steering them towards positions favoured by the Irish government. The second suggested that the Irish should work off, and on occasions against, the rest of the EEC to further their own interests. Such a policy, of course, would be inconsistent with the basic *communautaire* role articulated for Ireland by Irish governments. Indeed, Irish governments claimed that at all times they attempted to pursue the first approach of cooperation and consensus-building. Only when such a policy failed and on issues of vital national interest, or when the government was strongly committed to certain principles, they claimed, did they let Irish foreign policy diverge from that of the rest of the Community.

The latter formulation does amount to something more than a claim that, whatever its EEC obligations, the Irish government reserved the right to do what it liked when it liked. They were committed to the achievement of joint positions and, on occasions, as I have shown above, they surrendered their own policy preferences in the interests of Community solidarity, and cited this

122

reason rather than, for example, *force majeure*, to explain their change of position. The ambiguity in their foreign policy, however, left a standing opportunity or temptation to defect from Community solidarity to asserting an independent national identity in contrast to the rest of the EEC.

I shall show in the next chapter that three things increased the temptation to act in this manner. The first was the process by which a deepening international involvement put pressure at home on the basic elements of Ireland's independent identity. The demands of EEC membership in terms of economic conformity and political solidarity encouraged Irish governments to seek and take opportunities by which their national independence might be asserted. Secondly, the failure of the EEC to develop in accordance with Community principles also strengthened the temptation to defect. There was little incentive for the government of a small state to continue to absorb the costs and sacrifices implicit in a *communautaire* stance. It also operated, however, in the sense that the Community seemed to exact few penalties from its *demandeurs* and that, indeed, a strategy of this type appeared at times to be the most effective way of obtaining what one wanted from it. Thirdly, the inter-governmental character of existing EEC cooperation was made more attractive to the Irish by the development of the process of European Political Cooperation. The latter, while inconsistent with the *communautaire* desire for EEC development in a supranational direction, provided the Irish with opportunities for international role-playing of a more traditional kind.

Notes

1. For an example of this view see R. Ryan, Minister of Finance, 297, 259.
2. See 315, 1693-4 for details of this change up to 1979.
3. 319, 335-6, response to written question (20 March 1980).
4. 326, 1774 (12 February 1981).
5. 'Baxter Moore' in Orvik and Pentland, op. cit., p. 64.
6. These comments were based upon interviews conducted in Dublin in 1983.
7. 298, 1842-3 (28 April 1977). Dr Garret FitzGerald, formerly an economist and journalist, was Minister for Foreign Affairs in the Fine Gael/Labour coalition government of Liam Cosgrave, 1973–7, and Taoiseach 1981–2 and 1982–7. He is regarded as one of the most pro-EEC figures in public life in Ireland.
8. Ibid.
9. 308, 871 (19 October 1978).
10. 302, 1241 (8 December 1977). For a similar formulation by Charles Haughey, Taoiseach 1979-81 and 87–present, see 322, 1013 (8 June 1980).
11. 306-67 and 352-3 (4 May 1978). Michael O'Kennedy was Minister for Foreign Affairs between 1977 and 1979 in the Fianna Fáil government of Jack Lynch. He was particularly interested in Ireland's role in economic development in the Third World, and later became a European Commissioner.
12. O'Kennedy, 307, 299-300 and 314, 1918.
13. 330, 307.
14. 302, 957 (1 December 1977).

15. 328, 382.
16. 303, 1247.
17. 306, 341.
18. See 309, 721 for these data. See 315, 1440 and 318, 1136-63 for other statistics regarding overseas visits by members of the government. See 302, 1404 for details of the new Minister of State positions.
19. See O'Kennedy, 314, 233 for details of the Department's role in advising semi-state bodies and 312, 1153 for the Department's use of personnel from the Department of Agriculture. See *Ireland Today* (IT) (Bulletin of the Department of Foreign Affairs), No. 1001, September 1983 for the Minister of Foreign Affairs, Peter Barry's account of the role of the Department in negotiations with state-trading nations. See Keatinge (1978), op. cit., pp. 211-12 for a general account of the expansion of the Department.
20. 306, 344 (4 May 1978).
21. 'East' in Kegley and McGowan, op. cit., p. 143. 'The single most significant effect of interdependence seems to be the reduced influence of foreign ministries in foreign policy-making systems.'
22. 306, 341-2 (4 May 1978).
23. Keatinge, 'Ireland and the World 1957-82', in Litton, op. cit., p. 233.
24. 'East', in Kegley and McGowan, op. cit.
25. Interview with senior member of the Department in 1984.
26. 298, 1833-4 (28 April 1977).
27. Ibid.
28. 300, 30 (5 July 1977).
29. 302, 1254 (13 December 1977).
30. 300, 1263.
31. 302, 1254-5.
32. 307, 300-2 (31 May 1978); and 310, 1951 (15 December 1978).
33. 323, 1269 (30 October 1980).
34. Luxembourg, it was acknowledged, also had no imperial past, and after the accession of Greece to the EEC in 1981, the Irish claim was further undermined. 300, 281 (12 October 1977).
35. 302, 1461 (14 December 1977).
36. Private interview.
37. The 'veto', in effect, emerged from the French refusal to participate in the processes of the Community between 1965 and 1966. For further discussion of it, see Chapter 9 below.
38. 298, 1844.
39. *Ireland Today*, No. 990, July/August 1982.
40. Dennis Swann, *The Economics of the Common Market*, Penguin Books, Harmondsworth, 1978, p. 58.
41. Treaties of Rome, 1957.
42. 302, 1460.
43. This section borrows heavily from Swann, op. cit., pp. 69-70.
44. R. K. Carty, 'Towards a European Politics: The Lessons of the European Parliament Election in Ireland', in *The Journal of European Integration*, Vol. 4, No. 2, Winter 1981, p. 230. See also *The Economist*, 2 May 1979 for Senator Yates' (Fianna Fáil) view that the European Parliament was dominated by urban interests unsympathetic to the CAP.
45. 297, 1292 (10 March 1977). He was referring to the EEC treaty of 1975.
46. 300, 1263 (25 October 1977).
47. 297, 1320 (10 March 1977).
48. 298, 1844 (28 April 1977).
49. 325, 434.
50. Fourteen after January 1981.

8 EEC politics and the *demandeur* role

The original intention of the six founder members of the EEC had been to create a supranational authority, an integrated economy and common policies for certain issues to all of which they would subordinate their national policies. By signing the Treaty of Rome, they committed themselves to achieving these objectives over a twelve-year transitional period. Of crucial importance was not only the policy content, but also a commitment to establishing new processes by which subsequent policy would be formulated. The formal intention was to establish a unified, European political and economic entity.

Despite, or perhaps because of, the success of the first twelve years, there was a marked decline in the political will of the member governments to achieve further integration in the political processes of the Community. At the end of the first twelve-year period, therefore, the member governments did not sign a new treaty committing them to further integration over the next twelve years. Rather, they instituted a more modest process of deciding subsequent steps at summit meetings attended by heads of government. The intention was to pursue further economic integration which could be agreed upon while leaving political control of the process in the hands of the member governments. At the Paris summit of 1974, it was decided by the heads of government meeting there, that this process should be formalised and that they should meet at least three times a year to discuss either the business of the Council of Ministers or matters external to the Community coming under the heading of political cooperation. Meeting as such, the heads of government would be called the European Council, an institution distinct from the Council of Ministers although they could choose this forum in which to meet.[1]

In matters of internal Community policy, the European Council still receives proposals from the Commission and instructs it to implement its decisions, but it would seem that such policy is now much more the product of a regular process of coordination and negotiation between national governments, rather than the product of the Community institutions' own dynamics. In this chapter, therefore, I shall examine the Irish experience with two areas of policy-making in the EEC. The first, the process known as European Political Cooperation (EPC), was supposed to be, and remains, explicitly inter-governmental in character. The second, the way in which the Community's budget is set, may be regarded as a failed exercise in establishing integrated and supranational policy-making in the EEC. In the next chapter, I shall examine the Irish experience with successful areas of Community policy-making.

In the mid-1970s, inter-governmental cooperation became particularly associated with the effort to create common EEC foreign policies towards the outside world. The latter was an activity with which the integrated institutions of the Community have never been directly involved, mainly because no easy strategic or foreign policy consensus has existed among the members of the Community. In terms of military policy, the debate has been between those who wished to strengthen Western Europe's capacity to defend itself and act as a force in world politics, and those who wished to do nothing which might weaken the American security guarantee. The heat of the debate, however, has been generated by the sense that those wishing to integrate European defence and foreign policy have been out to dominate the Community in terms of traditional alliance politics. Hence, there exists a paradox in that the elaboration of schemes to integrate or coordinate these areas of 'European' policy has been seen as an attack on the supranational elements of the Community.

By the late 1960s, however, both the hopes of a continuing march towards full integration, and the fears of a Gaullist drive for some form of French hegemony in Europe, had largely disappeared. As a consequence of a decision taken at the Hague summit in 1969, the Foreign Ministers of the Six produced a report suggesting procedures for political cooperation which was accepted by their governments.[2] This process of European Political Cooperation (EPC) emphasised inter-governmental consultations and exchanges of information, for the purpose of coordinating their positions and taking joint actions on foreign policy matters where this was possible. Since 1974, therefore, the European Council has met, backed by regular meetings of Foreign Ministers. Serving these is a Political Committee comprised of senior foreign service officials from each country and a system of permanent and *ad hoc* working groups on a series of foreign policy issues.[3]

EPC presented Irish governments with a difficult choice to make or, more properly, it created a tension in Ireland's European policy. On the one hand, it may be seen that such processes potentially undermined the development of supranational policy-making in the Community. This was something that, presumably, Irish governments should have opposed, both on the basis of their commitment to *communautaire* principles and on the calculation that any system retaining the power of decision among the member governments would favour the more powerful of those governments. On the other hand, these same processes were regarded as presenting Irish governments with an opportunity for effective action which they would not otherwise have had.

According to FitzGerald, accepting his nomination for Taoiseach in 1981, EPC was an 'invaluable process' because it gave the Irish 'an input into foreign policy-making in disproportion to our size'.[4] It was not, however, simply the right to participate in joint decision-making as one among nine or ten governments that proved so important. The institutional arrangements of this form of cooperation were also attractive to them. These meetings were chaired and coordinated by one of the members who held the Presidency of the Council for a period of six months at a time, the office rotating alphabetically. It provided the holder with the usual privileges of the chair and a measure of influence derived from the functions of agenda-setting and guiding the discussion of policy. In addition, however, it provided the opportunity of hosting the spectacle of a major diplomatic conference when the Council met.[5] Recognition, as well as influence, could be obtained from participation in EPC. According to Kelly, speaking for the government in 1977, the period of holding the presidency which had just passed had demonstrated the 'greatly expanded role' which Ireland played in 'international affairs' as a 'direct result of membership of the Communities'.[6] O'Kennedy, speaking as Foreign Minister in 1979, claimed that the way in which Ireland held the presidency later in the year would 'have implications for our reputation abroad'. He went on to say that he intended 'to ensure maximum impact in the international media'.[7] Indeed, a major concern of the Dáil at one point during the second Irish presidency was whether a strike of post office and telephone workers could be settled before the heads of government of the EEC descended upon Dublin for a summit meeting with all the demands upon communications facilities which that would entail.[8]

Despite their enthusiasm for the opportunities offered by the European Council, however, Irish governments were aware of the difficulties which inter-governmental cooperation presented for the evolution of the Community. According to O'Kennedy, speaking earlier that same year, while the European Council provided a chance for heads of government to come together to discuss Community problems and foreign policy, the Irish were concerned that it should not 'disturb the institutional balance of the Community as laid down in the Treaties'.[9] And Kelly, speaking in 1977, claimed that the way in which the Council dealt with both internal and external matters courted the risk of moving the Community towards 'intergovernmental cooperation at the expense of its supranational character'. The protection of the latter he described as a 'vital interest to Ireland'.[10]

The Irish response to this problem took three forms. The first was an assertion that they would resist any tendency of intergovernmental cooperation to erode Community processes. Thus, O'Kennedy stated that European Council discussion should take place in accordance with the provisions of the Treaties, particularly with regard to the right of initiative of the Commission. This, according to Kelly, was 'the cornerstone of our approach to the European Council'.[11] Implicit in this position was the assumption that the Council system posed only a potential threat to supranationalism and that, as it presently operated, it was consistent with the principles of the Rome Treaty. This was supported by the second tactic of emphasising the lack of formal status of the process of inter-governmental cooperation. According to Lenihan, speaking as Minister for Foreign Affairs in 1980, EPC was a 'non-institutionalised intergovernmental arrangement' derived from 'political commitment' rather than treaty obligations. As such, it operated 'pragmatically and by consensus'.[12]

Thirdly, members of the government attempted to argue that intergovernmental cooperation applied mainly to policy areas external to the EEC, that is, the effort to establish a common foreign policy. Thus, in his discussion of political cooperation above, Lenihan maintained that its field of application was external. A serving minister elaborated on this point in a private interview by offering the following distinction. He stated that, on the one hand, there were 'economic and social problems' and the need to develop a 'greater union in the economic and social sense'; these were the preserve of the Commission. On the other hand, there was the question of 'international political cooperation both within and outside Europe'. With regard to 'within' Europe, it was clear that he was alluding to the process of establishing common positions on the conduct of relations with countries outside the EEC. This distinction between internal and external matters on the basis of the processes by which they were handled was not, however, watertight. Later, in the same interview, discussing measures taken to circumvent British obstruction of a CAP price review, the minister emphasised very strongly that this was a 'political content area' handled by the joint action of the other member governments.[13]

The existence of the EPC 'side' of the Community did not confront Irish governments with major problems. They treated it as a separate process and attempted to make the most of the diplomatic opportunities which it presented. From an integrationist or supranationalist point of view, however, EPC's intergovernmental character was merely symptomatic of deeper failings in the EEC's internal policy-making processes. It was the intergovernmental character of the latter which exposed the limitations of both the *communautaire* strategy and the *demandeur* alternative which the Irish employed. They tended to explain their difficulties as arising from intergovernmental collaboration *per se*. Where the latter existed, they argued, the bigger powers would win out and common policies regulated by regimes could not develop. The case of the EEC budget seems to bear out their position on this. However, as I shall show in the next chapter, even where inter-governmental collaboration enjoyed a measure of success in establishing regime-governed common policies, the Irish did not feel particularly pleased with the results or empowered by the process by which they were achieved.

Ireland's *communautaire* policy was addressed to furthering the economic, social and political development of the Community. This was expressed in two ways. First, there was the general notion of preserving the Community's 'momentum'; like a cyclist, the EEC had to keep going forward if it was to avoid a collapse. Secondly, Irish governments spoke of a political struggle in which they worked with their allies (the Commission and like-minded governments) to mobilise the sympathetic but faint-hearted many in the struggle against the obstructionist policies of the recalcitrant few. In practice, the debate about the direction of the Community became, in great part, reduced to arguments over the extent, nature and purposes of its budget. As a consequence, Irish policy, while frequently couched in terms of a contribution to these arguments based upon *communautaire* principles, was increasingly directed at justifying and defending Ireland's existing share of the finances of the Community.

The EEC, regarding it now as an entity in itself, required money for three purposes: to cover its own organisational expenses; to finance its common policies; and to give assistance to regions of the Community, both as compensation when common policies disproportionately hurt certain areas or sectors, and on the general principle of achieving convergence in levels of economic development throughout the Community. It was raised within the member states by their governments and transferred to the Community. The question of Community finances has produced a series of disagreements between member governments which became increasingly important during the period and which were not resolved during it. The debate is complicated and revolves around three related themes.

First, and ostensibly most important, have been the differing conceptions of a 'fair' approach to the raising and spending of these monies, activities which are necessarily redistributive and interventionist in their character. The most prominent conflict, that largely between the British and the rest, has been over the way in which, as a consequence of the CAP, revenue flows from industrial sectors to agricultural sectors regardless of whether the former are 'capable' of rendering the assistance or whether the latter 'need' it. There has also been a more general, if less prominent, debate about whether the richer and economically more developed areas of the Community are transferring sufficient resources to the less so, particularly in view of the widening gap

129

between the two.[14] The debate has been couched in terms of contending Community philosophies and sectoral and regional imbalances. In practice, however, member governments have attacked or defended particular aspects of the existing system on the basis of whether it serves their own national interests as they see them.

As a consequence of this national emphasis, a second problem has emerged regarding the status of EEC monies and, in particular, the control or influence a member government should exert over the portion which it has collected. Those hostile to the current system or aspects of it have claimed that the monies collected by a government constitute a national contribution to the finances of the Community. This being the case, they argue that these finances should be used in accordance with the principle of *juste retoure*: contributors should receive benefits commensurate with the scale of their contributions to the Community. Supporters of the system, in response, argue that the Community has its 'own resources' and that governments merely serve as the collectors of money to which they have no title. Indeed, they argue that the principle of *juste retoure*, taken to what they regard as its logical conclusion, would be an absurdity in that member governments would be entitled to reclaim any and all money which they had transferred to the Community.

More important for Ireland than either of these two difficulties has been a third theme, the question of how these differences between governments should be resolved. In principle, dissenters are obligated by treaty to conform to Community law and policy after due process of appeal and adjudication. In practice, the measures for enforcing such compliance are very limited. This is not simply a question of the weakness of formal procedures. More important is the absence of any stable collective or even majority political will for enforcing compliance either through the use of Community procedures or more conventional diplomatic pressures. The member governments have not been uniformly for or against the Community finance system on all areas of policy in which it deals and are, hence, reluctant to support strong measures against another government which might in the future be used against themselves. Further, they have been unwilling to precipitate conflicts in which the most likely outcome has been the immobilisation of the Community as a whole rather than the compliance of dissenting governments to Community policy.

As a consequence, they have attempted to resolve disputes within the Community by a process of inter-governmental bargaining over the establishment of common policies. This process works in two ways: it may seek to adjust policies to the demands of the dissenter(s); or it may seek to offer them sufficient incentives for abandoning their opposition. This system has worked reasonably well when it is possible to appease or accommodate the demands of a dissenter and where it is clear that such a government or governments are a minority in the bargaining process. Where the first condition is absent it is very difficult for the Community to do anything. Where the second condition

130

is absent one may get a political process which works, but the character and outcomes of which it is very hard to argue are consistent with the principles upon which the EEC is supposedly based.

In purely monetary terms, Ireland was and remains a major beneficiary of the system. The position of Irish governments throughout this period was that the principles upon which the system was based were sound and they emphasised its redistributional elements, in particular, the regional and social polices. They argued, however, in the words of one Taoiseach, that 'progress towards Community aims [had] generally been disappointing'.[15] According to O'Kennedy, speaking to the Dáil as Minister for Foreign Affairs in 1977, there was neither a 'comprehensive regional policy' nor an 'adequate regional fund' for meeting the problem of the increasing gap between the 'richest and poorest regions in the Community'. He went on to say that 'the elimination' of this gap was 'an essential step on the road to economic and monetary union'.[16] The linkage between an effective regional policy and progress towards economic and monetary union was offered in the first instance not so much as a tactical threat as a statement of mutually consistent principles. The Community was about the development of fair as well as common policies. As Lenihan argued in 1980, it was 'natural' that the 'requirements of the common purse should grow' along with the Community. To deny this would be to deny the 'Community's *raison d'être*' and to impose 'unreal and artificial' limits on its 'possibilities'.[17] What was required to solve the problem of regional imbalances, according to another spokesman for the government, was 'something on the lines of a new "Marshall Aid" programme which would transfer resources from the rich centre to the poorer periphery regions'.[18]

By claiming that regional imbalances hurt all the members of the EEC and not just the worse off, it was possible for Irish governments to articulate their efforts to seek redress in terms of a broad *communautaire* strategy. For example, FitzGerald, speaking from opposition in 1978, argued that

It is of interest not merely to this country – we are not simply pursuing a single national interest here...in putting forward our views on the whole subject, that we should not appear to be pressing a narrow national interest. It is in the interests of the whole Community that there is a convergence of the economies of the member states without which the existing Community arrangements could indeed at some point be endangered.[19]

Reporting back to the Dáil in 1980 on a European Council meeting, the then Taoiseach, Charles Haughey, stressed the global significance of the efforts of the EEC to solve its internal, and principally British, problem. He said that while many issues had been discussed, the 'main concern' was with the 'proper functioning' and cohesiveness of the Community so that in an increasingly dangerous world it can exercise its great influence in the interests of moderation'.[20]

The formal Irish position on the status of the EEC's finances was stated on several occasions and remained largely unchanged throughout the second period. According to Lynch, reporting to the Dáil on a European Council meeting in 1979, there had been agreement on 'certain essential principles'. First, 'own resources' was a fundamental Community principle which had to be retained. Second, there could be no question of Community expenditure being directed on the basis of *juste retour*. Third, solutions to the problem of convergence had to come from within the Community budget but finally, the VAT ceiling of one per cent should not be breached.[21]

The only major substantive change in the Irish position was with regard to the latter ceiling. Lenihan stated the following year that this had become a 'major problem' and that the budget for 1981 had almost reached this ceiling. He maintained that the CAP could not continue 'in a meaningful way' unless the one per cent ceiling was breached, and he cited with approval, the argument of the McDougall Report of 1977 to the effect that the members' contributions to the Community budget would have to increase from their current average of around 0.9 per cent to 2.5 per cent of GNP if any significant reduction of the inequalities in the standards of living within the Community were to be achieved.[22] This comment reflected an increasing tendency on the part of the Irish government to express its policy on what they called the 'convergence problem'[23] in simple monetary terms and with reference to fairness for the disadvantaged members, rather than by reasserting the need to strengthen the institutions and uphold the principles of the Community. By 1981, the then Taoiseach, Haughey, was referring to Irish policy on possible solutions to the CAP and the budget not so much in terms of *communautaire* principles but rather in terms of Irish preconditions. Any such solution, he argued, would have to conform to such principles but it could not: add to the problems of farmers already in difficulties; it could not make the economic problems of any member government worse, particularly with regard to the question of unemployment; it could not sharpen the disparities in living standards between regions of the Community; and it would have to respect the role of the EEC as an exporter of agricultural produce.[24]

The major problem with Ireland's *communautaire* strategy on the budget was not the failure of the Community to resolve its difficulties in this respect. It was, rather, with the mode by which the member governments attempted to resolve these difficulties. This process was characterised by inter-governmental bargaining over the existing resources of the Community rather than by a struggle to increase these resources or extend the role of the Community with regard to them. On the one side were those attempting to further their interests through the achievement and maintenance of some sort of cooperative system. On the other were those who sought either exemption from these collaborative efforts or compensation for their participation in them. This process depended on the former group continuing to regard the costs of satisfying the *demandeurs* as being offset by the value of preserving some form of cooperation. As such, it presented the Irish government with two problems. First, the *communautaire* strategy, with its emphasis on preserving momentum in the development of the institutions and common policies, had little relevance to actual Community processes on this question, other than as a statement of remote principles. Secondly, it could be seen to imply a role for Ireland as one of the system maintainers, that is, one of the governments prepared to pay, rather than extract, a price for its support of Community policies.

Since joining the EEC, Irish governments had never been averse to pursuing a *demandeur* approach on specific issues. They had, for example, threatened a veto in 1974.[25] As a consequence of the way the members of the Community attempted to resolve the question of the Community's finances, however, and despite the continuing articulation of a *communautaire* role for Ireland, the government developed its own *demandeur* strategy. This emphasised Irish national interests and was directed at preserving Ireland's existing share of Community resources rather than reforming the processes by which those resources were generated and distributed.

The policy was not entirely new. As I have argued above, the *communautaire* stance had its calculating component in that it was regarded as a basis for day-to-day influence as well as an instrument of long-term reform. FitzGerald had claimed with regard to the Irish position on Community finances that 'we should not *appear* to be pressing a narrow national interest'[26] (my emphasis). On other occasions, however, spokesmen for the Irish government had elaborated a policy which implicitly or explicitly emphasised national rather than regional or sectoral criteria for determining the distribution of Community assistance. For example, in discussing the evolution of the Community's industrial policy in 1978, O'Kennedy stated that the application of sectoral policies on an 'apparently' even-handed basis across the Community would have to cease. There was a need for policy to be seen to 'actively differentiate in favour of poorer regions' since there was a 'legitimate fear' that the 'restructuring of the central industries' was taking place at 'the expense of the regional and social funds'.[27] Nor was he simply arguing that it was more important to assist disadvantaged regions rather than struggling sectors like the coal, steel or textile industries of France and West Germany, however. By criticising the even-handed principle and referring to central industries, he was focusing on the way in which Community funds went to needy regions or sectors *per se*, without taking into account the relative wealth or poverty of the country within which they were located. Depressed sectors in West Germany, according to this argument, should not get the same level of assistance as similarly depressed sectors or underdeveloped regions in Ireland.

The government's emphasis on a peculiarly 'narrow national interest' was particularly in evidence when they dealt with domestic criticisms of their approach to the Community's regional policy. On one occasion, Neil Blaney,[28] a prominent deputy from County Donegal in the north-west of Ireland, suggested that the government should argue before the Community that the west of Ireland was in itself a region requiring special assistance. Colley, the Minister for Finance, replied that the government was not prepared to change Ireland's status from that of a 'single developing region'. Doing so, he argued, would interfere with Ireland's existing national quota, annoy those providing the funds by tinkering with a mechanism which was already the product of hard negotiations, and would obscure the point to be made about the 'economic imbalance' which existed between 'the State as a whole and the other more developed regions of the Community'.[29] A month later, in November 1979, another spokesman for the government rejected the suggestion that they should work to establish a single authority to administer regional funds for the whole island of Ireland. He stated that the British did not seem to be interested in such a proposal, but more importantly, he argued that such an agency would detract from the planning authority of the Irish government.[30]

The most important impetus to the elaboration of a more obviously self-interested and *demandeur* strategy on the part of Irish governments, however, was the manner in which the other members of the Community attempted to deal with British objections to the Community's system of finances. The British argued that this system was unfair in that, in effect, it transferred money from industrial sectors to agricultural sectors and, hence, from predominantly industrial countries to those in which agriculture played a large part. These transfers took place, the British argued, regardless of whether the donor country could afford to help, the recipient needed help, or anyone wanted what their agriculture produced at the price. The other members had accepted the British case in principle, and at the Community summit held in Dublin in 1975, a complex 'Budget Correction Mechanism' had been agreed to.[31] According to this, if the financial contributions to the Community raised in a member country exceeded the payments to that country from the Community by a specified amount, and if the performance of the economy of that country satisfied certain criteria measured in relation to average Community performance in terms of GNP per capita and growth rates, then it would be entitled to a rebate of a proportion of the contributions raised within it.

This mechanism was a characteristic product of the process of solving Community problems through inter-governmental cooperation. As a consequence of the strenuous objections of a government, a measure of consensus regarding the inadequacy of certain aspects of the Community system had been achieved amongst all the members. In the absence of any consensus among them regarding the nature or extent of the necessary reforms, however, the problem was 'solved' by maintaining the system and attempting to compensate the protesting member for its continuing acquiescence in this state of affairs. For a number of reasons, this solution was ineffective and did little more than postpone the problem or, rather, transform it into a drawn out, grumbling conflict about the size of British payments to and rebates from the Community. In general terms, the major difficulty was the economic recession being experienced by the Community and its member governments alike by the second half of the 1970s. Economic stagnation combined with rising inflation in most of the EEC had two consequences. First, the Community required more money simply to maintain its common policies and price supports at their existing level. Secondly, the member governments were reluctant to spend more money either to maintain the Community system directly or indirectly by financing the continued participation in it of its more reluctant members. Economic pressures, therefore, gave an increased sharpness to the political debate about 'fairness'.

The problem took the particular form it did because the British government was increasingly prepared initially to threaten, and then to obstruct, both the mechanisms of the Community's bargaining processes and, eventually, the means by which its common policies were funded. They enjoyed considerable success in this policy, because the processes of inter-governmental cooperation were sensitive to this kind of dissent, and also, because their actual contributions represented a significant proportion of the resources of the Community. As such, the British problem presented the Irish government with a number of difficulties.

In response to these, a *communautaire* stance would have suggested that the Irish government would oppose the British claim that they were being unfairly treated, their manner of obtaining redress and the way in which the Community attempted to accommodate them in this respect. The value of membership of the EEC, as Irish spokesmen were fond of saying, was not simply a matter of balance sheets.[32] The real problem with the Community's common policies as far as they were concerned were not the injustices, real or imagined, in the details of such policies as existed, but in the fact that there had been insufficient development of such policies. The way to restoring or improving fairness, therefore, was to restore the political will which would provide the momentum for further integration.

Such a strategy, however, did not address the immediate demand which the rebate system put upon Ireland. Quite simply, any money which went back from the common fund to Britain was not available for other uses or had to be made up from other sources. It was argued, therefore, that indirectly Ireland was paying to solve Britain's problems.[33] However, this argument was not incorporated into a confident projection of Ireland's place in the EEC, emphasising how times had changed and how Ireland, with one of the fastest OECD growth rates, was now in a position to contribute to helping Britain out. Nor, even, was it presented in terms of Ireland as the European 'good citizen' willing to make economic sacrifices for higher principles. Rather, according to Lenihan, speaking in the Dáil in 1980, the Irish had supported the establishment of the rebate system during the Dublin summit so long as it remained consistent with Community principles and, in particular, the principle of 'own resources'. More importantly, however, he stated that the Irish position had been that countries with a lower GNP than the UK (Ireland and

Italy) 'should not be penalised in any way'. The government hoped, he went on to say, that Ireland would be 'more than compensated' by alternative mechanisms designed to increase regional aid.[34] As FitzGerald put it, the Irish position should be that anything the third poorest country in the Community (Britain) got, should go also to the second and first poorest countries (Italy and Ireland respectively).[35]

The success of this policy is hard to assess. While it was usually in the political interests of Irish governments to give prominence to the cash benefits which accrued from membership of the EEC, it was not so clear whether they should emphasise their diplomatic success in achieving compensation for the rebate system, or the extent to which British obstructionist policies entailed costs for Ireland. Typically, they emphasised this 'cost' to Ireland, according to Lenihan, about £7 million in 1980 and £8 – 9 million in 1981, and then pointed out that the overall balance sheet was still overwhelmingly favourable to Ireland.[36]

The point is, however, that in responding to the budget issue, the Irish government increasingly adopted its own *demandeur* position, emphasising a national definition of what was 'fair' and requiring its own set of exemptions from Community policy. 'Fairness' was increasingly defined not in the general terms of the need for convergence between core and periphery, but in specific terms related to Irish interests. Thus, FitzGerald, generally regarded as the most *communautaire* of all leading Irish public figures, by 1979 was emphasising not only the costs of the rebate system to Ireland, but also setting this in the context of the 'price' Ireland had paid to enter the EEC. While core EEC principles, rather than Ireland's special circumstances, should be stressed, he argued, the fact remained that Ireland had lost between 72,000 and 200,000 jobs during the transitional period.[37]

Similarly, Lenihan, speaking in 1980 on increasing the Community budget, argued that those who paid the most into the budget (which he pointed out constituted less than one per cent of the Community's total GNP), did the best out of intra-Community (which he valued at 25 per cent of the Community's GNP). Not only this, but those who did the best out of this trade were also those who were responsible for the agricultural surpluses. The farmers in the industrial countries, he argued, imported feeds to take advantage of the CAP. Ireland, on the other hand, had a self-sustaining, rather than an 'artificial', agriculture. This was of vital interest to the Irish economy and yet it was doubly penalised because the rich countries refused to fund the CAP adequately while at the same time they gave direct assistance to their own agricultural sectors which competed with that of Ireland both for markets and for Community resources.[38]

The rebate system, it may be argued, imposed direct costs upon Ireland, but it is also clear that Irish governments became increasingly worried during the period with regard to what it signified for the future of the Community system. In particular, they feared that the other governments had settled for a system

136

of collaboration between themselves based upon a narrow definition of national self-interests and the principle of *juste retour* in any collaborative efforts. If this was the case, then according to FitzGerald, speaking from opposition in 1980, it

> could be absolutely fatal for this country as the biggest single net beneficiary of EEC membership, with something like 8 per cent or 9 per cent of our current budget year after year coming from that source.[39]

The problem for Irish foreign policy was that the Community no longer clearly constituted a situation in which the lethargic, though fundamentally sound, *communautaire* majority could be mobilised against the uncooperative minority. This uncertainty with regard to the changing character of the system is reflected in the wide range of prescriptions for policy offered both by spokesmen for the government and the opposition. Reporting to the Dáil in 1979 on the deliberations of the Joint Committee on Secondary Legislation of the European Communities, Deputy Quinn argued for a course of action which was consistent with the established principles of Irish foreign policy as an active independent. The EEC, he claimed, was in a state of 'budgetary crisis' in which the CAP and Irish interests were under heavy attack. It followed that the Irish government, as the government of a peripheral state which was currently holding the Presidency, should defend the CAP since there was 'no better country' with a 'moral right to advocate action on behalf of all the members of the Community'.[40] This approach was also echoed by FitzGerald, speaking the following year on the ceiling on VAT. He argued that Ireland's role had to be 'to mobilise support for the expansion of the Community's role with the smaller countries on this issue'.[41]

Unfortunately, it was no longer clear who were and who were not Ireland's allies in such a crusade. Speaking to the Dáil in 1979, a spokesman for the Department of Agriculture stated that Ireland's 'main concern' was to make sure that the *Commission* (my emphasis) stayed 'within its mandate' in any negotiations on the future of the CAP.[42] FitzGerald, a few days later, argued that Ireland should ally itself with France against the Commission on CAP proposals which, he said, favoured the British.[43] With the perceived drift of France and Germany away from the CAP and towards the *juste retour* principle, however, alliance politics gave way to a discussion of the veto. Speaking in 1980 on the outcome of the Venice summit, FitzGerald argued that the consensus on holding on to what the EEC had already achieved was gradually disappearing. In such a situation, in which matters which are of 'vital interest to us' are at stake, he advised the government to 'use the veto power we have in regard to a new president unless he is committed to Community policies'.[44]

The government, understandably, was more cautious regarding the options open to it in seeking to preserve the CAP or restore the momentum of the

Community. In response to the demands for an Irish leadership role, Colley, the Minister for Finance, replied that 'political skill' as well as 'pounding the desk' must be used to get what the Irish wanted from the EEC.[45] What they wanted was clarified by their position on the majority voting system adopted on setting farm prices in the Council in 1982. Despite the establishment of the rebate mechanism in 1975, British governments had continued to object to both the principles on which the Community's finance system worked and the size of their rebates relative to the size of 'their' contributions . In the absence of satisfaction on these points, they had embarked on a strategy of obstructing the workings of the Community. In particular, they had linked their approval of new agricultural price rises to obtaining a larger rebate. The voting procedures of the Council of Ministers were intentionally ambiguous. In theory, a qualified majority, but a majority nevertheless, was sufficient to have a measure adopted . In practice, since the Luxembourg compromise of 1966, the unanimity principle had been dominant, although not exclusively so.[46] As a consequence of British objections, therefore, the business of setting new agriculture prices had been blocked. This blockage was removed by an effective decision on the part of the other Council members to proceed by majority voting.

Lenihan, serving as Minister for Agriculture and Fisheries at the time, explained that the new farm prices would not have been possible without 'an initiative taken by our Government and other Community Governments' to defeat the 'blocking mechanism' being used to 'frustrate and prevent' them. Since the British 'total blocking abuse' of the Luxembourg Formula was leading to a 'legal vacuum and complete breakdown' in Community policy-making, he went on to say,

> It was eventually decided, by a reluctant agreement amongst seven member countries of the Community, to invoke the basic legal protection of the regulations of the Treaty of Rome to implement Community policies – in this case the common agricultural policy price fixation – by way of a qualified majority vote.[47]

Of significance here is the fact that this decision was not, nor was it presented as, a triumph of Community will over narrow, national self-interests. It was, rather, a calculated diplomatic manoeuvre by a number of governments with shared interests, designed to exploit both the preoccupation of the British government with the Falklands War and its desire to preserve the sanctions which the Community had imposed upon Argentina. As such, the Irish government presented its own part in this decision in very restrained terms and certainly not with any reference to Ireland's *communautaire* role in the EEC. Rather, according Lenihan, majority voting had been adopted by 'reluctant agreement' and, as he put it, ' 'I am glad we played a part in making that decision'.[48]

The caution with which the government had approached this decision was underlined by a serving minister in a private interview conducted shortly after. He said that he saw the use of a qualified majority vote against Britain as a 'major Community decision' which had 'political connotation right across the board' since they were trying it 'for the first time'. While the Irish had decided that for 'the overall interest' they were going 'with six of the member countries', this was, as he put it, 'the sort of area where we weigh a lot of considerations'. The conditions which the government had to weigh were certainly complex. The central problem was with regard to their policy on the place of the veto in Community decision-making. In principle, the retention of the veto by member governments constituted a major obstacle to recovering the momentum which Irish governments claimed was necessary if the Community advance in accordance with its stated objectives. Consistency with a *communautaire* strategy, it might be supposed, would have dictated that the Irish government strongly support the principle of majority voting on the setting of new farm prices. This was, after all, one of the few areas where there was an effective Community policy as far as the Irish were concerned.

On the other hand, much of the strength of weak actors in conditions of complex interdependence is supposed to be derived from the equalisation effects of the rule-governed character of regime politics. The Irish government was aware of this. Whatever their general principles, they had continued to argue in practice that the retention of the veto was necessary to preserve both vital Irish national interests and, increasingly, Community principles from attack by majority coalitions of hostile governments.[49] This concern over the veto was reflected in Lenihan's presentation in the Dáil of the decision to support majority voting. He claimed that unanimity was preferable on such matters and emphasised that the Irish, French, Italians and Germans all agreed that the power of the veto still remained, but it was 'not to be abused by bringing in extraneous matters'.[50] Indeed, it may be noted here that the governments of two other small Community members, Denmark and Greece, had sided with the British not so much on the substance of the Community's decision on new prices but on the manner in which it was taken.

These difficulties were resolved, however, by what was clearly a more pressing concern, namely the delay in obtaining the first payments of a total of £235 million which the Irish government estimated it would be receiving that year once the delay was removed.[51] In the face of a Community process characterised by bargaining between governments over the size an allocation of its financial resources, Irish policy became principally directed at doing what was necessary to secure and obtain their share. They did this not by trying to restructure the regime, nor by performing a good citizen role in the sense of FitzGerald's diplomacy-for-cash formula. The performance of a distinctive role was discarded in favour of becoming one of seven in a winning coalition of governments.

Further, the government were prepared to put at risk their principal tactical asset in regime politics, the veto, in order to obtain the money. However, the role of domestic factors in producing this concentration upon obtaining cash transfers should not be overestimated. While the Irish economy was in difficulties, and while £235 million is a considerable amount, it was still small relative to the scale of the economic difficulties which were confronting the Irish government.[52] It should also be noted that the *communautaire* strategy, both in its general principles and its tactical application, had been designed to safeguard and maximise these kinds of transfers. The narrowing emphasis of the government, therefore, was much more a product of the deterioration, as they saw it, of Community processes from which the government was determined to salvage what it might.

As these processes were seen to deteriorate, the emphasis in Irish policy shifted away from the effort to procure influence through the manifestation of a *communautaire* national identity, to the familiar concern of the first period, attempting to minimise the adverse effects upon Ireland of uncertainty and instability in its external environment. What was different from the first period, however, was that the Irish government was no longer restricted to the pragmatic and discreet incrementalism which had characterised their negotiations with the British in the early 1960s. Membership of the EEC enabled them to adopt, in addition, the tactics of joining shifting bargaining coalitions and exploiting regime rules and processes, even if this was in a manner which was inconsistent with their foreign policy principles. As I shall show below, however, the Irish continued to use role-playing in their attempts to play regime politics. In particular, they developed the role of Ireland as a *demandeur* whose participation in joint policies would have to be bought. Further, they performed this role not only in areas of policy where the Community was failing, but also in those where some success in the establishment of common policies was being achieved.

Notes

1. Swann, op. cit., p.48.
2. The Luxembourg Report on *The Problem of Political Unification*. The system of cooperation was known as the Davignon process after the Belgian diplomat.
3. Swann, op. cit., pp. 48-51.
4. 330, 306-7.
5. The first such meeting was in Dublin in 1975.
6. 298, 1297.
7. 314, 1902.
8. See 315, 763 for the adjournment debate on this problem (20 June 1979).
9. 314, 208-9 (9 May 1979).
10. 298, 1281.
11. 314, 208-9 for O'Kennedy, and 298, 1281 for Kelly.
12. 322, 969.

13. Private interview, 1982.
14. According to Lynch, speaking in 1978, Irish GDP per capita was 64 per cent of the Community average in 1972, and 60 per cent in 1976. 308, 406.
15. Lynch 305, 339
16. 300, 500.
17. 323, 1175.
18. 302, 551 (1 December 1977).
19. 305, 354 (11 April 1978).
20. 320, 424.
21. 317, 623.
22. 323, 1263 (30 October 1980).
23. 308, 406-7 (11 October 1978).
24. 328, 385.
25. 'Keatinge', in Litton, op. cit., p. 233.
26. 305, 354 (cited above).
27. 306, 356.
28. One of the Fianna Fail ministers dismissed in the early 1970s as a consequence of his alleged involvement in a plan to smuggle arms into Northern Ireland, Neil Blaney formed his own small republican party, Aontacht Eireann.
29. 316, 300 (18 October 1979).
30. 316, 2355-6. .
31. See Swann, op. cit., pp. 53-4, for the following details.
32. See, for example, FitzGerald, 331, 904.
33. See, for example, FitzGerald speaking in opposition, 319, 112–13 (19 March 1980).
34. 318, 333 (21 February 1980).
35. 320, 433 (1 May 1980) speaking from opposition.
36. See 322, 714–15 for these estimates of the 'cost'. See also Haughey 322, 1011 for this way of balancing these costs against an overall picture of benefits accrued from EEC membership.
37. 317, 625. See also 331, 904 for similar arguments.
38. 323, 1264.
39. 320, 440 (1 May 1980).
40. 316, 2420.
41. 325, 674 (9 December 1980).
42. 312, 716.
43. 312, 1583.
44. 322, 1026.
45. 316, 2427 (22 November 1979).
46. See 315, 1195–6 for an account by an Irish government spokesman on the place of the veto in the Community system.
47. 334, 1744-5 (19 May 1982).
48. Ibid.
49. See, for example, 333, 1685 (28 April 1982) for FitzGerald's justification for retaining the veto. He said it should not be 'abused' but used only when matters of 'vital national interest' were at stake.
50. 334, 1776.
51. Ibid.
52. According to a spokesman for the short-lived coalition government of 1981–2 speaking on 18 December 1981, the current budget deficit had risen from 4.4 per cent of GNP (£194 million) in1977 to a projected deficit of 9.5 per cent (£947 million) in 1981. Exchequer borrowing was projected to be cut by the government's budget from an estimated 20 per cent in 1981 to 16.5 per cent of GNP. The rate of inflation was in excess of 20 per cent.

141

9 Regime extension and Irish foreign policy

Where the EEC failed to make progress in terms of its evolution from inter-governmental bargaining to an integrated decision-making process, Irish policy shifted from the *communautaire* role-playing strategy to an attempt to manage the impact of the external environment on the internal affairs of the country by concentrating on the demands of the moment rather than the presentation of a consistent image. Where the EEC developed procedures for inter-governmental collaboration on the high politics of a common European foreign policy, I shall show below that Irish governments maintained and extended the activist role of the international 'good citizen' developed at the UN. Small power regime politics of the kind envisaged by some theorists of interdependence were little in evidence in either of these two spheres of Irish foreign policy and Community activity.

It may be claimed, however, that the way in which the Community attempted to solve its budget problems and the emergence of EPC were both symptoms of the failure to achieve its original objectives. If this is so, then the question of whether joining the EEC constitutes a legitimate test of what happens to a country when it experiences an increase in the conditions and relations of complex interdependence of its external environment must be addressed. Unfortunately, it cannot be definitively answered, but I shall make two points. First, while the EEC is, by virtually any criteria, a very imperfect organisation, it must be seen as embodying an attempt to move *from* a system, the relations of which approximate those of the realist model, *to* one characterised by interdependence and integration. This certainly seems more supportable than seeing it as representing a movement in any other direction, or no change at all. Secondly, for all its imperfections, the EEC has achieved some successes in its own terms, even if the manner of their achievement may seem stubbornly unchanged.

Developments in the EEC during the second period did not merely consist of institutional decay and the failure to establish common policies. The decision, in effect, to proceed by inter-governmental cooperation made at the Hague summit of 1969 also affirmed the intention of the members of the Community to achieve Economic and Monetary Union, and this was reaffirmed by the Tindemans Report on 'European Union' in 1975. While progress, in the terms called for in this report, was uneven, there were some institutional developments and common policies in certain issue areas were established. It is in these areas that one might expect one of two developments. First, the *communautaire* strategy of the Irish government might become more in evidence, because regime strengthening was a major objective of this aspect of Irish foreign policy. Failing this, one might expect the abandonment of all role-playing strategies in these areas of policy as the Irish began to take full advantage of the opportunities for 'the revenge of the weak' with which regime politics allegedly abound. In this chapter, therefore, I shall examine the Irish experience with regard to the European Monetary System (EMS), the Common Fisheries Policy (CFP) and the question of enlarging the Community.

The EMS established at the end of 1978 was intended by its supporters as a step in the direction of the long-term objective of achieving a united Europe. As a political and economic entity, it was envisaged that the EEC would have a single currency system.[1] In more immediate terms, it was designed to stabilise the exchange rates between the currencies of the member states and between them and the US dollar, the argument being that this would create a more stable trading environment within the Community and within the OECD. It was also hoped that through EMS there would be established a common European fund which could extend credit to its members.[2] It was intended that each member of the EEC should deposit 20 per cent of all its reserves in the form of gold and dollars in a common fund and, in return, they would receive an equivalent amount in European currency units (ECUs). Each ECU consisted of a so-called 'basket' of the currencies of the member countries, the size of each country's share of the basket reflecting the importance of its economy. Stability of exchange rates was to be achieved on the basis of each participating currency being pegged to a maximum 2.25 per cent variation above or below its original set value in the basket. As this limit was reached by a national currency, then the respective government was obligated to take measures to raise or depress its value as appropriate.

As such, the EMS politically was a very controversial matter for two reasons. First, in terms of the general principle of European Monetary Union (EMU), any step in that direction necessarily eroded the capacity of governments to adjust the value of their own currencies as an instrument of their economic policies, for example, to make their exports more competitive or to reduce the level of their imports. Secondly, whatever a government felt about the general principles of EMU, any particular step in that direction had to be evaluated in terms of its immediate effects on the national economy. Hence, the Community debate on particular steps once again revolved around the question of 'fairness' to particular countries. At its simplest, the problem was that weak trading (open) economies, and particularly those with high rates of inflation, would always participate in such measures or enter such a system, at a disadvantage. The tendency would be for fixed exchange rates to render their exports increasingly uncompetitive and they could 'solve' this only by deflating – which in turn would cause unemployment – or quitting the system.

The EMS did not constitute the first step which the Community had taken in this direction. Originally, there had been proposals to tie European currencies fairly tightly to the dollar in a so-called 'tunnel'.[3] After 1971, however, with major changes in US economic and financial policy, these proposals gave way to the 'snake' system in which the emphasis was increasingly upon fixing the value of European currencies relative to each other rather than the dollar. This system was hampered by the decision of the British, Italian and Irish governments not to participate and by the inability of the French to maintain their place in it. The problem, it was argued at the time, was that the snake system forced the governments with weaker currencies to deflate their economies in an effort to maintain their rates of exchange with stronger currencies, in particular the German mark. Indeed, one purpose of the basket system employed in EMS was to transfer part of the burden of maintaining the exchange rates to the governments with strong currencies by imposing an upper, as well as a lower, limit on fluctuations in the value of their shares in ECU.[4]

The Irish government wished to participate in EMS as a step which they regarded as being consistent with their support for the general principle of monetary union. In his report to the Dáil on the Bremen EC meeting which had taken the EMS decision,[5] the Taoiseach, Lynch, in effect established the priority of concerns with which the government addressed the issue. The first of these, he said, was the problem of economic divergence. What was needed, he had argued at Bremen, was a 'strong, coherent regional policy'.[6] Secondly, he pointed out that monetary stability contributed to stable trading markets and that, 'other things being equal', the more trade expanded, the better things were for Ireland. Finally, he argued that setting up the system would represent a 'significant step towards closer economic integration in the Community'. Such moves would have 'profound implications for the political development of the Community'. This was so because in any monetary union there could 'only be one monetary authority' and with such authority would come 'also a degree of political authority'. The implications for Irish policy, therefore, were that, while safeguarding their own national interest, the Irish had to 'play our part' in a development which promised to 'further the cause of Europe'. As O'Kennedy, speaking as Minister for Foreign Affairs, expressed it later in the same debate, Ireland's guarantee was in the EEC's 'political and institutional development', as opposed to a loose framework of cooperation and EMS represented a step along the road to 'greater cohesion'.[7]

Ireland's participation in EMS was also presented as a major act of national assertion by the government. The decision to participate, according to O'Kennedy, had been difficult, and required the same kind of courage and confidence which had made possible the decision to join the EEC itself. In a candid account of what Irish foreign policy was about, he stated that,

> From time to time we have to take decisions in relation to our international relations both in the economic and in the political spheres. Sometimes these decisions derive entirely from our own prior decisions but, as often as not, indeed almost always, the decisions we have to take from time to time derive from movements that have occurred within a general group of nations, be it in Europe or elsewhere.[8]

With regard to joining the EEC, he continued, it was the government's objective 'to try to influence decisions which would inevitably influence us'. Participation in EMS offered the same kind of opportunity, the chance to participate in decisions which would, in their turn, influence Ireland, and the decision to join, he claimed, was based on the confidence of the government that Ireland did have the 'capacity as a nation to influence directions within the EEC'.[9] Indeed, it was Professor O'Donoghue, the Minister for Economic Planning and Development, rather than the Foreign Minister, who, under pressure from the opposition, offered a more red-blooded, nationalist defence of the policy of the government when he confessed that in taking Ireland into the EMS, the government stood 'convicted as romantics' if

> to be romantic implies having some sort of conviction, some sort of ardour, some sort of vision of the future. It implies having a belief in the Irish people, a commitment to shaping our own affairs, to exercising the power that has been conferred on an independent Government, to adopting a truly republican stance and say 'It's government of the people for the people'.[10]

Despite the fact that there were difficulties and mistakes might be made, the important thing, he argued, was to believe that there was a way in which Ireland could 'play its part among the nations of the earth and make a contribution'.

The government's articulation of their EMS policy in terms of an act of national self-assertion was largely a product of the increasing difficulties with which it confronted them. The general problems confronting a weak, open economy have been outlined above. According to Lynch, the Irish government feared that the establishment of a monetary system would possibly result for Ireland in: an over-valued pound; increasing unemployment in an underdeveloped economy already confronted by a surplus of young people entering the labour market; a drain of Irish capital and labour towards the centre of the Community; and, a need to reduce Ireland's balance of payments deficits more quickly than had been originally planned.[11] While these challenges had to be met by the Irish people's own efforts, Lynch also argued that Ireland required Community action to make sure that membership did not result in 'an even greater flow of resources away from peripheral regions', or the need to slow the fast rate of economic growth which Ireland had achieved in the late 1970s by extensive borrowing. In general principles, the government linked participation in EMS to the establishment of an effective regional policy. In practice, Lynch argued that Ireland would need £130 million a year for five years to cover the costs of participating and assuming Britain became a member.[12]

Herein lay the second problem – the extent to which Ireland's EMS policy depended upon what the British intended to do and the fact that the British looked like they were not going to participate in EMS to its fullest extent. The question as it presented itself to the Irish government was what should they do if the British decided to stay out. A major departure from the past was the fact that it was no longer simply a question of having to follow Britain's lead. According to Colley, the Minister of Finance, the decision whether to join in the event of Britain staying out had to be based on 'a thorough assessment of where the balance of economic advantage would lie'. In favour of joining, he argued, were the following points: Ireland would link itself to stronger economic growth; the government would be better able to reduce inflation; the economy would attract more non-British investment; the government could pursue a more independent monetary policy; and Ireland would receive more credit and assistance from the Community.[13]

The principal problem with joining EMS, if the British stayed out, was that in all probability this would involve a break in parity between sterling and the Irish pound and, hence, the loss of a stable currency relationship with what was still the country's major trading partner. The assumption was that the Irish pound, linked as it was to stronger currencies, would rise above sterling, which had not at that time begun its sharp rise to the briefly held status of a petro-currency. If this were the case, then Irish exports to Britain and tourism might be hurt, while British exports to Ireland would be relatively cheaper and the Irish government might be forced to take measures to control currency speculation.[14]

An additional problem was the fact that any break with sterling would establish a further barrier between the Republic and the North. As an opposition spokesman pointed out, this would not only create the practical problem of dealing with different currencies on both sides of what had been a highly penetrated border, but would also be at odds with the established government policy of regarding the country of consisting of the whole of Ireland.[15] This

146

problem, a particularly difficult one for Fianna Fáil, was acknowledged by the government. According to Lynch, if the British stayed out of EMS, then they would weigh 'the implications for people's consciousness of the country as a unit ....relative to other elements' that influenced their attitudes towards unification.[16] The assessment of the government was clear, however. As O'Donoghue argued, Ireland could not lock itself into the sterling system simply to maintain the status quo with the North. Echoing de Valera's earlier strategy, he claimed that by joining EMS and enjoying, thereby, a faster rate of economic growth than the North, Ireland would convince the people of Ulster of the value of both Irish unity and independence.[17]

The British decided to remain outside EMS and the Irish eventually decided to join it. This outcome has been cited as evidence by the Irish government and commentators alike of the extent to which circumstances had changed from the time when Irish governments followed British policy with regard to the question of joining the EEC. It should be noted, however, that it is the break with sterling, rather than the process by which Ireland entered EMS, which is emphasised. A closer examination of this process makes the extent to which Ireland's external circumstances had been transformed by EEC membership less clear. It will be recalled that the Irish government had supported the principle of EMS but had argued that the process of joining would have to make economic sense. They estimated that transfers to the value of £650 million spread over the following five years would cover the costs of membership for Ireland, or at least would constitute sufficient compensation to secure its participation.[18] In November 1978, Lynch told the Dáil that he had made this position clear to the French President, Giscard d'Estaing, the British Prime Minister, James Callaghan and Chancellor Schmidt of West Germany. He had also discussed the possibility of new German investments in Ireland with Schmidt once the EMS had been established.[19]

The £650 million figure had been set on the assumption that the British would join; presumably if they did not, then the Irish would require a larger transfer. In the event, the Community made available a total of £670 million per annum as soft loans for five years to all the 'less prosperous' states through the European Investment Bank. Of this total, two-thirds would go to Italy and one-third to Ireland, that is £225 million a year in soft loans. Lynch claimed that since, if they took the whole amount available through interest subsidies and moratoriums, they would be obtaining £45 million of it in a lump-sum grant, then the total deal roughly corresponded to the £130 million which the Irish had asked for in the first place. Only an £85 million disparity remained! On the basis of this, he stated, the government would think it over. As a consequence, EMS was launched in early December without Irish participation.

By the start of the New Year, however, they had joined the system. The reasons why they had changed their position, according to Lynch, were as follows. First, a restriction on the use of the available money for infrastructure projects rather than other government programmes had been lifted. Secondly, some of the 'more prosperous' countries, impressed by Ireland's 'unique difficulties', had agreed to make resources available on a bilateral basis which were 'substantially in excess' of the original amount.[20] According to *The Economist*, Ireland was to receive an extra £50 million consisting of £26.7 million from West Germany, £16 million from France, £4 million from the Netherlands, £1.3 million from Denmark and £660,000 from Luxembourg.[21] On the basis of this, the Taoiseach claimed that he was satisfied that 'sufficient additional resources' had been provided to overcome 'the critical initial two-year period'.[22]

Other factors, however, no doubt played a part in the decision. In particular, the economic growth rate had been slackening by the end of 1978 and in November, a national agreement between the government and the workers in the public sector had fallen apart.[23] While the taunts of the opposition to the effect that the government was bringing Ireland into the EMS principally to obtain immediate resource transfers were an exaggeration, the tough budget the government was due to present in the New Year was certainly helped by the availability of an extra £50 million. Externally, the decision was probably facilitated by the fact that the Italians had decided to join the system, although with a wider band through which the lira was permitted to fluctuate.[24] Further, the British had declared their intention to keep sterling stable while not actually joining EMS, and on the basis of this, the Irish government expressed the hope that parity between the Irish pound (punt) and sterling could be maintained for a time.[25] Finally, as Lynch told the Dáil, not only had they settled for terms that 'might not be available later', but in so doing, he believed that they had 'enhanced the status of our country within the Community'.[26] It is the first part of this statement which is significant. The Irish government had decided to join EMS, held out for its best deal and entered when it considered that this, although far short of its declared requirements, had been achieved.

The first point to note about the approach of the Irish government towards participation in the EMS is the virtual absence of the *communautaire* strategy in the tactical sense of procuring influence with other members of the Community. The *communautaire* articulation was restricted to general statements of principle preceding and following accounts of the nitty-gritty of negotiations. On what was a policy issue clearly addressed to the future of the EEC, and acknowledged by the Irish government as such, they pursued a strategy of demanding compensation on the basis of particular national attributes – Ireland's relative poverty, lack of size and open economy. On this, there was a consensus between the major parties; no one faulted the *demandeur* strategy as such, only the way in which it was handled.

In doing this, the government pursued a strategy apparently consistent in some respects with the predictions of the complex interdependence thesis. The issues were certainly complex in their form, witness Lynch's transformation of the assistance in the form of loans offered by the Community into a sum approximating the government's original request. As Kelly pointed out, the

EMS debate in the Dáil was a 'pretty empty' exercise because between the Dáil and the Senate there were 'not five people capable of debating this subject with adequate professional knowledge'.[27] It is also possible to argue that the episode constitutes an example of a weaker actor playing regime politics and exploiting the rules of the regime, the commitment of other major actors to the regime, and Ireland's own position in it, to its own advantage. This, however, would be to focus on the form, rather than the character, of what was actually going on. In point of fact, the Irish government found itself with very little real ability to extract concessions from other governments in return for its cooperation. Instead, the familiar picture of a Taoiseach reporting to the Dáil on his bilateral discussions with several, rather than one, governments directed at obtaining special consideration for Irish problems in the face of changes in their external environment, presented itself. Lynch, like Lemass before him on the British import levy, was forced to return from such negotiations, after the initial decision to stay out of EMS, empty-handed, saying that other governments were sympathetic, understood Ireland's concerns, but had their own problems and could do nothing for the time-being to help Ireland.[28]

The major exception to this, of course, was the break with sterling and all that that might imply about the changing nature of the Anglo-Irish relationship. Opposition deputies criticised the nationalist articulation with which the government presented its policy – as one Deputy taunted, 'the pikes will be together at the rising of the moon to break the link with sterling'.[29] However, this was extremely important and a goal worth achieving in itself, even if the economic consequences were unclear. Nevertheless, these changes were the product of Britain's decline, not an increase in Irish capabilities caused by increasing interdependence or a transformation in the character of international relations between the governments of the Community. As Cluskey, speaking for the Labour Party, argued, breaking the link with sterling had a 'romantic' appeal, but the Irish should be under no illusion that it would result in 'full monetary control, or in a position where we could determine our own economic future independently and without regard to any other power'. Rather, joining the EMS would entail 'exchanging economic dependence on one economy, one currency, for dependence on another'.[30] This being the case, and for all the 'modernity' of an issue such as the EMS, it was the ideological and symbolic aspects of the issue as an opportunity for asserting national independence and identity, that became of prime importance to the Irish government. The need to take opportunities such as these was underlined by the sense of an absence of any real influence over the external developments and changes in which Ireland was necessarily involved.

The way in which the EMS was established underlines how limited the power of Irish governments remained when confronted by the process of regime extension. If the EMS showed how little control they had over the process of change, however, then their experience with the Common Fisheries Policy suggests that even once it is established, an international regime *per se* is not necessarily better for the interest of a small state than the preceding 'anarchy'. The emergence of the exploitation of ocean resources as an international political issue serves as one of the strongest pieces of evidence in the case which theorists of complex interdependence make about the transformation of international relations. Classically regarded, perhaps as *the* low political issue, fish have become the subject of major international conferences and exchanges of naval gunfire. From the point of view of a complex interdependence perspective, fishing and the wider question of the exploitation of ocean resources of which it is part contain all the elements of a 'modern' international political issue: first, the development of technologies which both exploit, ever more quickly and effectively, a limited and threatened resource, and also allow sustained access to previously inaccessible areas, in this case, the sea; second, the expansion of the external interests of governments, dictated by the demands of internal economic growth and facilitated by technological developments, into exploiting and controlling ocean resources; and third, the attempts by governments to establish rules by which their exploitation of these resources should be governed, so as to avoid conflict between themselves and the destruction of the resource. The fisheries issue is interesting, therefore, for this examination of Irish foreign policy because it is clearly concerned with regime, or rule-governed, international politics, and as such, contains at least one reasonably spectacular instance of their predicted 'equalisation effects' – the outcome of the 'Cod War' between Iceland and Britain in the mid-1970s.

Prior to the London Fisheries Convention in 1964, the oceans, with the exception of territorial waters within the three-mile limit, were in principle open to all who cared to fish them. This convention extended the exclusive area to twelve miles with a provision that foreign fishermen who had 'traditionally' fished in the newly-excluded areas still enjoyed access to the outer six miles of the belt. In the Irish case, for example, British, French, Dutch, Spanish and Belgian trawlers could continue to operate in certain parts of the 6–12-mile belt.[31] In contrast to much of the subsequent regulation of the ocean regime, which largely consisted of legitimising the claims of states to ever-widening bodies of adjacent waters, the original members of the EEC committed themselves to achieving a common fisheries policy. This consisted of allowing each other equal access to their waters 'up to each other's beaches'.[32] When Ireland, Britain and Denmark joined the EEC, their governments committed them in the Treaty of Accession to both this principle and allowing continued access to non-EEC countries with 'traditional' rights in their waters. In recognition of the greater interest of the three new countries in fishing and the fact that there were shortly to be major changes in the international law of the sea, however, the members of the Community agreed to a period of ten years' derogation from the principle of 'equal access'. Instead, a version of the six-and-six formula was retained.

The ten-year derogation from the principle of equal access was not really a transitional phase for new members, but rather a breathing space in which new arrangements could be put together. Fish and the control of waters had become more important because of the future law of the sea. Governments were going to be able to claim an exclusive economic zone (EEZ) extending out to at least 200 miles. The immediate consequence of this measure would be to transform the scale of the sacrifice to be made by countries with long coastlines facing open seas in accepting the principle of equal access. As the British were fond of observing, 60 per cent of the 'Euro-pond' consisted of what would otherwise be, they claimed, British waters.[33] Hostility to the equal access principle, however, was not simply the product of national greed directed at making the most of the windfall of the 200 mile zone. Another consequence of the pending law of the sea was that the deep-water fishing fleets of Britain and West Germany, in particular, would be denied access to their 'traditional' grounds by the application of the 200 mile rule elsewhere. Hence, the sea area available to the EEC became even more valuable. As a consequence of these developments, the effort to achieve a common fisheries policy for the EEC became a ten-year period of intermittent bargaining and conflict, the object of which was to determine the extent of the access enjoyed by the rest of the Community to the waters around, principally, Britain and Ireland.

Ireland's fishing industry was very small at the beginning of the period, and this despite Ireland being, by some calculations, 'the nation with the largest potential seabed territory in the EEC'.[34] The Irish took less than 10 per cent of the total EEC catch, 90 per cent of this being caught within their own zone.[35] A better idea of the size of Ireland's fishing industry relative to the resources available to it was given by the then Minister for Fisheries, Lenihan's, estimate that in1976 some 15 per cent of the total catch of fish within Ireland's 200-mile zone was taken by Irish fishermen.[36] From a CFP, the Irish government wished to maximise the financial and technical resources made available to it from the EEC while maintaining as much control as possible over the waters around Ireland. According to FitzGerald, speaking as Minister for Foreign Affairs in 1977, the development of the Irish fishing industry should be recognised as 'a natural part of the economic development' of what, apart from part of southern Italy, was the 'least developed part of the Community'[37]

The central assumptions upon which Irish fishing policy was based, therefore, were that the industry was of special importance to Ireland and that with regard to any CFP, Ireland constituted a special case within the EEC. This claim enjoyed a measure of recognition by the rest of the Community embodied in what the government called the 'Hague Agreement', accepted by the members of the Community in October 1976. According to a spokesman for Fine Gael reviewing the policy of his party in government six years later, they had obtained four concessions. First, as a special case, Ireland should obtain special treatment even in comparison to other seapowers such as Britain. Second, the Irish fishing industry should be permitted to double its catch between 1976 and 1979. Thirdly, it was recognised that Irish government had the right to take unilateral measures to preserve fish stocks until a CFP was agreed upon. Finally, the Irish fishery protection effort should receive what he called 'massive aid' from the Community.[38]

The heart and sticking point of Irish policy, however, was the claim to a 50-mile exclusive zone. According to Lenihan, what the Irish basically wanted was 'a preponderant share of the catch in the waters adjacent to our coast out to 200 miles, but in particular as far as 50 miles for our fishermen'.[39] In return, the Commission was prepared to offer twelve miles, the rest of the Community, apart from Britain and Denmark, nothing. The CFP which was finally agreed to by all the members except Denmark, incorporated many things which the Irish had wanted. A three-year aid programme worth £150 million was established, and Ireland had already received assistance for air and surface patrolling of its sea area.[40] A system of national quotas on catches was agreed to and Britain and Ireland retained preferential access to the 12- and 50-mile belts off their shores. Most importantly, the Irish catch increased by 166 per cent between 1973 and 1978, and Ireland's share in the total, and shrinking, agreed-to Community catch rose from less than 2 per cent to a target of 4.3 per cent set for 1983.[41] These successes, however, were restricted to the quantities of fish caught. With regard to its claim to the control or the exclusive use of the seas around Ireland, the government was less successful, despite the fact that they employed a range of tactics in their efforts to achieve this objective.

Least in evidence was the *communautaire* strategy of either straightforward support or attempting to gain exemptions and compensation by portraying Ireland as a major supporter of the Commission's proposals on the CFP. The reasons for this are quite clear. The CFP was a particular international order or regime which did not suit Irish interests. It did not present the Irish government with the usual task with which the establishment of a common policy confronts a weak actor, that is, attempting to smooth the process of adjustment to sharper competition in the domestic market while preparing to take advantage of the larger external market to which one now has access. Rather, the Irish government saw the CFP as presenting a threat to one of its few potential commercial strengths. A CFP based on the principle of equal access to all the waters of the Community would, in effect, legitimise the existing rate of exploitation of Irish fish stocks by other countries without offering Ireland very much in return. A *communautaire* approach would have implied that the Irish government agreed to a common policy based upon the sharing of resources, a disproportionate amount of which were 'provided' by Ireland.

The only time that a *communautaire* position was elaborated at any length was at the beginning of the period when the coalition government was still in power. The Minister for Foreign Affairs, FitzGerald, addressing the Dáil in 1977, argued that Ireland was not permitted to take unilateral action on establishing an exclusive zone because of the terms of the Accession Treaty which the previous government had signed. Nor, he claimed, had it been possible for the government to block the establishment of a joint 200-mile limit by the EEC, until they received satisfaction on their own demands. He argued

152

that if they had not declared the zone, this would have been 'extremely disruptive of Community solidarity' and would have been both offensive and irritating to Ireland's Community partners. This, he went on to say, would have weakened 'the moral validity' of Ireland's case as a poor nation with vital national interests at stake.[42]

Two things may be noted here, however. First, FitzGerald cited *communautaire* principles only with regard to the restraint with which Ireland's tactical position was handled, not with regard to the central issues at stake in the CFP. Secondly, it is not altogether clear that the Irish did not threaten to block the Community's 200-mile extension. According to *The Economist*, the package of concessions embodied in the Hague Agreement and outlined above were granted at about the same time as an Irish block on the joint 200-hundred mile extension was removed. Further, according to the same source, the Irish maintained their opposition to the agreements between the Community and third parties in order to extract concessions.[43] If the Irish government did pursue such linkage strategies, then it would seem quite likely that FitzGerald's *communautaire* rationale for Irish diplomatic restraint is to be understood principally in domestic terms. The government had, after all, removed its objection to the 200-mile extension without obtaining its most important demand, a 50-mile exclusive zone around Ireland.

The Irish government regarded the international regime embodied in the CFP as both unfair and hostile to Irish interests. Their policy was increasingly directed, therefore, at protecting those interests from the common policy by blocking it, and pursuing them by taking measures of their own. In doing this, the government had three strategies available to them: they could pursue alliances with other governments which shared their interests; they could take conservation and protection measures on a unilateral basis; and they could use the veto in the policy-making processes of the Community.

While they had adopted a policy of opposition to the EEC over CFP, the Irish government were by no means diplomatically isolated. The British, and to a lesser extent, the Danes were hostile to the CFP for similar reasons. Both the British and the Irish wanted exclusive coastal zones,[44] and failing that, a licensing system rather than national quotas, for catches. According to Lenihan, such a system ought to be 'very strongly under the control of the coastal state'. This was the position that both the British and the Irish would take at the negotiations.[45] However, even though at one stage Lenihan characterised the dispute as being between 'seven Community countries' on the one hand, and 'the two island countries' on the other,[46] any appearance of an 'Anglo-Irish ' alliance,[47] presented the Irish government with problems both at home and abroad. For obvious reasons, any overt cooperation with the British was always vulnerable to domestic criticism. More importantly, while Britain and Ireland did have similar problems with the CFP, the Irish government did not regard cooperation with the British as being a likely method of achieving their own objectives. As Lenihan argued in 1977,

One of our problems is that the British, although they have a certain interest with us in a large part of our case, do have other interests which disturb our other Community partners. One of our problems is to ensure that Ireland's special case which is generally recognised, survives through the whole situation.[48]

British opposition was taking a particularly abrasive form at the time and the British had already caused the Community a number of other problems. The dangers to which a too close association with the British tactics threatened Ireland's case for special treatment, however, were not really the problem. More important was the fact that any solution purely on the basis of the principles for which the Irish and the British had both argued, was likely to be so expensive to the rest of the Community that they would not permit it. Concessions in terms of increases in catches and control of sea areas which were feasible when a country took only some 2 per cent of the total were prohibitively costly in the case of a country which took 25 per cent.[49]

The important task, therefore, according to Lenihan, speaking in February 1978, was 'to detach Ireland from the British position' and to emphasise the Irish claim not in terms of the operating principles of the CFP, but in terms of the particular character of Ireland's circumstances. Thus, he stated that while 'some aspects' of the British and Irish positions coincided, he was 'out there' in Brussels 'fighting Ireland's case'. The British had additional problems in the North Sea but that was their problem. Ireland was not interested in fighting 'Britain's war...against Denmark and Germany...on what sort of coastal band exists in the North Sea'. That, he said, was a 'separate ballgame'.[50] That same month, the Irish attended a meeting organised by the West Germans to which the British did not go, and received further concessions in line with their own particular demands.[51]

As well as the different scale of their respective problems, the British and Irish also had divergent interests to satisfy in their fishing policies. As early as the autumn of 1976, they had differed over the willingness of the Irish to block the establishment of a common Community 200-mile limit. The Irish fishing fleet was a largely inshore one which was not immediately affected by the establishment of such zones elsewhere in the world, whereas the British possessed a deep water fleet which was looking for its own 200-mile zone as it was increasingly excluded from its traditional fishing grounds.[52]

Finally, the Irish and the British were in conflict themselves about access to one another's waters and, in particular, about the ownership of Rockall, an outcrop to the north and west of Britain and Ireland, and the status of the waters surrounding it.[53] If, as the British argued, this point could be used for determining control of the continental shelf around it, then the sea area belonging to whoever owned it was greatly expanded. Britain, Ireland and the Faeroes all laid claim to Rockall, but the Irish government emphasised a difference in the nature of the claims. According to Kelly, the British regarded all islands, whatever their size or habitation, as generating maritime zones. The

Irish, in contrast, were only prepared to accept 'inhabited islands within three miles of the mainland' for these purposes.[54] They had the new law of the sea and a ruling of the Commission on their side with regard to this,[55] but the dispute had lasted since 1964. The Irish had suggested third party *ad hoc* arbitration in 1976 and the British had finally agreed to this process in 1980.[56] However, as a spokesman for the government had argued in 1979, they 'were pressing on apace' to obtain Britain's agreement to this process but they could not 'do anything more'. As he put it, 'We are doing our bit and we have performed well to date in this regard. It is now a matter for the British to come clean on this matter. That is as far as we can go'.[57]

These differences with the British and, more importantly, the fact that Irish policy towards the CFP was based upon emphasising their own special circumstances rather than problems with the general principles of the common policy entailed that the government pursued its interests, in the main, by acting alone. They did so in one of two ways. First, in the absence of concessions from the Community on the Irish demand for a 50-mile exclusive fishing zone, the government took unilateral measures in an attempt both to safeguard fish stocks and to indicate the extent of their commitment to the exclusion zone to the rest of the Community. Under the terms of the Hague Agreement, in the absence of established CFP conservation measures, the member governments were permitted to take their own temporary conservation measures, provided that these did not discriminate on the basis of nationality. In January 1977, the Irish government announced that it was banning the operation of boats 110 feet or more long or with an engine capacity in excess of 1100 brake horse power, within the 50-mile zone.[58] According to the European Parliament's study of the effects of EEC membership on the Irish economy, 'this measure effectively excluded fishermen from other Member States'. After ten Dutch trawlers were arrested by the Irish fishery patrol for ignoring this ban, the Commission brought an action against Ireland on the measure before the European Court of Justice.[59] While the Irish measures did not formally discriminate against any particular country, according to *The Economist*, since Ireland possessed only two vessels over the designated size, the intentions of the ban were clear. In July, the Court ordered the Irish government to suspend the measure and in its final judgment decided that it was illegal. The Irish government complied with the decision of the Court.[60]

More successful for a time than this single example of unilateral action was the second tactic pursued by the government acting alone, exploiting their ability to veto Community decisions. The veto may be regarded as one of the most important weapons of regime politics. Its presence indicates the primacy of rules over the distribution of conventional attributes of power in determining outcomes (always assuming that possession of the veto is not simply restricted to those participants in a regime who are powerful in conventional terms). As such, the Irish government made considerable use of this measure, not so much to block decisions it did not like, but in a linkage strategy by which they blocked progress in other areas in an attempt to extract concessions on their own concerns. The Irish threat to block the Community's joint 200-mile extension has already been noted. They also threatened its use on the establishment of EEC fishing agreements with third party countries in retaliation for the Community's insistence on controlling total catches by a system of national quotas rather than allowing governments to regulate their own sea areas on a preferential basis.[61] According to FitzGerald, speaking for the opposition in 1977, but obtaining Lenihan's agreement on his view of Irish policy, the veto was 'the trump card' which the Irish held. They could

> and must veto any agreement entered into or purported or attempted to be entered into by the Community with third countries for reciprocal fishing rights unless and until our claim is satisfied.[62]

As the ten-year derogation period drew to a close in 1982, however, the limits of the veto were exposed. It became clear that most of the members of the Community were probably going to achieve agreement on the CFP, and that major Irish objectives would not be achieved. In a debate on a private member's motion, the opposition drew attention to domestic concern about the state of the Irish fishing industry. They argued that cheap imports from Iceland, Norway and Germany had depressed the price of fish on the Irish market and that because they received no subsidies, Irish boatyards were not competitive with those abroad. While Irish catches had been good, they claimed these gains were largely comprised of cheap mackerel from off the north-west coast caught by approximately 24 trawlers, or only some 10 per cent of Ireland's fishermen. Abroad, meanwhile, subsidised, well-equipped and wealthy foreigners were poised to descend on the Irish fishing grounds as soon as the principle of equal access came into force. Because of this, one opposition deputy argued, it was essential that the final agreement should provide minimum prices and protect the Irish fishing industry from third countries. The minimum which the Minister should obtain from any agreement on CFP should be a 12-mile limit.[63]

The problem was, however, that there was very little the Irish government could do to insist upon these demands. As Daly, the Minister for Fisheries and Forestry, made clear,

> At this stage the exercise of the veto would have the opposite result to what we seek in as much as it would merely block agreement on a revised fisheries policy, permitting fishing vessels to fish right up to our shores.

This would be 'an intolerable situation for us', but because of the commitments entered into at the time of the Treaty of Accession, free access would occur in the absence of an agreement being reached. The influence of the government was limited, therefore, by the fact that countries favouring equal access 'had the law on their side'. It was in their interest that 'there be no agreement reached on a revised policy'.[64] All he could do, therefore, was to assure the Dáil that extensive bilateral negotiations were going on to avoid a free-for-all which very few governments actually wanted. While Ireland's needs had yet to be met, a number of reasonable proposals were being discussed, and he mentioned with approval a suggestion by the Commission that a further ten-year derogation with another ten possibly added to that might be adopted.[65] What he and his minister for state emphasised, the following day, was that the Irish government had little power to influence these negotiations about regime change to serve Irish interests and that the proposals from the Commission looked like Ireland's best bet.[66]

In its fisheries policy, the Irish government did not pursue a *communautaire* strategy designed to procure influence and favours through the performance of 'good citizen' roles. They did not regard the CFP as a situation in which short-term adjustment pains would be compensated for by the longer-term benefits of participation in a common policy. The costs of the CFP were regarded as prohibitive to the Irish fishing industry unless certain exemptions were obtained. As a consequence, the government pursued a policy which focused on their own interests in two senses. First, they pursued their interests to the exclusion of all others; they were not interested in working with other governments nor with altering the general principles of the CFP for the good of all. Secondly, they projected a specific articulation of this self-interest as a tactic designed to convince other governments of the special nature of Ireland's case. Ireland, they argued, was poorer than the rest of the EEC and struggling to develop its industries. It therefore deserved special treatment. Besides, by uncoupling themselves from other *demandeurs*, notably Britain, they hoped to make a settlement of their own requirements more financially acceptable to the rest of the Community.

This projection of a deserving identity, however, was coupled with an attempt to exploit the rules, procedures and issue linkages of Community politics to obtain their objectives. The results of their efforts to play regime politics were mixed. The attempt by the government to make their point through unilateral protection measures failed, despite the efforts of the government to present the outcome of the CFP negotiations a 'test of the bona fides of the Community and the Commission' as far as Ireland was concerned.[67] It was they, the weak actor, who were forced by their need to continue participating in a regime, into accepting the decision of the European Court of Justice. Their use, or threat, of the veto was more successful. Concessions such as the Hague agreement or the raising of Irish quotas during the discussions in Berlin, seemed to flow after the Irish had threatened to block the joint 200-mile extension or third party agreements. By the same score, however, the Irish block was always removed without obtaining their 50-mile exclusion zone, and to settle for national quotas, no matter how generous, rather than control of their own seas, always represented a concession by the Irish. In the end, the

157

structure of the problem and the rules of the game the Irish were playing, themselves rendered the veto useless.

Ultimately, the fisheries policy of the Irish government was a failure in that it did not achieve a major objective, the 50-mile exclusion zone. It is tempting to conclude, however, from the important concessions which they did extract and the fact that they maintained a struggle for ten years, that this episode does provide an example of the equalising effects of regime politics. However, the importance of the British resistance to the CFP in preserving the situation in which the Irish could attempt to extract side payments cannot be ignored. For despite the efforts of the Irish government to decouple their position from that of the British, the duration of their own struggle was probably dependent on the willingness of the British to continue resisting. If they had any doubts about this, then they were removed, presumably, by the way in which the Community dealt with protracted Danish resistance once the CFP was agreed to by the rest. Rather than establish the policy by a majority overrule (the British, but not the Irish, objected to this), the rest of the Community simply took national measures in line with the agreement. Once the British and French agreed to a compromise on French access to British waters in the summer of 1982,[68] therefore, the process of achieving the CFP gathered momentum and the Irish were returned to the familiar position of saying what they would like and then seeing what the latest round of restructuring in their external environment would give them.

A similar pattern developed in Irish policy on the question of admitting Greece into the EEC. According to the Treaty of Rome, any European country may apply for membership. The success of their application, however, is contingent upon their unanimous acceptance by existing member states. Greece applied for membership in 1975, followed by Spain and Portugal in 1977. While enlargement is not an issue of regime extension in the strictest sense, one would expect it to be one which called forth a similar *communautaire* response on the part of the Irish.

During the second period, the question of Greek membership of the EEC provided the Irish government with a number of problems. In terms of general *communautaire* principles, the Irish government should have supported Greek membership. The EEC was supposed to be about *European* unity, prosperity and orderly relations, not about the establishment of a narrow and convenient trading bloc of advanced Western European states. As O'Kennedy put it in 1979, the Community was 'incomplete' without Greece, Spain and Portugal.[69] In terms of regime politics, however, not to mention more immediate Irish national interests, the situation was not as straightforward. As a small, underdeveloped country similar to Ireland, Greece could be viewed as either a potential ally in the political processes of the Community or as a rival for its scarce resources.

The strategy of the Irish government consisted of linking the admission of Greece to the implementation of reforms in the Community which would restore its momentum in the direction of further integration. Speaking for the coalition government in 1977, Kelly stated that Ireland supported the enlargement of the EEC, but not at a cost to the latter's capacity 'to develop its full potential'. The government had two 'preconditions' which would have to be satisfied before it could agree to the admission of Greece. First, enlargement, and particularly its financial implications, should not hamper the attainment of other EEC objectives. Secondly, the decision-making structures of the Community would have to be strengthened before negotiations on new members were concluded.[70] By the latter, he was referring to fundamental Community problems. Kelly argued that the Irish government wished to see an end to the principle of unanimity voting 'in cases where no vital national interest exists'. Further, he declared that the government was opposed to the development of any two-tier structure which would treat the large, rich states in a different manner from the small, poor ones. This had been proposed in certain quarters as a way of coping with the increased diversity of an enlarged Community. Kelly argued that,

Under no circumstances would we agree to any changes that would weaken the role of the smaller States in decision-making or would give any privileged position to larger countries in a directory-type system.[71]

Indeed, according to FitzGerald, the Irish government had taken a leading role in pressing for a representative of the Commission to be present at the Western Economic Summit held in London. This was not simply to represent the EEC as a whole, but also to represent the member states which were not asked to participate in the summit.[72] Later that same year, the new Taoiseach, Jack Lynch, stated that enlargement was desirable and that 'political considerations outweigh the institutional and financial difficulties – large as these are'.[73] The Foreign Minister, O'Kennedy, however, made it clear that Irish policy still emphasised the link between enlargement and reforms within the Community by stating that in the government's view, enlargement had to be a way of moving the Community on to a 'higher plateau'. This required an

efficiently working Community with the additional resources required to maintain and expand the benefits of common policies to new entrants and existing member states alike.[74]

Despite linking the question of enlargement to these major concerns, however, the substantive issue which concerned the Irish government was, perforce, much narrower. Speaking for the government in 1979, Andrews stated that Ireland continued to support the accession of Greece to the Community because it entailed no cost to Ireland. The Community had agreed to an Irish proposal made in 1976 that funding adjustments would be made as soon as the Greeks joined, and he pointed out that Greek agriculture posed no threat to Ireland.[75] In the final Dáil debate on the accession of Greece to the European Community, the potential financial consequences were very much in evidence. O'Kennedy emphasised the government's efforts to ensure that a short transitional period was given to Greece in sectors important to Ireland such as beef and dairy products, and reiterated the government's interpretation of the 1976 agreement by which the Community was committed to not letting enlargement damage the common policies or efforts to correct regional imbalances.[76]

It was left to an opposition spokesman, O'Keefe, to attempt to emphasise the broader implications of the issue. Greece, could be 'regarded as the cradle of democracy' but of late, as he put it, 'they have had their ups and downs'. Nevertheless, he suggested that the country would be an 'ally' of Ireland in the fight against the 'two-tier system' because of its similarities in population size and problems confronted.[77] Quinn, the spokesman for the Labour Party, was not so generous. He claimed that 'The accession of this state, which is as poor as, if not poorer than we are, is the largest single threat to the few miserable pounds we get out of the regional fund as it is'.[78]

This concern with Community finances in the final debate may be explained in great part by the fact that, the following day, a European Council meeting chaired by Ireland was to be held in Dublin to discuss the 'British problem' and the wider difficulties of which it was a part. Defending Ireland's share of the existing Community budget had, however, been the major preoccupation of the government throughout the period. While the Fine Gael spokesman above argued that Greece would be a valuable addition to the coalition of weak states opposing the proposals for a two-tier system in the EEC,[79] this had not always been the priority of his party. Speaking back in 1977, FitzGerald had claimed that Ireland had pointed out to its fellows that the then 'five smaller countries' of the Community should unite to protect both themselves and the 'Community System' from the bigger members and a too hurried enlargement. While there was no opposition to the principle of Greek entry *per se*, these other Community problems had to be solved first.[80]

The grand strategy of linking enlargement to the prior implementation of major Community reforms was neither successful nor particularly credible as a *communautaire* policy. Threatening to block the accession of Greece would be scarcely likely to have caused the British to relent in their obstructive policies or the other members to get tougher with them. It is also highly unlikely that the Irish would have actually placed themselves in the position of vetoing the entry of another small state into the Community. The choice of this strategy would also seem to indicate that the Irish were not primarily concerned with acquiring another ally for the pursuit of their interests in the regime politics of the EEC, either. Until the decision was taken to let the Greeks in, the emphasis of the Irish government was on the danger that Greek membership would entail that Community resources would be spread more thinly. The

160

Greeks, then, were presented as potential rivals, albeit through no fault of their own.

The principal objective of the Irish government's policy on enlargement was to draw attention to the fact that they did not want their share of the resources of the Community to suffer from it. It was to this end that they articulated a *communautaire* stance as the basis for virtuous criticism of the Community's faltering momentum and talked of mobilising the small states of the Community on a policy of insisting on reforms as a precondition of enlargement. Even so, the policy was largely unsuccessful. Responding to a question on Ireland's reduced share of the regional development fund in 1980, the then Minister for Foreign Affairs, Lenihan, replied that he expected Ireland's 'percentage' to be reduced as a result of Greek membership and the 'consequent division of the fund between ten rather than nine member states'. However, he continued, there would be 'no question of a reduction in our cash receipts from the fund'. That would be 'unacceptable'. Everyone had taken cuts to 'facilitate Greece' and it was very difficult for the Irish government to oppose these cuts strongly when Ireland's reduction was 'easily the lowest' of the nine members.[81]

To conclude, in pursuing their objectives within the EEC during the second period, Irish governments operated with two basic strategies: the projection of a *communautaire* identity; and the attempt to exploit the rules of regime politics by adopting *demandeur* positions. As it became clear to these governments that the Community was not in a process of transition from intergovernmental bargaining to integrated, supranational decision-making, the substance, if not always the articulation, of Irish foreign policy shifted from the former to the latter approach.

The *communautaire* role-playing approach rested, essentially, on the same assumptions about international order as those upon which the UN policy had been based during the first period. The more orderly and rule-governed a society was, the less outcomes within it were determined by the threat or actual use of force. Therefore it was in the interests of a weak state like Ireland to work for a more orderly society. There is, of course, a measure of irony in the prescription that a government which is too weak to get its own way in the existing system should direct its efforts to transforming the system as a whole. In the case of both the UN and the EEC, however, the Irish government applied this prescription with a considerable degree of what one of its senior diplomats, noted above, called 'intentional naiveté'. Whatever the prospects for reform in the international and regional organisations of which they were a member, and however unlikely it might be that Irish governments could lead or push the international community towards reform, they regarded the 'good international citizen' role as worth performing for more immediate reasons.

First, as the components of a national identity, these roles served as 'proof' both at home and abroad that Ireland was indeed a distinctive and full participant in international society, operating on the basis of the values of the

Republican tradition. Secondly, they were regarded as instruments of policy in the existing international or regional systems of which Ireland was a member. This was the policy of prestige, in its small state articulation focusing on virtue and utility rather than demonstrations of power, designed to procure influence through status. While this constituted a more tactical or calculative rationale for establishing and performing these roles, however, it too rested upon assumptions about the social nature of the international system, namely, that other governments were, for whatever their reasons, receptive to the interests of a state which they regarded as being both virtuous and useful.

This was by no means an entirely ludicrous assumption. It has been argued above that Ireland's UN policy did bring it a measure of influence, albeit in a highly restricted area of policy. The assumption that the EEC was like the UN only better, and that, hence, the strategy would work there too, only better, proved wrong. While useful in the loose and essentially static order represented by the UN, the *communautaire* version of good citizenship was inappropriate in the EEC, which constituted a particular and evolving (in the sense that it was changing and these changes had important consequences for Ireland), regional system. It was not that the other member governments were unimpressed by demonstrations of virtue and utility on the part of one of their weaker fellows. In the sense that one may point to the generally 'good feeling' about Ireland in the Community, they probably were. The problem was that the *communautaire* strategy *per se* did not begin to address the kind of issues that were continually at stake for Ireland in the politics of the EEC. The rewards at the UN took the form of occasional or remote flattery, for example, the call in times of crisis to participate in peacekeeping operations, or the achievement of influential participation in long-running attempts to tackle the problems of arms control. To defend one's share of the CAP, to block or change hostile Community proposals and to minimise the negative consequences to Ireland of participation in a new common policy, however, it was not sufficient to perform one's role and wait for the response.

As a consequence of the character of Community decision-making and what Irish governments wanted from that process, performing a *communautaire* role lost the centrality to Irish foreign policy implied for it by 'diplomacy for cash' formulations of the sort offered by FitzGerald. Good behaviour in these terms could not be offered as a *quid pro quo* for concessions when the other members wanted Ireland to go along with compromises which had little to do with the future evolution of the Community or, indeed, Irish interests. It was more likely to undermine immediate Irish objectives in that it might be expected that the genuinely *communautaire* government should be offering, rather than extracting, compensation in order to establish common policies. What happened, therefore, was that Irish governments attempted to incorporate this role into their second strategy of operating as a *demandeur*. They did this by arguing that the absence of economic convergence in the EEC signified that the rest of the Community – governments and the Commission alike –were increasingly failing to perform in accordance with the principles to which they were supposed to be committed. This being so, Irish governments would continue to speak up for those principles and to act on them where they could, but they would take the necessary measures to safeguard their own interests in the existing system. This involved different tactics, but Irish governments could continue to claim a happy coincidence between pursuing their own national interest in the economic development of Ireland and the broader *communautaire* principle of economic convergence between all the members of the EEC. Pursuing the former objective was presented as part of pursuing the latter.

The *demandeur* strategy was regarded as neither a counsel of despair nor even a reversion to business as usual by Irish governments. Whatever loss of momentum the EEC might have suffered, the fact remained that its past successes had produced a regime of rules and understandings within which the relations of its members were conducted. These were conditions which approximated to those specified by the proponents of the complex interdependence thesis. The extent to which inter-state relations and foreign policy behaviour were transformed by these conditions, however, was not so great as to increase markedly the ability of Irish governments to control their external environment and its impact on Ireland. Certainly, from the point of view of Irish governments, relations became more complex after they had joined the EEC; there were more of them with more actors. Also, the distinction between domestic and external policy was eroded as economic issues became more obviously important. Irish ministers participated in decision-making in Brussels which would have a direct impact on domestic legislation and policy. Sectors of Irish society, notably farmers and fishermen, mobilised around not just trying to influence government policy in Dublin, but also how the government conducted Irish relations with the other members of the EEC. Most importantly, regime politics gave the Irish government an environment in which its fellows were formally committed to strengthening the regime, and a veto over major decisions which it could not accept.

The way in which these two assets were used, however, and the limited success Irish governments enjoyed from their use, indicated how little the essentials of their external circumstances had changed. While they gained, for example, compensation for their participation in the EMS, exemption from certain restrictions on the CAP, and special help from the CFP, it cannot be said that Irish governments participated as co-equals with the more powerful members of the EEC in shaping Community policy. This was because interdependence, in so far as it could be said to define relationships in the EEC, was largely restricted to the area of formal, institutional interaction. Nye and Keohane's underlying power structure did not exert remote or occasional control over regime outcomes but, rather, permeated the regime itself in the sense that policy outcomes were principally determined by the extent of the consensus among the major participants. Irish policy in this regime took the form of exploiting rules to extract concessions. The success enjoyed, however, was as much a product of the fact that it did not cost a lot to settle their claims or the absence of agreement among the major actors, as any equalising effects conferred by regime rules.

Beyond the realm of institutional equality, Ireland remained a weak, peripheral actor which needed the Community and what it offered more than the Community or anyone in it needed Ireland. This fact was reflected in the restraint with which Irish governments used or threatened to use their formal right to block Community decisions. The efforts of the Irish government, therefore, were principally directed at the familiar task of attempting to minimise the particular costs to them of each change in their external environment and these changes were the product of decisions effectively arrived at by others. As an exercise in damage control, either through prevention or, more often, seeking exemption and compensation, this approach applied equally to those areas of policy where the Community could be said to be failing or succeeding.

The *demandeur* strategy did not consist of a managerial approach to external relations in which the Irish government cultivated a shifting group of state and non-state allies in an effort to shape the EEC or its policies in accordance with Irish objectives. Its chief weapon was the threat to block Community decisions and this right, as well as the right to membership of the EEC *per se*, derived from Ireland's standing as a sovereign independent state. The emphasis on inter-governmental cooperation, therefore, and not any other characteristic of the regime, was the basis for any enhanced influence which Ireland enjoyed within the EEC. The chief objective of the strategy was to limit the negative consequences of Community decisions to Ireland in particular. Because of the care with which the veto had to be used or threatened, however, this was attempted in the main by emphasising the extent to which Ireland was a special case in the Community, underdeveloped and deserving of assistance.

Once again, therefore, Irish policy was directed at pursuing objectives through the projection of a particular definition of Ireland's national identity as a sovereign, independent state. The country was virtuous, self-sacrificing and hard done by. The instrumentalist rationale of the *demandeur* strategy increasingly gave way to asserting and demonstrating Ireland's independence as an end in itself. It did so for a number of reasons. First, the Community failed to develop either in accordance with the expectations and hopes of Irish governments or in a way responsive to their *demandeur* strategy. It did, however, develop and in a way which both increased and made more explicit the extent to which the external environment determined Irish domestic policy. Irish governments could no longer refer to Aiken's universe of vast impersonal forces 'out there' inevitably constraining Irish options. Rather, they were confronted by a particular organisation in which they were participants producing specific decisions which had major consequences for the Irish, but over which they exerted little influence. Threatening to a sense of Irish independence though this was, however, the EEC did not present Irish governments with a choice concerning their membership of it. They had to be in it, both to preserve Ireland's established trading relationships and to develop new ones. Since withdrawal was not an option, therefore, they responded to this sense of threat by attempting to reassert Ireland's independence both in the world and from the rest of the Community as an end in itself.

Secondly, if the *demandeur* strategy and regime politics offered few substantial gains to Irish governments, they provided them with important opportunities to distance themselves from the British. While it may be true that membership of the EEC altered Ireland's external economic situation from discreet dependence on one country to explicit dependence upon several, the political consequences of this shift for Ireland should not be underestimated. Throughout the second period, British policy continued to be the primary external reference point for Irish governments. On the CFP, for example, the Irish were at pains to uncouple their own position and claims from those of the British, and yet their struggle lasted only so long as the British remained in the field. On the EMS, the major economic case for or against Irish participation remained unclear. In the end, the decision of the government was predicated on incorrect assumptions about what sterling and the punt would actually do. The political consequences of breaking with sterling, and being in a position to do so were, however, considerable. Once again, the rewards of a strategy of emphasising national independence and identity were restricted to the same area, as in the case of the UN policy. It was important to Irish governments, however, that in seeking to modify the effects of regime change upon their economy, they looked to Brussels, or several capitals, rather than just London, and that in the process of pursuing their interests they could actually and openly distinguish them from those of the British and attempt to safeguard them, at times, at the latter's expense.

Finally, in contrast to the disappointments and sense of threat with which the internal Community system confronted Irish governments, the process of inter-governmental cooperation by which EEC policy towards the outside world was formulated offered them considerable opportunities for international role-playing of a more traditional kind. EPC was supposed to be separate from the processes by which the internal policies of the Community were formulated and to start with, the Irish government supported this distinction. The EEC, in this sense, was regarded as an enhancer of their ability to pursue their own political policy in the wider world. Increasingly, however, Irish governments viewed these opportunities first as a simple compensation for the disappointments of the Community processes, and then as a means of offsetting the negative consequences of EEC membership for their sense of Irish independence. These opportunities offered by the EEC for pursuing an Irish foreign policy in the wider world are examined in the next two chapters.

Notes

1. See Swann, op. cit., pp. 40–52, for a general description of developments in the EEC during the 1970s and details of the EMS.
2. For details of this see *The Economist*, 9 December 1978.
3. Swann, op. cit., p. 270.
4. See *The Economist*, 19 August 1978, for details.
5. Bremen, 18 July 1978.
6. See 308, 406–14 (11 October 1978) for the following discussion.
7. 308, 569-70.
8. Ibid., 562.
9. Ibid., 564.
10. Ibid., 1139–40
11. For Lynch's estimate of the impact of participating in the EMS see 308, 415 and 310, 981.
12. 310, 984 (7 December 1978).
13. 308, 431.
14. Ibid.
15. Peter Barry, the Fine Gael spokesman on foreign policy and later Foreign Minister. 308, 433.
16. Ibid., 418
17. Ibid., 1133–4.
18. See 308, 885 for FitzGerald's point on this.
19. 310, 412–15 (30 November 1978) and 984-5 for the following discussion.
20. Ibid., 1988.
21. See *The Economist*, 23 December 1978, and 315, 652-3 for further details of the transfers to Ireland.
22. 310, 1989 (15 December 1978).
23. For details of this see *The Economist*, 18 March 1978.
24. For details of this see *The Economist*, 16 December 1978. The band through which lira was permitted to fluctuate was 6 per cent rather than the normal range of 2.25 per cent on either side of the value allotted to the currency in the basket.
25. 310, 1989. Parity ended on 30 March 1979.
26. Ibid., 2045.
27. 308, 753.
28. 310, 1337-8.
29. 308, 751.
30. 308, 455.
31. For details of this, see 336, 1178 (22 June 1982).
32. See ibid., for Daly's (Minister for Fisheries and Forestry) account of this.
33. See *The Economist*, 6 March 1976. The Irish would have contested this claim.
34. See, for example, Sean O'Donnell, 'A Real Navy Soon?' in *Eire: Ireland,* Vol. 12, No. 2, p.132.
35. See *The Economist*, 6 November and 7 August 1976.
36. 302, 596. D.A. Gillmor, writing in the bulletin/magazine of the Department of Foreign Affairs, describes Ireland as 'an island country which has shown surprisingly little interest in its marine resources', *Ireland Today*, No. 1005, February 1984.
37. 296, 764.
38. 336, 1165 (22 June 1982).
39. 324, 967 (20 November 1980).
40. For details of the financial aid programme see *The Economist*, 6 November 1982. For details of other forms of assistance, see 336, 1165.
41. See *The Economist*, 8 January 1983, for details of these figures. However, 'Gillmor', in

Ireland Today, op. cit., points out that while the weight of fish caught between 1978 and 1982 went up 127 per cent, the real value of the total catch rose by only 7 per cent because most of the fish caught were cheap mackerel.

42. 296, 763-9.
43. *The Economist*, 23 October 1976.
44. Ibid., 6 March 1976.
45. 330, 860 (18 October 1977).
46. 301, 14 (2 November 1987).
47. *The Economist*, 23 October 1976.
48. 300, 862.
49. See *The Economist*, 6 November 1976 for this point. See 303, 1439, for FitzGerald's account of the British pressure on Ireland to support the British case for similar concessions to those which the Irish had obtained from the Community. He argued that the reasons for Ireland's success in extracting these concessions were the 'goodwill' Ireland enjoyed and the size of its catch (2 per cent of the Community total).
50. 303, 584-5 and 1427.
51. See *The Economist*, 4 February 1978, for details of the Berlin meeting from which the British were absent as a bargaining manoeuvre, and at which the Irish obtained further concessions. This was, itself, probably a similar manoeuvre on the part of the other members to 'punish' Britain and weaken its position.
52. *The Economist*, 23 October 1978.
53. For details of this dispute see 296, 1469, 1572 and 333, 555.
54. 296, 1409, Kelly (parliamentary secretary to the Taoiseach), 8 February 1977.
55. See *The Economist*, 28 August 1976, for this.
56. 333, 555.
57. 316, 2281-2.
58. *The Economist*, 7 May 1977.
59. *The Effects on Ireland of Membership of the European Communities*, European Parliament, p. 116.
60. *The Economist*, 7 May 1977.
61. *The Economist*, 2 October 1976.
62. 300, 527.
63. 336, 1175-6 (22 June 1982). This debate may be found in 336, 1169-82.
64. Ibid., 1180
65. Ibid., 1181-2.
66. 336, 1419.
67. Lenihan, 303, 1428 (15 February 1978).
68. *The Economist*, 8 January 1983 and 6 November 1982.
69. 314, 1909 (31 May 1979).
70. 298, 1285.
71. Ibid..
72. Ibid., 1847.
73. 300, 227.
74. Ibid., 490.
75. 316, 2365. See also 317, 259 for details of this.
76. 317, 255-60 (27 November 1979).
77. Ibid., 267.
78. Ibid., 276.
79. The idea behind the two-tier system was that those states which were most able and willing to proceed with common policies should go ahead leaving the rest to follow at a later date. The problem with this for a small state like Ireland would be that such integration would proceed without the need to offer compensation and assistance to those who could

participate in it only with difficulty. Despite its support for such moves in principle, Ireland would be likely to find itself among the weaker and less *communautaire* members of the second tier.

80.   298, 1849 (28 April 1977).
81.   323, 854-6 (23 October 1980).

10 The EEC as an instrument of Irish foreign policy

For a number of reasons, Ireland's foreign policy of international role-playing did not decline with its admission to the EEC. First, in the terms of interdependence theory, the EEC constituted an ambiguous environment. It offered both the integrated and rule-governed processes of an international regime and the bargaining opportunities and capability strengthening of an alliance between governments. While some commentators on Irish foreign policy regarded and continue to regard membership of the EEC as signalling the end of Ireland's 'pre-history' foreign policy and the beginning of a new era of pursuing 'real' external interests, Irish governments themselves did not share this view. They consistently claimed that membership of the EEC would both strengthen Ireland's ability to pursue its established foreign policy objectives and provide it with new opportunities for performing the good international citizen role. It should be noted that claims such as these pre-dated articulations of Irish disappointment with Community processes and the subsequent tendency to regard EPC as compensation for this disappointment.

Secondly, inter-governmental cooperation not only characterised the making of Community policy towards the outside world, but also policy within the EEC itself. As I have shown above, Irish governments adopted a strategy of performing roles that emphasised their claim to represent a sovereign, independent state with particular virtues and needs to extract what they could from these processes. Indeed, the emphasis of their approach was strengthened by the character of EEC regimes themselves. In so far as the EEC offered an equalising effect between strong and weak actors, it did so by emphasising the equality of sovereign states. The Irish government was on its strongest ground, therefore, in those parts of the Community process where this formal equality was most in evidence.

The limited character of these equalisation effects suggests the third and most important reason why international role-playing did not decline. The politics of interdependence were restricted, as far as the Irish were concerned, to the formal structures of the Community regime and were the product of a collective political will to create and maintain such structures. It was not the product of some deeper transformation of the nature of the relations between states. Ireland's relationship to its external environment, therefore, essentially remained one of dependence. In so far as things changed for Irish policy-makers, they did so because of Britain's decline in the existing system with its associated opportunities for diplomatic diversification and not because of qualitative changes in its external environment. As a result, the sense of a generalised threat to Irish independence remained, sharpened now by domestic economic difficulties and the fact that Ireland had been opened up to a significant part of the international economy. This was compensated for, in part, by a measure of diplomatic manoeuvre acquired *vis-à-vis* the British. Irish governments were presented, therefore, with both the need and the opportunity to demonstrate their political independence. They were so, however, in an environment in which their old distinction between 'political' foreign policy and 'economic' external affairs had become impossible to maintain and where manifesting an independent national identity became more important, both in itself and in its potential consequences, than it had been in the past.

None of the activities associated with Ireland's international role-playing in the wider world ceased as a result of Ireland's membership of the EEC, and several of them appeared to be strengthened as a consequence of it. Because of the wide range of international actions which Irish governments continued to undertake, therefore, I shall examine two specific issue areas in this chapter which illustrate different aspects of the attempt to use the EEC as an instrument of Irish role-playing foreign policies during the period: first, development assistance to the Third World; and, secondly, the contribution to international security through support for UN peacekeeping operations in the Middle East. Irish policy on development assistance is a new concern, largely made possible by Ireland's membership of the EEC. The contribution to international security is an example of continuity in policy, but I shall also show how formerly insulated areas of international activity became involved with other Irish interests as a consequence of EEC membership. In the following chapter, I shall examine the attempts of Irish governments to preserve the country's position of neutrality. This, of course, is not an issue area in any simple sense,

170

but rather, one of the central principles upon which, according to successive governments, Irish foreign policy is based. My purpose will be to demonstrate the extent to which membership of the EEC has placed considerable pressure upon one of the established components of Ireland's national identity, and to chart the variety of measures by which Irish governments have attempted to deal with these pressures.

Irish governments have claimed that their development assistance policies are rooted in fundamental national values. As citizens of a Catholic country, the Irish had a moral obligation to help the poor where they could, and a long and continuing 'missionary tradition' can be cited in this respect.[1] As a nation which had struggled to free itself from the material deprivations of colonial status, its people had a ready sympathy with others in the same predicament. Until the 1970s, however, there was little or no government policy with regard to development assistance. As Keatinge puts it, there was little

> beyond regular statements of admiration for the dedication of the missionaries, supplemented by nominal subscriptions to UN specialised agencies and intermittent contributions to disaster relief.[2]

In part, as he goes on to argue, government inaction was a product of the tension which existed between two fundamental values – anti-imperialism on the one hand, and anti-Communism on the other. There exists no simple ideological consensus in Ireland regarding the nature of international justice and the reasons for its widescale absence. Further, the slowness in creating a role for the state on questions of development assistance is related to a similar tardiness and lack of consensus about its role on questions of domestic social welfare.[3] More importantly, however, until the mid-1960s, development assistance was generally regarded as meaning foreign aid in terms of bilateral transfers, and since the Irish government had little money to spare, there was very little it could do.

Ireland's membership of the EEC, however, coincided roughly with major changes in the international community's professed understanding of what foreign assistance was supposed to be about. The emphasis shifted from bilateral cash transfers of 'aid' to a broader conception of managing the international economy to facilitate the economic development and welfare of all. The practicality of these schemes, given the very questionable degree of commitment which different governments had to them is not of concern here. What is important is that, in stressing the need to transfer production technologies and management techniques and the need to reform the terms of trade between the rich and the poor countries through multilateral negotiations, these changes provided Irish governments with opportunities for a role in development assistance which their lack of money had previously denied to them. In particular, these opportunities were presented in the extended process by which the EEC negotiated with the African, Caribbean and Pacific (ACP) group of countries to reform their overall trading relationship, and the consequences of these negotiations.[4]

Irish foreign policy was directed at acquiring and publicising a distinctive, indeed unique, role for Ireland in this process, both as an end in itself and as an instrument of other policies. This unique character of the role rested on two claims. The first was that, whatever the nature of Ireland's peripheral position in the economy of the EEC, by world standards it was a rich and relatively developed country. According to O'Kennedy, addressing the Dáil as Foreign Minister in 1977, Ireland was a 'relatively privileged' member of the 'International Economic Community' and as such, it was 'conscious of its obligations' to help 'the underprivileged of the Third World'.[5] He pointed out on a later occasion that the Irish were some twenty times richer than the poorest aid recipients, and FitzGerald, in a speech entitled 'The Role of the Irish Government in the Promotion of International Development and Justice' in 1983, classed Ireland as a 'relatively prosperous country', the 25th richest out of 160 countries in the world.[6] Secondly, however, they presented Ireland as a country which had been developed by the efforts of its own people over the last fifty years. O'Kennedy, for example, variously classed it as 'only relatively recently developed' or 'in a stage of recent development'.[7]

In Ireland, therefore, was both a developed country and one in which the people knew what it was like not to be so. Irish governments thus claimed a bridging role between the developed states of the EEC and the underdeveloped ACP countries. According to Lenihan, they could offer 'the capacity and skill' which their people had acquired in 'building up from what we were, a developing nation'. This could be translated in 'effective action' by giving developing countries 'advice and help'.[8] Further, according to a spokesman for the Labour opposition, because Ireland had no imperial past and, hence, no global network of economic interests, or 'no commitment to such industrial bases or consortia', as he put it, it was 'much freer' to provide 'unprejudiced and more professional help and skill to developing countries'.[9]

These components of 'acceptability' to ACP countries were also claimed as policy assets for Ireland *vis-à-vis* the other members of the Community. According to O'Kennedy, for 'historic reasons' countries like Ireland had much 'to contribute to the attitude' of other members of the Community. Ireland had the 'goodwill' of the Third World which it could exploit to its own advantage through 'various bilateral and multilateral agreements'. It could also use this goodwill to the advantage of the rest of the Community, 'not for all of which have the developing countries the same degree of admiration they have for our country'. Ireland, he continued, was in a position to bring about 'a closer liaison between Africa and Europe and the Far East and Europe' and the other members of the EEC should recognise this.[10] The role of the country on development assistance policy within the EEC was more clearly elaborated by the Minister for the Environment, Burke, to the Dáil in 1980. He stated that the Irish government were 'totally committed' to seeing the world's wealth

172

equitably shared between the 'Northern and Southern hemispheres'. He maintained that the Irish had 'no difficulty whatsoever' in determining which 'side' they were on in the North–South dialogue. They were there as members of the EEC with a 'very special place' in the Community because of their 'lack of empire'. Ireland's 'very important role' in this dialogue and the 'very special regard' in which it was held were borne out, he argued, 'by the honour which was bestowed on us at the signing of the Lomé 2 agreement, an agreement which we brought to finality because of our independent stand'.[11]

Despite the fact, therefore, that, as Lenihan put it, 'We do not have funds to distribute on a very large scale',[12] Irish governments elaborated a role for themselves between the EEC and the ACP countries composed of several distinctive tasks undertaken by them. While it was 'for wealthier countries to provide the cash',[13] Ireland, it was claimed, served as a western, liberal, capitalist model of successful development for the governments of new states. It was also an active model in that Irish governments were willing to communicate their expertise in economic development to the new states and, because of Ireland's colonial past, these new states could regard it as an 'acceptable' teacher. Finally, Ireland provided a sympathetic link for ACP states to the Community. This operated not simply in the sense of transferring information between the two groups, but also in the sense, it was claimed, that Ireland pressed its richer allies to be flexible with regard to Third World demands. Not only would the Irish government 'play our part in developing constructive policies towards the Third World', according to FitzGerald, it would also 'seek to influence other countries to do the same'.[14]

Despite the assertion that Ireland's contribution was to be made in the areas of expertise and facilitating negotiations, however, the cash transfers made by the Irish government also increased after they joined the EEC. In O'Kennedy's words, 'our level of aid took off'.[15] Speaking of this increase during the period of the coalition government of which he had been a member, Ryan claimed that it had been made possible, in part, by Ireland's membership of the EEC and the advantages which flowed from that 'year in and year out'. It was only right, he argued, that Ireland should share some of the resulting 'increased opulence', as he termed it.[16] A rationale more in accordance with the development role claimed by Irish governments was put forward by FitzGerald, however, speaking in 1983. He argued that only by contributing to the alleviation of the 'most pressing problems facing the Third World' could Ireland 'achieve a level of credibility' which would let it influence 'the solutions being formulated to the long-term problems of developing countries'.[17]

Following EEC membership, therefore, there was a steady increase in the amount of money which Irish governments allocated to development assistance. Ireland joined the other members of the EEC in committing themselves to the UN targets of 0.7 per cent of GNP in official aid and one per cent of GNP in all transfers. Between 1974 and 1976 aid increased from £2.5 million (0.083 per cent of GNP) to £4.6 million (0.104 per cent) and the target which the coalition government set for 1979 was 0. 23 per cent of GNP.[18] From 1977 onwards, with the election of a Fianna Fáil government, this rate of increase declined, and while the estimate for 1980 was 16.22 million Irish pounds, this constituted only 0.19 per cent of GNP.[19] Nevertheless, FitzGerald was able to claim in 1983 that, with official Irish development assistance standing at 0.23 per cent of GNP, Ireland had achieved a 'sevenfold' increase over a period of ten years.[20] As another measure of this increase, it may be noted that the total number of countries in which Ireland had bilateral aid programmes of assistance went from none in 1973 and three in 1974 to 35 in 1979.[21] This growth was also reflected in the expansion of the processes by which the government managed its development assistance policy and an increase in the level of its participation in multilateral organisations concerned with development assistance. In 1974, an agency for organising voluntary service overseas was established and the following year a coordinating organisation was set up 'to act as a clearing house for technical development aid activities of twenty-four semi-state agencies' involved in bilateral aid. In the mid-1970s a separate Overseas Development Assistance Division was established in the Department of Foreign Affairs.[22]

With regard to increased participation in multilateral organisations, the principal consequence of EEC membership was Ireland's involvement in the Community's negotiations with ACP countries. In addition to participation in the negotiating process, this also involved Ireland in making transfers to the European Development Fund. This was used both to channel assistance to associated countries and to stabilise the price which those countries received from the Community for their basic products.[23] On the basis of the frequent reports to the Dáil which these transfers made necessary, it would appear that Ireland contributed about 0.6 per cent of the Community total.[24] In addition, Ireland was involved in making a contribution to the joint EEC position within UNCTAD,[25] and this in its turn necessitated a series of small contributions on a regular basis to food aid conventions and common funds for commodities, either to facilitate their processing in Third World countries, or to maintain the price of specific commodities, such as cocoa, on the international market.[26] Membership of the EEC also had the consequence of changing Ireland's status in the International Development Association (IDA) in 1973. Ireland had originally joined the association in 1960 as a part II member, 'a mainly developing country', rather than a part I or 'donor' country. According to O'Kennedy, when the 'substantial economic progress' which the country had made since 1960 was taken into account and because Ireland was the only member of the EEC with part II status, it was decided to become a part I member of the IDA in 1973.[27]

The Irish government was generally very frank about the sort of considerations they took into account when adopting and pursuing their foreign aid policy. This is one area of foreign policy where it would seem that the parliamentary process operated with a measure of success in that it forced governments to demonstrate the extent to which self-interest as well as altruism lay behind a particular project or transfer. The major objective of their development assistance policy, according to most spokesmen for the Irish government, was to help poorer countries in their own efforts to develop. As Andrews, a Minister of State for Foreign Affairs, claimed in 1978, some countries might be motivated in their assistance policies by 'self-interest' rather than 'altruism'. Irish policy, however, 'in the final analysis' was motivated by 'concern for Third World endeavour, by idealism, by a will to help the less well-off sections of the nations of the earth'.[28] In support of this claim, it may be noted that the bulk of Ireland's foreign aid was channelled through multilateral organisations. In the early 1970s, about 50 per cent went through UN organisations, 35 per cent through EEC channels, and only 15 per cent went to the newly-instituted bilateral programme.[29] By 1983, bilateral assistance had increased to one-third of the total, but the majority of Ireland's effort still went through multilateral organisations, principally now the EEC.[30]

Further, it may be noted that Ireland's growing bilateral aid programme was, according to the government, focused on the poorest people in the poorest states. Five 'countries of concentration',[31] had been selected by the coalition government: Lesotho, Sudan, Tanzania, Zambia and India.[32] With the exception of the last perhaps, these constituted a rather unpromising group for commercial exploitation, and because the Irish emphasis was upon transferring their own expertise it would seem likely that the effects of their assistance would be to replicate Irish strengths in the target countries rather than create commercial opportunities there. According to O'Kennedy, bilateral aid was concentrated on a small number of countries simply to avoid its being spread too thinly, and indeed, India was dropped from the list by early 1978.[33] He claimed that in selecting the principal nations chosen, political criteria were not important, although he added that a few countries would not be helped for political reasons.[34] Ireland wished to give assistance to the rural poor and all that the government looked for was a social structure that could accept this kind of help and exhibited a potential for cooperation and partnership.[35]

More common than Andrews' claim to Ireland's purity of intention, however, were mixed-motive articulations of Ireland's development assistance policies. These took two forms: a justification in terms of their contribution to international stability; and a reference to the way in which they served Irish commercial interests. According to FitzGerald, speaking as Taoiseach in 1983, Ireland's development assistance effort served a 'fundamental objective' of Irish foreign policy, namely, the maintenance of a stable international system upon which all countries depended.[36] Lenihan, on the other hand, offered a systemic perspective which emphasised the Brandt Report's position on international economic interdependence. Development assistance, in his view, was a crucial instrument in revitalising international trade.[37] It was Colley, however, the Minister for Finance in 1977, who presented a narrower conception of the meshing of self and general interest. After going through the usual recitation regarding the relevance to the Third World of the Irish experience of economic development, he added that,

> it should not be overlooked that bilateral aid expenditure can provide potentially valuable outlets for Irish goods and services as well as giving many Irish organisations the required overseas experience to enable them to compete for other contracts funded by international development agencies, such as the World Bank and the United Nations Development Programme or the European Development Fund under Community auspices.[38]

Irish governments made no secret of the commercial gains which they hoped to make from their development assistance policy. FitzGerald, for example, stated that 'there was an element of self-interest' in that Ireland gained from Third World development both in terms of access to new markets for Irish exports and because the 'development process itself sometimes benefits us directly' when Irish firms won contracts from multilateral agencies. According to him, this presented no problem so long as it was remembered that the 'central' objective was the transfer of resources.[39] Similarly, O'Kennedy, after speaking in the Dáil in 1977 about Ireland's unique development role within the EEC, argued that global interdependence should be stressed 'if only for selfish reasons' and that Ireland hoped to 'maximise on the opportunity' that the Lomé agreements presented for 'consultancy contracts for appropriately qualified firms'.[40] The following year, he estimated that the value of involvement of Irish semi-state bodies in development projects neither partially nor wholly funded by the Irish government in 1977 was 'in the region of twelve million pounds'. He went on to say that the semi-states should be encouraged to increase their overseas earnings as this both created employment and improved Ireland's balance of payments.[41] He claimed in 1979 that Irish firms had won £1.72 million, and possibly as much as £2.18 million, from the European Development Fund (EDF) between 1976 and the termination of the fund in the late 1970s. This, he said, constituted 2.2 per cent of all such contracts awarded by the 'old' EDF.[42]

This effort was justified as being in accordance with proclaimed basic Irish values and directed at securing certain commercial benefits. However, it was also directed at the political objective of manifesting Ireland's distinctive independent identity in the international system. The political character of the policy may be seen from the government's insistence that overall control of it should be retained by the Department of Foreign Affairs. In responding to the suggestion that programmes should be administered on an *ad hoc* or functional basis by the semi-state bodies principally involved, O'Kennedy replied, in 1978, that he regarded development assistance as 'an integral and increasingly important part of foreign policy'. Therefore, it should remain under the control of his department.[43] This stress on the political character of the policy was also present in FitzGerald's explanation of the increasing emphasis on bilateral assistance. Speaking in 1983, he said that the government wanted to provide aid which would be recognised by 'the Irish people, as by the recipient countries, as distinctively Irish'.[44]

The problem was, of course, that Ireland lacked the surplus material resources required to pursue a conventional policy of prestige through development assistance transfers and projects. Accordingly, Irish governments pursued their political objectives through a strategy of international role-playing, articulating a bridging role for Ireland between EEC and ACP countries and rationales for their policy in terms of its contributions to global stability, prosperity and justice. Even so, their lack of money posed problems even for the political objectives of Ireland's development assistance policy. Most serious, perhaps, were the domestic difficulties engendered by the fact that the Fianna Fáil government of the late 1970s found it increasingly difficult to maintain the rate of increase of 0.05 per cent of GNP per annum in money spent on development assistance set by their predecessors. The domestic political pressure they underwent on this was particularly telling because the commitment was closely associated with FitzGerald, the leader of the principal opposition party.[45]

In 1980, Lenihan informed the Dáil that while total aid expenditures had risen by 12 per cent in the previous year, the bilateral programme had been cut back and the government was concentrating on maintaining existing commitments. He cited 'budgetary constraints' as the reason and claimed that Ireland was 'in line with what every European country is doing at present'. In claiming that Ireland's allocation was still about 0.2 per cent of GNP, he pointed out that while 'not in the same league financially as countries like Sweden and the Netherlands', Ireland gave about the same, proportionately, as Switzerland and more than Finland and Italy.[46] He went on to argue that, 'In the last analysis, our own self-interest as a nation is the paramount factor in any Government thinking on matters of this kind or any other matters.'[47]

Domestic criticism was blunted by the fact that Ireland, as well as the rest of the EEC, was in economic difficulties and the government's ability to claim that the actual amount of money allocated to development assistance had continued to rise each year.[48] There was the problem, however, that the government was committed to achieving the UN target of 0.7 per cent of GNP,[49] and to specific transfers to multilateral agencies. The sensitivity of the government with regard to the latter and the extent to which the development assistance programme was bound up with the question of Irish prestige, were reflected in their decision to cut back on their bilateral, rather than their multilateral effort. According to Lenihan, there were practical grounds for this choice in that multilateral agencies did not always spend all the money made available to them and, hence, donors could hope for a rebate at the end of the year which could be redirected toward their bilateral effort.[50] He went on to argue, however, that it was important 'as a State' to show 'our commitment and credibility' by making these contributions which were already committed to the multilateral efforts of the UN, the EEC and the IDA. It was important 'to show earnest of our credibility and *bona fides* in the matter to give the full percentage sought by them and agreed between Ireland and them'.[51] No doubt, the government was concerned that it should not jeopardise the chances of Irish firms or semi-state bodies in the competition for contracts offered by the multilateral agencies. It was not, however, the maintenance of its financial stake, *per se*, in these agencies which was crucial to the government's defence of Irish interests. They simply did not contribute that much and even this small amount in the case of EDF, outweighed the commercial benefits which flowed back from it.[52] Once again, it was the projection and protection of Ireland's reputation as a credible participant in these ventures which was regarded as important both as an end in itself and as an instrument of other policy objectives.

As such, development assistance became the vehicle for a very successful exercise in projecting the external identity of the state with a minimum of the appropriate domestic resources. There were a few difficulties with the policy. For example, economic difficulties forced the Irish into admitting that they could not afford membership of the Development Assistance Committee of the OECD.[53] Further, it was occasionally claimed by government spokesmen that Ireland's lack of an imperial past, the very factor which made the country so 'acceptable' to Third World governments, hindered the attainment of Irish commercial objectives. The poor performance of Irish firms and state-sponsored bodies in winning development consultancy contracts, for example, was sometimes attributed to the lack of 'direct historical association' with the Third World which some of their European rivals enjoyed.[54] On another occasion, however, Ireland's own former status as a British colony was indirectly proclaimed by a government spokesman as an asset in dealings with the Third World, not in the usual terms of a shared colonial experience, but because the Irish spoke English.[55]

In spite of these difficulties, the policy was successful for a number of reasons. First, it was largely made possible by Ireland's membership of the EEC. It was the latter which presented the government with opportunities for involvement in multilateral bargaining and provided them with both the projects in which their skills could be employed and the resources to finance these efforts. Secondly, development assistance was a suitable issue for mobilising support behind international activism. It had something for everyone in the domestic political process, or at least it seemed to cover the great divide between those interested in a commercially-oriented external policy and those who wished Ireland's efforts to be directed at some kind of international altruism. It was also useful to the government of a small state in that it was an external issue of 'substance' and an 'economic' one at that. Hours of debating time and pages of government documentation could be, and were, given over to itemised appreciations of projects initiated, Irish bodies involved and the multilateral agencies with which they liaised,[56] even if it could all come down to a few hundred pounds paid by someone else so that an Irish person could organise a seminar on trade fair participation in Greece or Latin America on a break-even basis.[57] This is not intended to decry the importance of such activities as cross-breeding Connemara ponies with their Basotho counterparts or running Masters programmes in development and export management for Third World students at Irish universities.[58] But in terms of the political significance of Ireland's development assistance policy, these activities were the ballast of an effort which also included more prestigious and incongruous projects such as Ireland 'aiding' Saudi Arabia to develop its dairy processing industry.[59]

Finally, and most importantly, in addition to being a consensual, substantial, economic and prestigious issue, development assistance fitted the role-playing criterion of being an area of policy in which independence and identity could be manifested without fear of immediate or dire consequences. As a political policy, it was projected at the same international society of states to which Ireland's other 'good citizen' activities were addressed, and for the same purposes. It was not a reformist effort directed at a tight regime within which Ireland had to participate. So long as Irish governments, like their OECD counterparts, continued to measure their development assistance efforts against the performance of other states, or their own previous performance, rather than against the scale of the problem of underdevelopment in the international system, then their efforts troubled nobody important either at home or abroad. This being the case, they could continue to congratulate themselves on a policy which, by OECD standards, was both thoughtful and distinctive, and which contributed positively to the idea of Ireland operating as an independent entity in the international society of states.

If Ireland's development assistance policy was a novel activity largely made possible by the country's membership of the EEC, then the contribution to international security which it continued to make during the period was not. 'Contributing to international security' is, of course, a very broad term. Irish governments claim that all their foreign policy is formulated with considerable attention to its consequences in this respect. They explained their development assistance policy, for example, in terms of its contribution to peace and security as well as development and justice. Even in the narrower terms of preventing armed conflict in the existing 'war system' as the precondition of all else, however, Ireland's contribution was not restricted to its continued support for and participation in UN peacekeeping operations. Irish governments also continued to pursue an active role in the UN's efforts on arms control and disarmament, and they attempted to develop new roles for themselves in the processes established by the Conference on Security and Cooperation (ECSC) at Helsinki in 1973,[60] and the 'Euro-Arab dialogue' which began shortly afterwards.[61]

The analysis here, however, will be confined to examining Ireland's peacekeeping policy in the Lebanon and discussing the consequences of the country's expanded interests in the Middle East for an established foreign policy activity. I shall argue that while much of the new Middle Eastern policy made possible by Ireland's membership of the EEC was directed at the same objectives as their peacekeeping contribution in the region, there was no easy compatibility between the two and that Ireland's capacity to serve as a peacekeeper may have suffered as a consequence.

UN peacekeeping, it was argued in the first section, was the substantial and distinctive component of the Irish attempt to perform a 'good international citizen' role. It was substantial in terms of the blood, treasure and important symbols of the nation's sovereignty and independence, its armed forces, which the government was willing to commit to an international activity over which they had little control. It was distinctive in that they proclaimed a reputation for impartiality which enabled them to participate in such forces, and a spirit of self-sacrifice with which they approached the problems and controversies generated by peacekeeping, as both being derived from attributes of national character and values.

The Irish government attempted to maintain this approach with regard to their contribution to the peacekeeping force in the Lebanon. They, and others, however, found it increasingly difficult to separate the peacekeeping policy from their wider effort in the Middle East. For the Israelis, in particular, the Irish briefly became one of the least acceptable components of a force to which they were generally ill-disposed, with the consequence that Irish soldiers were apparently singled out for special harassment by the militias sponsored by the Israelis. The Irish government, in its turn, did not respond to these difficulties as a selfless peacekeeper prepared to turn the other cheek, while trusting to the efforts of the Secretary General and the Security Council to alleviate their predicament. Rather, they attempted by their own efforts through bilateral and multilateral contacts to improve the circumstances of their contingent and the peacekeeping force as a whole. These efforts were largely unsuccessful, and Irish governments were spared the consequences of the tension between their role as a UN peacekeeper on the one hand, and the active representative of a concerned regional 'power', the EEC, on the other, only by the second Israeli invasion of the Lebanon in 1982. This effectively removed the immediate source of Irish problems by 'freezing' UN activity in the area and bringing even 'moderate' opinion in the UN into line with the Irish position.

While the formal commitment of Irish governments to UN peacekeeping remained unchanged during the intervening period, their ability to manifest this commitment with soldiers was put under considerable strain. This had nothing to do with the politics of complex interdependence, however; peacekeeping was not rendered irrelevant by the emergence of 'new' Irish external interests. The problem was that after the re-emergence of the troubles in the North in 1969, the Irish army had a much more pressing security problem on and within its own borders. Despite the withdrawal of the Irish contingent from UNEF II in 1974 after car bomb attacks in Dublin and Monaghan, however,[62] the main response to the security problems at home was not to abandon peacekeeping, but to expand the armed forces so that they could deal with both.[63] By 1977, the government was able to offer the UN a full contingent again for service in Cyprus,[64] although the Secretary General did not take up this offer.[65]

While Ireland's peacekeeping policy was presented by Irish governments as a continuing international role, the substantial component of the policy was necessarily reactive. It depended not only on a crisis, but also upon a rarely attained favourable conjunction of circumstances and attitudes on the part of great powers and involved minor powers alike. Because of the reduction of the Cyprus force and the problems presented for it by the Turkish invasion of 1974, and because the existing Middle East forces, UNEF II and UNDOF[66] were adequately manned, Ireland's next opportunity to manifest its rededication to peacekeeping came with the first Israeli invasion of the Lebanon in March 1978. Southern Lebanon had long been a relatively safe area from which the PLO had launched violent, but usually small-scale, attacks upon settlements in northern Israel. The Israelis claimed that the Lebanese government was increasingly unable, or unwilling, to control these attacks and that its authority in southern Lebanon was being replaced by that of the PLO and its local allies. Their invasion had the objective, therefore, of stopping these attacks by destroying the PLO's camps and supplies and driving all Palestinians and their sympathisers out of a limited area of southern Lebanon close to the Israeli border.

The UN Security Council established a peacekeeping force (UNIFIL) which was charged with confirming an Israeli withdrawal from this area, maintaining peace and security there, and facilitating the restoration of the authority of the Lebanese government.[67] It was clear from both the eventual size of the force and the weapons which it was permitted, that it was intended to be able to create the conditions of peace and stability in the area in the face of several heavily-armed groups already operating there. Their consent to its mandate, unlike that of the governments in the area, was not a precondition of UNIFIL's attempting to carry out the mandate.

Irish participation in the force was first officially discussed a little less than a month after the Security Council established UNIFIL.[68] They did not join it, however, until May when UNIFIL was expanded from 4000 to 6000 men. In the debate on the motion making Irish soldiers available 'for duties outside the State', spokesmen for both the government and the opposition reiterated Ireland's reasons for supporting peacekeeping and the significance of the fact that they did so. In his opening speech, O'Kennedy, the Foreign Minister, recounted the history of Ireland's participation in such operations, reaffirmed the Irish view that they not only supported UN peacekeeping, but regarded it as a duty and obligation that they should do so, and claimed that the UN request was an 'earnest of the confidence' that it had in the virtues of Ireland and its soldiers.[69]

The Irish had been asked to serve, it was generally agreed, because their attitude, foreign policy and history made them acceptable to all the parties involved. As FitzGerald put it, referring to a visit he had made to the Middle East in 1975, the Arabs and the Jews were confident of Irish impartiality and 'the one thing they were unanimous about was' having Irish troops between the antagonists.[70] There seemed to be few changes in attitudes from the debates which preceded the commitment of Irish troops to the Congo or Cyprus. There was a greater tendency to 'take a close look at the small print' of the UN mandate,[71] particularly with regard to what the force was allowed to do or was likely to do in the face of local opposition, and also with regard to its finances. The latter, according to O'Kennedy, posed no problems. The financing of the force by the members of the UN was mandatory and, hence, Ireland could not be placed in a position of having to pursue the UN for its operating costs.[72] With regard to problems in the field, the Foreign Minister gave an ambiguous but 'loyal' helpful fixer's answer. First, the whole enterprise was based on the assumption of 'maximum cooperation' from all concerned. If there was not, he continued, then the mandate ran out in September, and presumably would not be renewed. Secondly, O'Kennedy offered a 'strong' interpretation of the mandate of the force by claiming that 'self-defence' included 'resistance to attempts by forceful means to prevent it from discharging its duties'. Finally, he deflected the question of the government's own policy in the face of such difficulties by emphasising that UNIFIL was under the control, 'political or otherwise' of the Secretary General of the UN.

The one major departure from form was that, towards the end of an opening speech which had charted Ireland's principled and practical support of UN peacekeeping and emphasised its acceptability for such tasks, O'Kennedy introduced the theme of 'the overall problems of the Middle East'. While he did not spend much time on this, he did say that the Irish had

> joined with our partners in the European Community on a number of occasions in outlining our views on the elements which should form the basis of a permanent peace settlement in the Middle East generally and have encouraged negotiations to this end.[73]

O'Kennedy's remarks reflected the fact that, largely as a consequence of its membership of the EEC, there had developed both Irish interests and a policy towards them in the Middle East. This remark requires some sustaining. Writing in 1962, Conor Cruise O'Brien observed that, where foreign policy was concerned, the Irish press had a tendency to indulge in great debates over matters of very little substance. He had made his point humourously by simply invoking one editorial heading: 'Ireland's China Policy'.[74] Ireland did not have a policy on China then, nor, according to him, and several other prominent figures interviewed for this section, could it be said to have a Middle Eastern policy now. What one had, they claimed, were rows in the newspapers and the

Dáil about something in which Ireland had few direct interests and over which it had even less influence. This theme was echoed on one occasion by the Minister for Foreign Affairs, O'Kennedy, who when speaking in the Dáil on his estimate in 1978, argued that with regard to the 'fluctuating situation' in the Middle East, the Irish should not always 'express our opinion simply for the sake of expressing it'.[75]

It is, nevertheless, possible to chart the expansion of Irish commercial interests, formal diplomatic relations and foreign policy activity in the region during the 1970s. With regard to the former, basic trade statistics present an ambiguous picture. Between 1975 and 1981, the value of Irish exports to Israel as a proportion of all trade decreased from 0.3 per cent to 0.1 per cent. Over the same period, Ireland's exports to other Middle Eastern countries increased from 1.6 per cent to 6.2 per cent of all Irish trade. Imports from Israel remained constant at 0.2 per cent while the value of imports from other Middle Eastern countries fell from 5.7 to 1.5 per cent of all Irish trade.[76] Of particular concern to Irish governments was the securing of their oil supplies. During the late 1970s, Ireland's dependence on oil as a source of energy declined.[77] During this same period, however, Irish governments presented the problems created by their energy requirements in stark terms. According to O'Kennedy, speaking in 1979, because of its high growth rates, the Irish economy would find it impossible to conform to the EEC response to the oil shortage caused by the Iranian crisis – that is, relying on holding consumption at the 1978 level.[78] Speaking later that same year, the Taoiseach, Lynch, claimed that Ireland imported 80 per cent of its energy requirements, 75 per cent consisting of oil. Between 1972 and 1979, he continued, the proportion of Ireland's GNP spent on oil had increased from 2 to 5 per cent.[79]

Ireland's exports to the Middle East consisted largely of food and live animals. According to Keatinge, such trade is 'volatile', declining and 'is of doubtful long-term benefit to the economy'.[80] Despite the questionable importance of trade with the Middle East in the overall scheme of Ireland's overseas trade, however, Irish governments have chosen to emphasise their expanding interests in the area by the establishment of formal diplomatic ties and considerable publicity devoted to the attempt to develop commercial links. Between 1974 and 1977, Ireland opened formal relations with thirteen countries in the region. According to Keatinge, at the end of 1982 four of these countries had resident Irish missions (Lebanon, Egypt, Iran and Saudi Arabia).[81] Throughout the spring of 1983 and under the coalition government, a series of visits and exchanges took place between Ireland and the Arab states. In January, the Secretary of the Arab League visited Dublin.[82] In February, the Deputy Prime Minister and Foreign Minister of Egypt returned an earlier Irish visit. Throughout February and March the Minister for Industry and Commerce visited Saudi Arabia and Bahrain and discussed Irish technical assistance in the Gulf and schemes for empty tankers to return there with fresh water. In April, the 'largest ever' Irish trade mission (50 companies represented) visited Saudi Arabia, and the bulletin of the Department of Foreign Affairs claimed that Irish exports to there had trebled in three years. Finally, in May an Irish–Libyan joint commission on economic, industrial, scientific and technical cooperation met in Dublin, and Libya was described as 'one of Ireland's largest export markets'. It was on the basis of this kind of sequence, that the Minister for Foreign Affairs, Peter Barry, speaking to his estimate in 1983, could claim that,

> Outside of Europe, North America and those countries which are historically and ethnically offshoots of Europe, no part of the world is closer to us in terms of geography or political or trading links than those countries which together make up the Arab nation. It would be foolish to attempt to deny that part of the importance to us of the region derives from its vast resources of oil, but the links between the Arab world and Europe are older and deeper than any forged in a twentieth century oil crisis.[83]

The latter statement was not merely a reflection of the need to serve Irish commercial interests in the region, nor did it simply constitute the adoption of an EEC position simply because Ireland was a member of the Community. It was, rather, the product of a choice made by successive Irish governments to pursue, and to be seen pursuing, an active role in shaping the EEC's policy towards the region. The purposes of the policy were several. The formal objective was to harness the diplomatic weight of the Community to the effort to establish a just and lasting peace in the Middle East in accordance with Security Council resolutions 242 and 338.[84] Secondly, Irish governments wished to contribute to the improvement of relations between the EEC and the Arab states. Finally, they wished to avail themselves of the opportunity of playing a role within the EEC, both as a useful link between the two groups and as an initiator of policy as an end in itself. As Lenihan explained it, with regard to the EEC's policy on the Middle East, Ireland took 'a very positive initiative'. While in Bahrain, the Minister himself had made a statement which advocated 'a homeland for the Palestinians'. Shortly after this the Irish and the French, working together, secured 'the agreement on of the Nine in the Venice Declaration'. He regarded this as an example of Ireland playing a 'useful role' in the EEC by offering it 'constructive leadership'.[85]

The policy may be said to have originated in a joint proposal made by the Irish and Italian representatives on the political committee of the EEC in 1973 that the Community 'consider its long-term position on the Middle East'.[86] Four years later, according to Lenihan, the EEC position, to which 'Ireland fully subscribes' had evolved to support for the following: withdrawal from the occupied territories; the right of all states in the area to 'secure and recognised boundaries'; and

recognition of the legitimate rights of Palestinians, including their right to a

184

homeland and their right to participate through their representatives in any settlement affecting their future.[87]

The Irish government were at pains to emphasise their own role in contributing to that position on any occasion at which EEC policy towards the Middle East was discussed. Speaking again on the subject in 1979, for example, Lenihan stated that 'as a country' and as 'holding the presidency of the EEC', Ireland had made every effort to achieve a Middle East settlement 'which would embody a homeland for the Palestinians'. While the 'integrity of the State of Israel' was 'fundamental' to any Middle East settlement, he continued, the West Bank and Gaza were 'possible areas for the future homeland of the Palestinians' and the Irish government maintained contacts with anybody who was seeking such a homeland, including the PLO.[88] The following spring, the Irish position on the Middle East received a further elaboration during Lenihan's visit to Bahrain. Reporting to the Dáil on the joint communiqué which he had issued with the Bahraini Foreign Minister, Lenihan said that both sides had stressed that all concerned parties, 'including the PLO' should play a part in establishing a peace settlement. The communiqué had also recognised the right of the Palestinians to a 'state' rather than just a 'homeland' and, as Keatinge points out, it lacked the usual 'balancing clause' affirming 'the right to exist of all states in the region'.[89]

The leading role developed for Ireland, particularly by the Haughey government, and the 'Bahrain declaration' provoked considerable debate at home and abroad regarding the position of the country *vis-à-vis* the rest of the EEC on the Middle East.[90] Under criticism from the opposition that Ireland had been thrust into a dangerously exposed position[91] for short-term economic gain or out of incompetence, the government attempted to clarify, or minimise, the significance of the position. Lenihan, for example, emphasised that Ireland continued to condemn the use of violence to further the cause of the Palestinians,[92] and the government argued that the declaration had simply broken the path for the EEC's own Venice Declaration of June 1980 with which, they claimed, it was consistent. In subsequent elaborations, for example, they argued that the PLO was not the *sole* representative of the Palestinian people, that it did not constitute a provisional government, and that its role was recognised only in representing the Palestinians in the peace negotiations.[93] Their coalition successors were content to follow essentially the same policy expressed, however, in the much safer formula that they accepted the right of the Palestinians to self-determination 'with all that that implies'.[94]

During the same period in which Ireland's Middle East policy was evolving and running into difficulties, its soldiers in UNIFIL were experiencing problems of their own. In the spring of 1978, the Irish government sent 665 soldiers to the Lebanon.[95] While the number of personnel involved varied, the Irish contingent, which was comprised of an infantry battalion and a headquarters section, was regarded by the government as the best-equipped Irish contingent ever offered for UN service up to that time.[96] Eventually, it possessed its own communications equipment, transport, engineers, medical platoon, armoured personnel carriers, heavy mortars and anti-tank weapons.[97]

The presence of these heavy weapons was one indication that UNIFIL, like most other UN peacekeeping forces, had become politically controversial. Indeed, the Irish involvement as part of a reinforcement for UNIFIL was further evidence of this fact. Another way in which the controversies of peacekeeping manifested themselves was that UNIFIL, again like most of its predecessors, experienced financial difficulties because some members of the UN were slow in paying their assessed contributions.[98] By 1980, the government claimed that UNIFIL was working at 26 per cent below its required funding.[99] Because they were willing to calculate the 'cost' of UNIFIL to Ireland in terms of the balance between what the UN paid them and the money they had actually spent, rather than the money they were entitled to under the UN funding arrangements, however,[100] the government was able to claim that the real cost of participation in UNIFIL between 1978 and 1982 was only £300,000.[101]

More severe problems confronted UNIFIL in its area of operations. Armed factions in southern Lebanon wished to continue with their own activities and were prepared to fire on UNIFIL if it attempted to interfere. In particular, a force of mainly Christian militiamen known as the '*de facto* forces' had been established by the Israelis in a narrow strip of territory along the Lebanese–Israeli border. The Israelis had done this because they professed little confidence in the ability or the inclination of the UN forces to prevent the infiltration of PLO guerrillas from the north and also because they wished to continue influencing directly events in southern Lebanon. In the view of the Irish government and the UN, this group constituted the principal obstacle to UNIFIL's fulfilment of its mandate. First, its existence was regarded as demonstrating the extent to which the Israelis and groups not recognised by the Lebanese government continued to exert their control over this part of Lebanon. Secondly, the '*de facto*' forces had appropriated UNIFIL's interpositionary role for themselves. Thirdly, and most importantly, the militia attempted to harass UN contingents and to force them out of their positions by snipings, kidnappings and a series of armed confrontations.

While these took the form of small crises and exchanges of fire, it did seem that there was a pattern of escalation, intended or not, to the level of violence and that Irish troops were heavily involved. Initially, the government declared that while it was concerned at these exchanges, it had no intention of withdrawing Irish troops.[102] In May 1979, however, a government spokesman acknowledged that the Irish contingent 'in particular had come under severe artillery fire on several occasions'.[103] That same month, Irish troops came into direct confrontation with Israeli forces wishing to search a village occupied by the Irish,[104] and in July, the opposition in the Dáil were asserting that the militia were no longer firing to harass, but to hurt Irish soldiers.[105] In April 1980, the

Irish contingent suffered casualties in a week-long engagement with the militia in which each side deployed armoured fighting vehicles.[106] In addition to these direct confrontations, the Irish contingent also became the victims of a series of abductions and murders intended, in part, to exert pressure on them, but also, apparently, the product of a code of blood feuding in the area.[107]

The Irish were not new to these kinds of difficulty. Their first experience of peacekeeping, in the Congo, had exposed Irish troops to considerably heavier fighting, and sharper political controversy. Despite an undercurrent of feeling at that time that there were limits to the level of casualties which were acceptable, the formal response of the government had been that this was the price of peacekeeping and that it was up to the UN and the Secretary General, not the Irish government, to deal with particular problems. In this, they largely enjoyed the support of the Dáil. There was no such consensus in the Dáil, however, regarding the problems of UNIFIL. There was agreement that the Irish had been somehow singled out for special treatment by the militia, if not by the Israeli government itself. The question was why.

According to the government, the answer was to be found in the specific deployment of Irish troops in UNIFIL's area of operations. Speaking in the Dáil in 1979, O'Kennedy argued that the problems of the Irish contingent were largely a product of the Israeli decision to hand over the border zone to the 'de facto' forces. Most of the Irish battalion was deployed immediately to the north of part of this border zone. Others manned outposts in the zone itself and at UNIFIL's headquarters in a coastal town located in territory controlled by the 'de facto' forces.[108] The Irish troops, therefore, had a difficult time because they occupied the important and exposed UN positions. The government also claimed that the 'de facto' forces singled out different national contingents of UNIFIL for rough treatment at different times.[109]

Much of the opposition did not accept this view. They argued that the difficulties of the Irish contingent were attributable to the more opportunistic or ill-advised elements of Ireland's broader Middle Eastern policy. These, they claimed were undermining the credibility of Ireland's reputation as a UN peacekeeper. Somewhat inconsistently, however, they then asked the government what initiatives it intended to take to reduce the problem, and they recommended that the Irish troops should be more heavily armed and react more aggressively when fired upon.[110] The extent to which Ireland's Middle Eastern policy did actually undermine its peacekeeping effort is very difficult to assess. The Israeli government and press did react to developments in Irish policy, particularly the 'Bahrain Declaration',[111] and the heaviest combat in which Irish troops were involved followed that declaration by about two months. Wounded Irish soldiers, however, continued to be treated in Israel, and the Irish contingent was never accorded the degree of formal hostility meted out to others, for example, the Poles. On balance, it is probably fair to argue that Israeli hostility to UNIFIL as a whole and the dictates of military logic were the principal causes of the difficulties of the Irish contingent, and that Ireland's Middle Eastern policy merely became an additional source of tension in local confrontations between the Irish and the militia that had developed for other reasons.

While their role as an initiator of Middle Eastern policy within the EEC may have had little influence on Israel, however, it is clear that it did have an influence upon how the Irish government responded to the difficulties of their contingent in UNIFIL. First, the fact of a Middle Eastern policy itself indicated the extent to which circumstances had changed since the time of the Congo operation. At that time, Lemass had specifically refrained from making any comments on the political situation in the Congo because, he argued, doing this might put the lives of Irish soldiers in more danger than they already were. Ireland's contribution to peace there was soldiers on the ground; the rest was left to the UN. In the case of the Lebanon, however, the Irish government neither accepted that it was the lot of the peacekeeper merely to endure, nor that their only appropriate channel of action was through the Secretary General or the Security Council of the UN. Rather, they increasingly regarded the Irish contingent as one aspect of Ireland's effort in the Middle East and attempted to solve its problems in the context of that foreign policy by a series of multilateral and bilateral contacts and initiatives.

The principal target of the Irish government's bilateral effort was Israel itself. While, according to Lenihan, there was 'no question of a bilateral dispute between Ireland and Israel',[112] it was clear that they regarded Israel as being the power behind the efforts of the '*de facto*' forces to interfere with UNIFIL's mandate. In 1979, O'Kennedy informed the Dáil that he had made representations to his Israeli counterpart, Dayan, and that the Taoiseach, Lynch, had exchanged letters with Begin.[113] In 1981, the Irish Defence Minister, visiting the troops in the Lebanon, went to Jerusalem for talks with the Israeli Prime Minister,[114] and there is also evidence that the permanent representative at the UN was used to make contact with the Israelis.[115] While spokesmen for the government were generally positive regarding the response that they got from Israel on each of these contacts,[116] it is clear that they were largely unsuccessful in terms of their main objective of ending the harassment of the Irish contingent and the UNIFIL as a whole. They were, however, more successful according to Lenihan in their attempts to get the United States to exert its influence on Israel in the interests of restraint. Speaking to the Dáil in 1980, he claimed that the US had been 'very helpful'. A recent release of Irish soldiers held hostage by the militia was 'due in no small measure to United States intervention' with Israel on Ireland's behalf.[117]

With regard to the use of multilateral channels, Ireland's policy within the EEC has already been commented upon. The EEC was regarded as a vehicle or instrument of Ireland's broader Middle Eastern policy and an arena in which the Irish government was taking the lead. It is thus unlikely that they would have wished members of the EEC to help them out of their particular problems in the Lebanon, nor that they would have regarded its members as being capable of offering effective help in this regard. They did, nevertheless, secure a condemnation of attacks on UNIFIL from the European Council in April 1980.[118]

The principal target of their efforts in this respect remained the UN. Here, however, the tension between their role as a peacekeeper and their role as an active initiator of Middle Eastern policy within the EEC was most in evidence. On the one hand, Irish governments attempted to maintain the established position that resolving UNIFIL's problems was the preserve of the UN. Participation in the force was presented as 'the practical expression' of Irish support for UN peacekeeping.[119] As Lenihan responded in 1980 to an opposition suggestion that the Bahrain declaration had destroyed any leverage the Irish government may have had over the Israelis, the Irish were not in the Lebanon 'in an Irish capacity'.[120]

Similarly, under pressure from the opposition to persuade other countries to punish Israel's obstruction by cutting off its supplies of arms, O'Kennedy replied such questions would obviously 'have to be resolved in the UN'.[121] Clearly, spokesmen for the government were willing to assign responsibility to the UN for taking initiatives which they either disagreed with or which they felt were too dangerous for Ireland to take. Even when the question was phrased in more precise terms, however, for example, FitzGerald's inquiry as to whether the minister would not agree that his function was 'to protect the lives of Irish soldiers and the United Nations rather than to try to whitewash the situation?' O'Kennedy replied that FitzGerald, of all people, as a former Minister of Foreign Affairs, should recognise that it was not the function of the minister 'to protect the forces in operation'. He went on to say that the government could make protests but that it was the function of the UN and the UN commander-in-chief to try and protect the forces.[122]

On the other hand, the United Nations was also used as a forum in which Israel could be isolated as a target of Irish protests about the treatment of their soldiers[123] and to publicise its wrongdoings in the Lebanon. This was particularly the case after the second Israeli invasion in June 1982. Prior to that time, Ireland's formal UN activity was principally directed at Israeli policy in areas of the Middle East other than southern Lebanon,[124] and at attempting to condemn specific actions without joining the prevailing Assembly consensus on producing blanket condemnations of Israel and questioning its status at the UN. After the invasion, the Irish government pursued an active role both in the UN and the EEC. According to the Taoiseach, Haughey, speaking in June 1982, Ireland, along with its EEC partners, had condemned the Israeli invasion and the preceding bombardment, called on the Israelis to withdraw and let UNIFIL carry out its mandate, and had declared that future action would be contemplated if the Israelis did not comply. He went on to say that prior to this decision, the UN Security Council, on which Ireland was serving, had unanimously adopted 'a resolution sponsored by Ireland' which called for a complete and unconditional Israeli withdrawal.[125]

The tension between these two approaches is exemplified by the following explanation of Irish foreign policy offered by two different ministers in the same debate in 1980. According to the Minister for Defence, Faulkner, the basis for Ireland's success as a peacekeeper lay 'in the fact that as a small nation Ireland has no ambition to involve herself directly in conflict elsewhere in the world'.[126] Ireland's success, therefore, was based on its lack of interests and ambitions in the troublespots of the world. Later that same day, however, the Minister for Foreign Affairs, Lenihan, stated that 'Irish foreign policy in the Middle East or elsewhere,...is dictated by Ireland's national interest, as the Government of Ireland see it'.[127]

These remarks were made in a debate in the Dáil about an initiative taken by the Irish government, which may be seen as an attempt to reconcile Ireland's Middle Eastern policy with its role as a peacekeeper. As has been noted already, the level of violence increased in southern Lebanon during April 1980, culminating in the abduction of three Irish soldiers and the murder of two of them by militia from the '*de facto*' forces.[128] As a consequence of these events, the Irish government made representations to the Security Council and also suggested that all ten countries supplying soldiers should meet with the Secretary General to discuss the adequacy of the existing mandate.[129] This meeting was unusual for two reasons. First of all, it was intended to be at the ministerial level;[130] lower-ranking representatives of the donor countries met frequently with officials of the Secretariat in New York. Secondly, it was to be held in Dublin. Lenihan expressed his purpose for the meeting in the following terms. He hoped that 'moral pressure' exerted by the ten countries which had provided troops for UNIFIL 'acting together' upon the UN would 'operate as a diplomatic lever' on Israel's policy towards the '*de facto*' forces. In addition, he argued that the meeting was intended to obtain a 'sense of solidarity' among the donors regarding their commitment to remaining in the Lebanon and the uniformity with which they should interpret the mandate and deal with incidents in the area.[131]

According to Lenihan, the meeting was a success. Eleven countries were represented[132] and Brian Urquhart attended as the representative of the Secretary General. Agreement was achieved, despite Lenihan's professed fears to the contrary. The donors would continue to operate as a group with 'continued contact' to maintain their solidarity, and the meetings already being held with the Secretary General would be 'intensified and take place regularly'.[133] The next meeting was arranged for Oslo and representatives of the group were given the responsibility of presenting the text of the Dublin communiqué to the Secretary General, the President of the Security Council and the governments of the Lebanon, Israel and the United States.[134]

The Dublin meeting represented an uneasy blend of support for the UN and initiative-taking in the context of Ireland's Middle East policy. The Irish government emphasised that the meeting was called to facilitate the efforts of the Secretary General and to maximise the effectiveness of UNIFIL. They also

190

emphasised their own adherence to the established peacekeeping conception of UN forces rather than an enforcement role for them. With regard to suggestions for the development of the latter, Lenihan said that Ireland would view that as a 'mistake'. What was required was the cooperation of all concerned so that UNIFIL, 'one of the bricks in a very shaky edifice', could establish control over the whole of its mandated area.[135]

Nevertheless, considerable emphasis was also placed on the facts that this was an Irish initiative and that Israel was the problem. In announcing the decision, Lenihan said that *he* had invited the other contributors and the Secretary General to Dublin. He presented it as an Irish initiative and claimed

> with respect to our international standing at present, that there was a very immediate and full response from the other countries concerned, all of whom congratulated us on the initiative we were taking.[136]

According to the Minister of Defence, Faulkner, the Dublin meeting was what 'one might term a landmark in peacekeeping' and he claimed that regular monitoring meetings would take place in the future.[137] On being asked in an interview for this section if the Dublin meeting represented a major development in Ireland's approach to international security or whether it was an *ad hoc* response to a particularly tense situation, a serving minister replied that it was 'a little bit of both' but that it was 'our initiative' to which the UN had responded immediately, considering it to be an excellent idea, but 'an Irish idea'. Subsequent developments, or rather the lack of them, were to show that Faulkner's estimation of the significance of the Dublin meeting was somewhat inflated. While Keatinge's view that it constituted merely one aspect of a run 'for collective cover' in the aftermath of the Bahrain declaration may be a little harsh,[138] it certainly did demonstrate the limits to what a weak state, even with respected status, can achieve by unilateral initiatives.

There were a number of reasons why there was no real follow-up to the Dublin meeting at the level of representation and with the level of publicity which was achieved on that occasion. First, as one member of the Irish foreign service pointed out, there really was very little of substance which could be achieved at such meetings. If one were concerned with the practical operation of UNIFIL, then there was plenty of opportunity for cooperation on the force committee at the UN in New York. If one were interested in higher-level contacts, for example between Foreign Ministers, then these too could be undertaken at New York. Indeed, that was the easiest venue for getting all the ministers concerned together.[139] If one wished to protest at the treatment of UN soldiers and the failure of members of the UN to allow it to fulfil its mandate, then the point had been made at what could have been a one-off meeting.

Secondly, however, there were political difficulties with what the Irish seemed to be trying to achieve in establishing regular, high-level meetings of peacekeepers. These difficulties could be traced back to the attempts of other countries, notably Canada and the Scandinavian states, to increase the UN's peacekeeping 'preparedness' by efforts made outside the UN, in order to circumvent political problems within the organisation. These efforts had met with a very cautious reception from the UN Secretariat because, it would seem, they regarded them as potentially politically controversial. Put simply, it was not worth annoying permanent members of the Security Council for the kind of gain which might have been obtained through 'preparedness' measures. And these were measures to be taken to improve the effectiveness of peacekeeping in general, not just a particular operation. Viewed in this context, therefore, it was highly unlikely that an Irish initiative, taken with regard to a particular force and the problems caused by a particular country, and promoted by a government with a distinctive broader policy on the problems of the region, would be welcomed by the UN.

Membership of the EEC broadened Ireland's role in the Middle East in the way that Irish governments had hoped and predicted that it would. It did this by providing them with an opportunity to be active in the processes of European Political Cooperation and by letting them speak 'for Europe', on occasions, to the wider international community. As far as interdependence theory is concerned, however, these changes constituted a regression. Before they joined the EEC, the policy of Irish governments in the Middle East had largely been restricted to participating in the international security 'functionalism' of peacekeeping. This had been regarded as a good thing in itself and as a means of acquiring prestige in the eyes of the international community as a whole by performing an 'international good citizen' role. Membership of the EEC, however, permitted the development of a policy directed at acquiring prestige and securing specific interests for Ireland in two regional systems: the EEC itself and the Middle East.

As a consequence, in terms of their role-playing rationale, Irish governments were no longer principally interested in using the Middle East as an opportunity for manifesting their support for the international security functions of the UN. Rather, they wished to use their reputation in that respect and their position in the EEC to make a specifically Irish contribution to the solution of the problems of the Middle East, both as a prestige policy and to secure material interests. Membership of the EEC, in other words, provided Irish governments with an opportunity to pursue a policy in the Middle East that was more concerned with asserting Ireland's ability to perform as an independent and distinctive actor than had been the case in the past.

The expansion of Ireland's role in the Middle East made possible by membership of the EEC was not matched, however, by any notable increase in the ability of Irish governments to achieve the objectives they set for themselves in the region. They failed to bring peace to the Middle East, or even to southern Lebanon, although in this respect they were in the company of much more powerful governments that, arguably, achieved a good deal less. More interestingly, the rewards of their expanded Middle Eastern policy, in terms of the prestige acquired, were also questionable. This was so because Middle Eastern role-playing was more vulnerable than simple peacekeeping alone to the unfolding events over which the Irish government had no control. Status as a peacekeeper was acquired by the fact of participation. More status was acquired by simply enduring when things went wrong and the mission became difficult. Indeed, to do anything else could be regarded as inappropriate.

On the other hand, once, like the Irish government, one was supposed to be contributing actively to the creation of a peaceful settlement in the Middle East, by bilateral and multilateral negotiations, policy initiatives and the pursuit of leadership roles, then two things followed. First, by taking a series of actions, the success of the government's role-playing policy could be judged by the outcomes of these actions. Secondly, the government had to react to the events in which they were participating. They could not, therefore, simply endure the latest Israeli act of aggressive self-help or an Arab statement which did not recognise the right of Israel to exist; they had to formulate a specific policy response to such events. Unfortunately for the Irish government, because their initiatives and responses had very little influence on the behaviour of the governments at which they were directed, then the attempt to play a Middle Eastern role could be seen to be ineffective.

The wider Middle Eastern role also had unfortunate consequences for Ireland's peacekeeping policy in the Lebanon. Any intervention in the problems of the region which went beyond contributing to the preservation of the circumstances in which the antagonists could reach an agreement if they so wished was necessarily a political intervention, if only because it could be interpreted as such by the parties concerned. The Irish government's view of a fair settlement in the Middle East was regarded as a hostile position by Israel, and this hostility was compounded by the unfortunate, to say the least, coincidence of the evolution of an Irish policy on Palestine and the publicised development of commercial and diplomatic relations with Arab countries.

The uneven efforts of the Irish government to deal with this problem by separating their contribution to UNIFIL from their broader Middle Eastern policy were not successful for two reasons. The first was the fact that the Irish government regarded Israel as the principal obstacle to the success of the peacekeeping force. Thus, while they emphasised the fact that they were in Lebanon in a UN capacity, and reiterated their support for a peacekeeping, rather than a peace-enforcing, interpretation of the mandate, Irish proposals for improving the effectiveness of the force always involved some targeting of Israel.

Secondly, while Irish governments proclaimed a separation between their peacekeeping role and their broader Middle Eastern policy, they attempted to resolve the problems of the former by the unilateral initiative-taking methods which characterised the latter. The Dublin meeting was the product of the hope of one government in particular; that their Middle Eastern role should have

193

some utility in improving the lot of UNIFIL. There is nothing to suggest that their motives were not of the highest in taking this initiative; they were responding to a local crisis in the Lebanon in which Irish troops were heavily involved. While the Irish government were happy to emphasise the prestige aspects of their role in orchestrating a response to the crisis, they were not attempting to use UNIFIL as an instrument of the more substantive elements of their Middle Eastern policy. Nevertheless, their willingness to make even this kind of connection between their two roles in the region was evidence of the way in which the two could not but be regarded as connected by others.

The Dublin meeting may be regarded as a useful example of the extent to which Irish capabilities were enhanced by their membership of the EEC and the broader Middle Eastern policy that this made possible. Regime politics allowed the government of a small state to become more active in the part of those politics which were addressed to an external high political issue – the Middle East. On the basis of that activity, the government could even feel emboldened enough to take initiatives outside the immediate regime context – in this case, the Dublin meeting of concerned peacekeepers. The success was that the meeting occurred and that an immediate point was made. The limitations of Irish power were demonstrated by the fact that, in terms of their own professed objectives for the initiative, little else occurred, except that there was now tangible evidence of the Irish government playing a game in the Middle East in which they were really out of their depth and which had questionable effects on their established role as a UN peacekeeper. This broke what might be said to be the first rule of small state prestige policies – that one should know one's own limitations or, more importantly, never lay oneself open to the charge that one does not.

The separation between Ireland's Middle Eastern and peacekeeping roles was only properly achieved after the second invasion of Lebanon by Israel in 1982. This had the effect of temporarily moving the centre of controversy north towards Beirut and away from UNIFIL. From that point on, the Irish government was able to proclaim both its adherence to UN peacekeeping by supporting the maintenance of UNIFIL as a symbolic and practical manifestation of order in the midst of chaos,[140] and to pursue a highly critical line at the UN on Israeli actions in the Lebanon which were no longer primarily directed at UNIFIL.

Notes

1. Keatinge (1978), op. cit., p. 182.
2. Ibid., p. 182.
3. The controversy over the social programme (known as the 'Mother and Child' scheme) of the Inter-Party Government in the late 1940s is the most obvious example of this lack of consensus regarding the role of the state. When the government attempted to institute a welfare programme for mothers and their children, it provoked fierce opposition orchestrated

by the Catholic Church, on the grounds that such a policy constituted an attack on the institution of the family. For details, see Lyons, op. cit., pp. 575–8.

4. The Lomé agreements (1975 and 1980) gave the exports of the ACP states free access to the EEC on a non-reciprocal basis, set up a fund to stabilise the level of earnings which the ACP countries obtained from the export of their staples and made financial aid available to them.
5. 300, 272.
6. O'Kennedy, 306, 376 (4 May 1978). FitzGerald, *Ireland Today*, No. 1000, July/August 1983.
7. 302, 128 (24 November 1977).
8. 324, 426 (4 December 1980). See also 300, 282, for O'Kennedy, speaking in 1977, on the way the experience of the semi-state agencies in building up the Irish economy could be used in the Third World.
9. Deputy Quinn, 302, 123 (24 November 1977).
10. 302, 1461 (14 December 1977). See also 300, 281 for another example of this argument.
11. 325, 426. The signing of both conventions took place at times when Ireland held the presidency of the Council of Ministers. See 317, 1059 (4 December 1979) for O'Kennedy speaking on this.
12. 325, 426.
13. 323, 1163 (30 October 1980).
14. *Ireland Today*, 1000, op. cit.
15. 306, 414 (4 May 1978).
16. 302, 114–15
17 *Ireland Today*, op . cit .
18. Keatinge (1978), op. cit., pp. 183-4.
19. 326, 1757 (12 February 1981).
20. *Ireland Today*, op. cit.
21. See 322, 743–4, for details of aid programmes.
22. Keatinge (1978), op. cit., pp. 184-5, the Agency for Personal Service Overseas (APSO) and the Development Cooperation Organization (DEVCO), respectively.
23. In addition, FitzGerald maintained that Ireland had made a major contribution to preparing the EEC's position on international trade at the Williamsburg Summit. *Ireland Today*, op. cit.
24. See, for example, 317, 1058 and 328, 2553.
25. See O'Kennedy, 300, 4950, for the joint position adopted by the members of the EEC.
26. See for details of these: 315, 1005; 334, 1637; and 322, 1765. The latter example was a wheat transfer.
27. See O'Kennedy 302, 111–12 (24 November 1977) for this. Note, however, Ireland's refusal to apply for membership of the Development Assistance Committee of the OECD because of the costs involved (Lenihan, 323, 845, 23 October 1980).
28. 307, 85. Andrews speaking on Ireland's support for the fourth extension of the 1971 Food Aid Convention.
29. Keatinge (1978), op. cit., p. 184. Donors have little or no control over how their contribution to multilateral aid is spent and, hence, cannot use it as an instrument of their own specific interests.
30. J. O'Keefe. Minister of State for Foreign Affairs, in *Ireland Today*, No. 1002, October 1983, p. 10. See also 336, 179, for other aid statistics.
31. See Colley, Minister of Finance, 302, 1322 (13 December 1977) for the use of this phrase.
32. See 303, 1310 (15 February 1973) for a list of the countries of concentration.
33. See 306, 373 for an amended list without India.
34. 303, 1310. See 317, 1079 (4 December 1979) for O'Kennedy's statement that political criteria were involved in the delay and suspension of aid to Uganda when Amin was in power.

35. 303, 310.
36. *Ireland Today*, No. 1000, op. cit.
37. Lenihan, interview.
38. 302, 1322-3 (13 December 1977).
39. *Ireland Today*, op. cit.
40. 300, 282–3.
41. 305, 263–4.
42. 317, 1058-60. He estimated that Irish contributions had amounted to 0.6 per cent of the old EDF over an eight-year period.
43. 306, 376.
44. *Ireland Today*, op. cit. FitzGerald also stressed Ireland's preference for committing their multilateral assistance to the EEC rather than other international organizations, because this provided the government with a 'much greater degree of control'.
45. Keatinge (1978), op. cit., p. 184.
46. 319, 477-81 and 2114 (24 April 1980) . See 326, 1757 (12 February 1981) for a table showing Ireland next to last in the EEC both in terms of absolute cash transfers (to Luxembourg) and as a percentage of GNP (to Italy).
47. 319, 2114.
48. 319, 477 . See also 322, 905 and 333, 575.
49. See 323, 575 (21 October 1980) for Lenihan's reaffirmation of this commitment.
50. See 322, 904 for this argument. In 1980, Lenihan informed the Dáil that Ireland had received a rebate of over 1.5 million Irish pounds, most of which he was going to redirect to bilateral programmes, 323, 1130 (29 October 1980).
51. 322, 905 (18 June 1980).
52. See 317, 1058-60 for details. Speaking in 1979, O'Kennedy said that Ireland had contributed £18.6 million to the European Development Fund over an eight-year period. Irish firms had obtained between 1.72 and 2.18 million pounds in commercial contracts during the same period.
53. See 323, 845 for this.
54. See, for example, O'Kennedy 300, 283 (12 October 1987).
55. 303, 1310.
56. See, for examples: 305, 263-72, 1725-38; 311, 981-88; and, 313, 1441-44.
57. 305, 1731-4.
58. For details of these, see Michael Moloney, 'Irish State Agencies and Developing Countries: A Sharing of Experience', in *Ireland Today*, No.993, November/December 1982.
59. Ibid.
60. See Keatinge (1978), op. cit., pp. 197-88; and Patrick Keatinge, *A Singular Stance: Irish Neutrality in the 1980's*, Institute of Public Administration, Dublin,1984, passim. See ch. 11, n.2 for a comment on this work.
61. One major area in which the countries of the EEC have attempted to develop a European foreign policy is with regard to the Middle East. This effort has been based upon an obvious concern, the dependence of most EEC countries on oil from the Middle East, has been justified by the experience of some of the members in the area, particularly the British and French, and has been directed at articulating support for diplomatic proposals on the Palestinian problem. In particular, the Venice Declaration of June 1980 recognised the rights to self-determination of the Palestinian people.
62. Keatinge (1978), op. cit., pp. 159-60.
63. See 306, 643 for details.
64. FitzGerald, 298, 942.
65. O'Kennedy, 306, 597 (9 May 1978). It should be noted that even after the withdrawal from UNEF II, Ireland continued to be represented in peacekeeping operations by a few officers

and NCOs and, for a time, by an Irish commander of UNFICYP. See 304, 437 (28 February 1978) for Malloy, the Minister of Defence, giving details of this commitment.

66. The United Nations Emergency Force of 1973 (UNEF II) was established in the aftermath of the Middle East war of that year to separate the Egyptians from the Israelis. The United Nations Disengagement Observer Force (UNDOF) was created shortly afterwards from UNEF troops to supervise the disengagement of the Israelis and the Syrians. The United Nations Truce Supervision Organisation (UNTSO), established in the late 1940s, remained operational.

67. The United Nations Interim Force in the Lebanon (UNIFIL) was established by the Security Council in March 1978. For a study of its operations see Alan James 'Painful Peacekeeping: the United Nations in the Lebanon 1978–83', in the *International Journal*, Vol. 38, No. 4, Autumn 1983.

68. 305, 342 (11 April 1978).

69. 306, 595–9 (9 May 1978).

70. 306, 300.

71. Keatinge's phrase, in Keatinge (1978), op. cit., p. 161.

72. For this section see 306, 612–13.

73. 306, 598.

74. O'Brien (1962), op. cit., p. 25. He was referring to the UN debate about who should occupy China's seat at the UN.

75. 307, 318.

76. Patrick Keatinge, 'Ireland, Political Cooperation and the Middle East', in David Allen and Alfred Pijpers (eds), *European Foreign Policy-Making and the Arab-Israeli Conflict*, Martinus Nijhoff, The Hague, 1984.

77. Ibid. According to Keatinge, it fell from 74.5 per cent of energy requirements in 1975 to 62 per cent in 1981. According to Job Langbroek and Paul Burke, Irish natural gas was accounting for 11 per cent of Ireland's energy needs in 1982. *Ireland Today*, No. 992, October 1982.

78. 314, 560.

79. 315, 972-3.

80. 'Keatinge', op. cit.

81. Ibid.

82. For details of this diplomatic activity, see *Ireland Today*, Nos. 993, 996, 998, 999, 1001.

83. *Ireland Today*, 1001.

84. 316, 1939 (20 November 1979), Lenihan in response to a question about the PLO.

85. Interview.

86. For this see William Wallace, Helen Wallace and Carol Webb, *Policy-Making in the European Communities*, John Wiley, NY, 1977, p. 238.

87. 314, 1929 (31 May 1979).

88. 316, 1936-8 (20 November 1979).

89. 318, 424-5 (26 February 1980) and 'Keatinge'', in Allen and Pijpers, op. cit.

90. See, for example: 318, 423; 320, 1116; and 'Keatinge', ibid.

91. See, for example, FitzGerald, 322, 1019 (8 June 1980).

92. 318, 426 (26 February 1980).

93. Lenihan, cited in 'Keatinge', in op. cit.

94. See Peter Barry's foreign policy estimates speech for 1983 cited in *Ireland Today*, No. 1001, September 1983.

95. 306, 599.

96. 320, 1140 (8 May 1980), Faulkner, Minister of Defence.

97. Ibid.

98. See 314, 1933 for O'Kennedy's comments on this.

99. Lenihan, 320, 38.

100. See ibid.; and 328, 717 for details of this.
101. Reply to parliamentary question, 25 March 1982 (333, 553).
102. 311, 1157 (14 April 1979).
103. 313, 1693 (1 May 1979).
104. Smith, op. cit., pp. 204-5.
105. 315, 2261–2.
106. For details of this action, see Lenihan 319, 1261 (16 April 1980); and Smith, op. cit., pp. 219–26.
107. Ibid., p. 229.
108. 314, 234. For further details of troop deployments, see Lenihan, 320, 1113.
109. Ibid. (8 May 1980), Lenihan.
110. See 320, 160 and 1127, for examples of these suggestions.
111. See 'Keatinge', in op. cit.; and 320, 1161 for details about the treatment of Irish troops by Israeli television and newspapers.
112. 320, 1112 (8 May 1980).
113. 315, 2610.
114. 328, 734.
115. 315, 2610.
116. For examples, see 313, 1694; 315, 2263; and 315, 2544.
117. 320, 1169.
118. See 'Keatinge', in op. cit.; and Lenihan 320, 25 for the role of the Foreign Ministers' Meeting in this.
119. Colley, 313, 1695 (1 May 1979).
120. 320, 32 (29 April 1980).
121. 314, 236 (12 June 1979).
122. 315, 2267 (12 July 1979)
123. See 319, 1262 for Lenihan's account of the use of the UN in this respect.
124. For example, on the status of the PLO, the occupied territories, events in Beirut and the attack on the Iraqi nuclear reactor carried out by the Israelis.
125. 336, 357.
126. 320, 1136 (8 May 1980).
127. Ibid., 1163.
128. For details of this see: 320, 22, 1142-3; and Smith, op. cit., pp. 229–30.
129. 320, 28-9 (29 April 1980).
130. This section comes from 320, 28, 1111.
131. Ibid., 1105–7.
132. There were the ten participants in UNIFIL and Sweden which was about to join the force.
133. Ibid., 1111.
134. Ibid.
135. 320, 333 and 1108-9.
136. Ibid. 31-7.
137. Ibid.
138. 'Keatinge', op. cit.
139. Lenihan stated in the Dáil that the Irish had originally wanted the meeting in New York, but that Dublin had been decided on so that high-ranking officials might attend. 320, 1105 (8 May 1980).
140. This was the interpretation put forward at the Permanent Mission to the UN in the aftermath of the second invasion. See also Haughey speaking as Taoiseach, 16 June 1982. He described UNIFIL as 'an important potential for order in a fundamentally disturbed region', and as 'a core of stability'. 336, 361-2.

11 Irish neutrality and the EEC

EEC membership enhanced Irish role-playing efforts in areas of policy like development assistance where there was little likelihood of costly consequences for the country and where the government's actions were directed at satisfying general values rather than specific, substantive objectives. Even where Irish role-playing was directed at achieving more substantial goals, membership of the EEC provided an extended and flattering degree of participation in regime politics. However, this enhanced 'run for their money', which enabled Ireland, for example, to have a Middle Eastern policy, did not permit the achievement of very much beyond the act of participation itself. This spectacle was an important Irish objective, but it became very difficult for the Irish government to pursue a prestige policy in a situation where the unfolding of events clearly and continually underlined their lack of real influence. Further, role-playing, in terms of shaping an EEC policy on the Middle East, possibly hampered the effectiveness of the Irish in performing their more traditional role in the area as a UN peacekeeper.

I shall now examine the idea of the EEC acting as a constraint upon Irish foreign policy in more detail by looking at its impact on the neutral orientation of the country. As many spokesmen for the Irish government have argued, membership of the Community has involved a trade-off for Ireland between gaining an enhanced ability to pursue certain objectives and an overall reduction in the number of policies which they used to be free, at least to attempt. While they are a good deal less forthcoming about precisely what it is they can no longer do, one aspect of Irish foreign policy which may be clearly seen to be under pressure in this regard is Irish neutrality. It may be seen to be threatened both by the fact that Irish membership of any organisation other than the UN could be said to constitute a violation of previously articulated principles of Irish neutrality and, more importantly, because all the other members of the EEC are in NATO.

As a consequence of this, Irish governments have been forced into a series of difficult reformulations of the meaning of Irish neutrality. They have, for example, attempted to emphasise the extent to which it is restricted to 'purely' military considerations or the refusal to join alliances. On other occasions, it has been presented as a useful, distinctive instrument of Irish policy within the EEC and as an attribute which makes Ireland useful to the EEC. None of these, I shall argue, has been very successful because Irish neutrality is intimately bound up with the ideological presentation of what Irish independence means – in the words of one commentator, 'independence' and 'neutrality' in this context are virtually interchangeable.[1] Irish governments, therefore, are caught in a constant pull between demonstrating their loyalty to the original meanings of Irish neutrality at home, and arguing to outsiders that it is really not very important or controversial and should be regarded as a useful instrument of, rather than obstacle to, anything which the Irish wish to achieve in the EEC or the world beyond. In this, they have been aided by a series of academic treatments of the subject which demonstrate that Irish neutrality has little substance in fact (voting records, trade patterns and the like) and is 'only' of symbolic or declaratory nature.[2]

Tinkering with a basic component of the meaning of Irish independence has not been successful because the character of the international system and Ireland's place in it which made the ability to pursue a neutral policy so important have not been transformed. Ireland remains a weak, dependent state in a world of powers. Attempts to 'modernise' Irish neutrality for the 1980s or for the EEC, attempts to give it an instrumental character as an heirloom dusted off and put to use as a distinctive, if mildly eccentric, national attribute, would have been risk-free only if the material gains of the alternative, 'modern' articulation of Ireland's future within the EEC were unambiguous. This they have not been, and as a consequence, the pressure has mounted upon Irish governments to reassert independence in its established terms. This should not, however, be regarded as a descent into the cheap opportunism of exploiting loyalties to ancient symbols for short-term gains like the preservation of a particular government or even particular politicians. Such calculations have certainly played a part in the re-emergence to prominence of the question of Irish neutrality. Both, however, are more properly regarded as responses to the threat which membership of the EEC poses to the established conception of Irish independence without clearly offering something in its place.

Since Ireland became independent, its position of neutrality has been justified in a variety of terms with different emphases at different times.[3] During the period under examination, spokesmen for the Irish government offered versions of all these rationales. They may be reduced, however, to four basic conceptions: two articulations in terms of basic identity; and two in terms of neutrality as an instrument of policy. The most general explanation was that a commitment to neutrality was somehow lodged in the collective historical experience of the Irish people as one of the nationalist or Republican values which they continued to embrace.[4] While Sinn Féiners may have had geopolitical reasons and autarkic and isolationist preferences which explained their commitment to neutrality,[5] in this conception, the Irish people are presented as being wedded to this approach because of its nationalist-Republican antecedents *per se*. O'Kennedy's speech on the Foreign Affairs estimate for 1978 illustrates this view. Foreign policies, he argued, are neither arbitrary nor are they made in a vacuum. They are determined, in part, by situation, 'by what we are and how we see ourselves as a people' and by choices already made by the state. Material interests and external constraints were the important determinants of foreign policy, he continued,

> But this is not all. Our view of our own history, our efforts to assert our own identity, and the beliefs and outlook of our own people – all these things have given us a commitment to certain values. We believe that certain things are right and certain things are wrong for States as they are for individuals.[6]

Neutrality, in this view, was a choice of the past to which the Irish people remained morally committed. Such an articulation in itself provides no guide to whether a spokesman is for or against Irish neutrality (it should be noted, however, that it is impossible to be both an open opponent of Irish neutrality and occupy a prominent position in Irish political life).[7] What it does do is present neutrality as a pre-existing determinant of present Irish foreign policy, and as almost a constraint which has to be taken into account, rather than as a policy or instrument of policy in itself. Thus, one frequently finds formulations by Irish governments to the effect that they cannot take a certain course of action because Ireland is neutral, offered with an air of self-sacrifice and sense of burdens borne. Neutrality, in this view, does not dictate the thrust of Irish foreign policy on an issue; it prevents the government from doing certain things.

Secondly, neutrality was regarded as a basic Irish value, not simply on a moral basis, but also because it was regarded as both the proof and precondition of Irish independence. Fanning argues that

> The Irish commitment was to the ideology of independence, whether in the shape of Collins 'freedom to achieve freedom' or de Valera's republic. Neutrality, then, was not an end in itself, but a means to an end; the means whereby the end of

sovereignty might be freely expressed in the form of an independent foreign policy – a policy independent, above all, of British policy.[8]

In part, this followed the pre-independence tradition of interest in international affairs, which was noted in Chapter 3, when local authorities would pass resolutions on international affairs, their purpose being, as O'Brien puts it, to find out what Britain was doing and then 'say something different'.[9] As an extension of this tradition, therefore, the importance of neutrality might have been said to be derived from the extent to which it annoyed Britain. Fanning's instrumentalist conception of the role of Irish neutrality in acquiring and demonstrating Irish independence should not be allowed, however, to obscure the extent to which they became interchangeable. The point was that if a refusal to participate in Britain's imperial wars could be sustained in the face of British hostility, then Ireland could be viewed as truly independent. As O'Leary, speaking for the Labour opposition in 1982, expressed it, 'our neutrality derives from our independence and our independence is internationally sustained by our neutrality'.[10] Thus, any government considered to be moving away from neutrality could be confronted by the argument that this would amount to 'a total renunciation of our entire struggle for independence'.[11]

Thirdly, Irish neutrality was justified in terms of its contribution to the military security of the country. The Irish nationalists had realised that once independence had been achieved and Britain recognised this fact, then Britain itself would be the best guarantor of Irish security. Given, however, that Ireland was not going to play an active part in British defence policy, then the best way to secure this protection was to convince the British that no Irish government would permit its territory to be used as a base for attacks on Britain. Failure in this respect would result in Ireland becoming a problem to be planned against in British defence policy rather than a value to be defended. Neutrality, therefore, was a necessary security policy both to avoid participating directly in the British defence effort and to convince the British that Ireland posed no threat to them. If it was successful in this respect, then it also constituted a sufficient security policy, in that Britain could be relied on to do the rest.

The security explanation of Irish neutrality continued to be articulated during the second period by spokesmen of the Irish government. Speaking in 1981, the then Taoiseach, Haughey, referred directly to what he called de Valera's policy of not permitting Ireland to become a base for attacks upon Britain. He argued that in formulating their defence policies, every country had to take account of the 'attitudes and interests' of its neighbours. In Ireland's case this was 'particularly so in regard to Britain'. Therefore, the de Valera rationale, he claimed, was 'still our policy'.[12] More often, however, the security explanation of Irish neutrality was couched not in terms of reassuring Britain, or anyone else for that matter, but in terms of the fact that Ireland did not need any other kind of defence policy. One commentator explained the survival of Irish neutrality by the fact that the country was quite simply 'extraordinarily fortunate' in its security position. It is threatened only indirectly because it is 'at the heart of the NATO system'.[13] If there was a threat to Irish security, then it was the one posed to Western Europe as a whole by the Soviet Union and its allies. If this was the case, then nothing the Irish government could do or refrain from doing would significantly contribute to or detract from the level of security which NATO already, in effect, provided to Ireland. As one serving minister put it in an interview for this section,

> I can see why military alliances in many circumstances are necessary. I don't think it is necessary for us.... [We] are a small country and an ex-colonial country that doesn't have to get entangled in a military alliance, that is within the European Community and yet has many friends outside it, in the UN and elsewhere.

Finally, Irish neutrality was linked to the continued existence of Partition. This linkage emerged particularly during the Second World War, replacing the pre-war emphasis on sovereignty and the preservation of a certain freedom for diplomatic manoeuvre.[14] The immediate cause of this shift was that the Western Allies, if not exactly pressing Ireland to join them, were highly critical of its refusal to do so. Further, they expressed a *de facto* opinion on de Valera's constitutional claims to the whole island of Ireland by developing and making extensive use of military facilities in the North without consulting the Dublin government. By emphasising Partition in their turn, the Irish government attempted to give their own people something substantial to focus on in their support for what was, at times, a difficult policy. In addition, they also attempted to reduce American pressure on themselves by calling the attention of American public opinion, or the Irish-American section of it, to this particular reason for their refusal to participate in the war against Germany.[15] MacBride, the Minister for External Affairs in the post-war Inter-Party government, preserved this link between neutrality and Partition when he said that Ireland could not join NATO or any other alliance of which the country responsible for the division of Ireland was also a member.[16] And in 1951, de Valera argued that ' A free Ireland would probably have the same inducements to join as other nations'.[17]

During the period under examination, however, government spokesmen rarely articulated this conception of, or justification for, Irish neutrality. There are several probable reasons for this. First, the linkage policy had been developed as a defence against pressure to join the Western Alliance, not as a means of achieving an end to Partition. The attempt to use it in the latter sense, embodied in the post-war policy of the 'sore thumb', was a complete failure and seen as such by all but the most Republican and left-wing members of the Dáil. The consensus was, in the words of one commentator, that offering to join NATO in return for what one of its members would regard as the cession of part of its national territory, was a strange idea indeed.[18] Secondly, in the late 1950s,

Irish neutrality had become part of the proclaimed basis of a wide-ranging, active foreign policy. To have maintained the linkage would have suggested an inappropriate willingness on the part of Irish governments to indulge in horse-trading on the basis of offering up their principles and national values in return for territory. This was the kind of deal which de Valera himself, his remarks above notwithstanding, had ruled out; sovereignty came before unity at any price.[19]

The one time during the period when the link was openly articulated, therefore, was an occasion of considerable political controversy. At the end of 1980, the Taoiseach, Haughey, had met in Dublin with a British delegation led by the Prime Minister and including her Foreign Secretary and the Secretary of State for Northern Ireland. On the Irish side, this meeting was part of a new emphasis on contacts between London and Dublin as the proper way of dealing with the problems of Northern Ireland.[20] It became known that in the course of these discussions, a general review of the present and future of Anglo-Irish relations had taken place and that possible solutions to the Northern Ireland problem had been set in the context of developments in 'the totality of relationships within these islands'.[21]

While this pregnant phrase could be, and was, taken to mean any number of things, one recurring theme in speculation about the Haughey–Thatcher talks concerned possible changes in the security relationship between the two countries. As a consequence, the government scheduled a debate on defence policy in the following March to reconfirm the principles which had guided that policy in the past.[22] While spokesmen for the government went to some lengths to reiterate their commitment to the established principles of Irish neutrality, the Taoiseach, himself, persisted in making ambiguous, or even obscure, connections between Partition and the security of the British Isles and Ireland. While nothing had changed from the principles established by de Valera, he claimed, a solution to the problem of Northern Ireland would make a big contribution to the security of the islands. This, of course, could have referred to internal security conditions. However, he went on to suggest that once a 'political solution' was reached, a review of 'what would be the most appropriate defence arrangements for the island as a whole' would have to be undertaken.[23] More than this he would not say, and wisely so, for the policy, if policy there actually was, would have depended on a degree of flexibility and capacity for accommodation on the part of the British Prime Minister, not usually forthcoming in her conduct of foreign affairs. In the event, the Anglo-Irish détente evaporated in the face of the British government's handling of the hunger-strikers' campaign in the North.

No Irish government, in public at any rate, went so far as to offer participation in NATO in return for reunification. The formula was that the government of a re-united Ireland, once it was re-united, would be able to look at many issues, defence policy among them, in a new light. The controversy created in Ireland by Haughey's hints in this direction, however, is evidence of the continuing importance and sensitivity of the issue of Irish neutrality. It is not considered negotiable even for the cherished national objective of reunification. The tension between Ireland's membership of the EEC and its basic foreign policy orientation as a neutral state could not easily be reconciled either by trading off the latter for other values, or reducing it to the role of a distinctive instrument of prestige and influence within the Community. By the early 1980s, neutrality had again become a major political issue, and when it did so, basic questions about Irish unity, the relationship with Britain, the meaning of Ireland's independence and its place in the world, were quickly disinterred along with it. I shall now examine why this was so.

Membership of the EEC presented Irish governments with three sets of related problems as far as their policy of neutrality was concerned. First was the issue which has been discussed at some length in the 1960s of whether a neutral country could properly join anything other than a universal organisation such as the UN. In so far as neutrality had originated in a refusal to participate in defence efforts orchestrated by the British and a commitment not to join those directed at Britain, there was no particular reason why Ireland could not join other groups.[24] Between the wars, for example, in addition to its membership of the League, Ireland was also in the Commonwealth, and after the Second World War, it became a member of Organisation for European Economic Recovery (OEEC) and the Council for Europe.

With the development of an activist foreign policy at the UN in the late 1950s, however, neutrality was redefined in such a way as to open the question of participation again. In the context of this activist neutrality, the refusal to be involved in British security efforts was extended by Frank Aiken to a rejection of the system of opposing blocs, or participation in it, as a means of obtaining national or international security. Members of the political left argued that this neutrality also debarred Ireland from becoming a member of organisations such as the EEC. The position of other European neutrals such as Sweden, Austria and Switzerland was used to lend force to the argument that the credibility and, hence, effectiveness of such a country were closely related to its ability to avoid formalised entanglements with other states.[25]

The second major problem for Irish governments was with the extent to which the EEC could be regarded as a regional organisation free of military purposes. Questions of defence had been largely avoided by the architects of the Rome Treaty for two reasons: first, other efforts had demonstrated that no easy European consensus on defence policy existed at the time; and secondly, the defence concerns of the original six members of the EEC found expression in the wider NATO alliance of which they were all members. Nevertheless, it had been widely considered that a fully-developed Community ought one day to be able to take responsibility for its own defence on a collective basis. Very little came of this until the late 1970s when the West Germans, and then, the French and British, called for the development of European security cooperation outside the NATO context to be put on a firmer basis.

205

The reasons for this development are both uncertain and paradoxical. What is interesting is that they did not come as the last chapter in the story of European economic, social and political integration as had been envisaged by many, including Irish governments. They arose, rather, out of the success of the substitute inter-governmental process of European Political Cooperation. This new high political consensus was based upon unpromising foundations: a sense of their own weakness on the part of the governments of the old European powers; fear of Soviet power; unhappiness at the character of the US response to it; and perhaps most importantly of all, a desire to make the most of one of the few areas of consensus which was emerging between the governments of the EEC. As a consequence, very little of substance emerged. The Europeans worked for joint positions at the follow-up meetings to the ECSC and at the UN, attempted to coordinate some of their defence procurement policies, 'decided' to commit troops to the Multilateral Force and Observers operating in the Sinai after the departure of UNEF II;[26] and discussed German proposals to formalise EPC and include defence policy-making within its sphere of competence.[27] While these were small measures in themselves, they caused considerable problems for Irish governments who, although more or less committed to participation in the collective defence of a future united Europe,[28] had never expected defence demands to be made upon them so soon by a Community, the development of which was obviously incomplete and unsatisfactory for Ireland.

The third problem was also caused by the development of the EPC process. Along with the growth of 'habits' of consultation, cooperation and the formulation of joint policies and positions on certain issues, there also emerged the idea that a political solidarity ought to exist between the members of the Community. This was quite different from the painstaking creation of joint positions in which the Irish government participated as a formal equal, because it suggested the possibility that European governments should endeavour to support the unilateral foreign policy actions of their colleagues. While the Irish might have had their doubts about being marshalled into joint actions of the Nine or Ten, particularly when these dovetailed neatly into American-orchestrated responses to the latest Soviet or Iranian outrage, this was a different order of problem to the difficulties of formulating an after-the-fact response to, for example, the latest French adventure in Africa.[29] As I shall show below, the major difficulty for Irish governments in these terms, was the British decision to go to war in order to recapture the Falkland Islands in 1982.

During the second period, Irish governments rejected the argument that membership of the EEC was inconsistent with the principles of Irish neutrality in two ways. First, they claimed that such a view of neutrality was impractical. Ireland could not avoid dealing with other countries of which it did not approve nor issues which might have some military implications. Under pressure from the opposition in 1980 regarding the disappearance of 'our profile of independence' and the government's alleged failure to speak out on a number of issues, Lenihan replied that Irish foreign policy had to consist of a balanced combination of enlightenment and self-interest. This being so, Ireland was lucky to get on so well with the other members of the EEC because, as a small country, it could not afford to 'go around the world wearing the conscience of the world on [its] sleeve'.[30]

Secondly, they argued that such a conception of neutrality, debarring Ireland from membership of anything but the UN, implied a moral isolationism which did not accord with fundamental Irish values. In an interview for this section, a former Foreign Minister made a distinction between what he called 'positive' and 'negative' neutrality. Ireland was an exponent of the former which he said involved an active policy rather than 'opting out of the world'. This involved 'making practical and constructive international, diplomatic use of our particular positions'. With positive neutrality, he argued, Ireland could be neutral and at the same time have 'associations with other like-minded countries'. But it did not necessarily have to get involved in 'military associations with such like-minded countries'.

The Irish government, somewhat confusingly, rejected 'negative' neutrality for implying both an impractical excess and unacceptable lack of moral activity in the world. Further, they were not entirely true to their own conception of 'positive' neutrality. This was particularly the case in the variety of arguments they put forward for rejecting the idea that Ireland should become a member of the Non-Aligned Movement (NAM).[31] Speaking in 1979, O'Kennedy offered the argument from the 1960s that Ireland had neither requested nor been invited to attend a recent meeting of the NAM. While he did not think that Ireland would become a member, he added that it did have 'considerable sympathy' with the 'basic objectives' of the group, was in regular contact with some of its members, and that its position was respected by the group. In addition, he claimed that Ireland was better able to perform its bridging role between the EEC and the ACP states by staying out of the NAM and that membership of the group was not, in itself, any proof of neutrality.[32]

The next year, however, Lenihan characterised orientations in the international system in the following terms:

There are non-aligned groups, military groups and countries that are genuinely, totally committed to neutrality and we happen to be one of those countries of which there are very few.[33]

In 1981, he reiterated his position more clearly.

The status of Ireland internationally can be stated clearly and briefly. We are not a member of any military alliance. Neither are we a member of any non-aligned group. ...The non-aligned group are also a bloc. There is a bloc situation in the world: the eastern bloc, the western bloc and the non-aligned bloc.[34]

In an interview in 1982, however, a serving minister contrasted Ireland's positive neutrality with 'the negative neutrality of the kind you associate with the Non-Aligned Movement'.

Membership of the NAM, therefore, was rejected on several grounds: because it would interfere with the effectiveness of Ireland's own role-playing; because the NAM constituted an example of the negative neutrality which Ireland eschewed; and because it actually constituted a bloc with its own set of interests in the international system. The last argument, in particular, returned the government to the position of rejecting membership of a particular grouping by the suggestion that membership of any grouping was inconsistent with neutrality. For example, Lenihan argued in 1981 that with regard to its UN policy, Ireland was 'better off as a neutral' associated with countries like Austria and Sweden.[35] The problem with this formulation, of course, was that it applied equally to membership of the EEC. Indeed, the governments of the two countries mentioned had cited their own neutrality as one of several reasons for not becoming members of the Community. The inconsistency of the government's position in this respect was mitigated only by the tendency of the opposition from the left to use exactly the same kind of argument to establish that Ireland should join the NAM and leave the EEC. For them, membership of the former was consistent with 'positive' neutrality. Membership of the EEC violated the stricture that Ireland should avoid all groupings other than the UN and the NAM.

It became increasingly difficult, however, to square EEC membership with even the 'positive' conception of neutrality as the government understood it because of the developments within the Community noted above. They responded to these changes by re-emphasising the third principle set out by Cosgrave in 1956, that Ireland was a Christian-Western country committed to supporting the principal upholders of those values. This was rendered consistent with neutrality by pointing out that Ireland was not 'indifferent to the major issues which face the international community as a whole'. It would continue to work for 'order and justice' and the reduction of tension and armaments in the world.[36] Thus, Lenihan argued in 1980, neutrality should not be a reason for refraining from supporting the United States in the hostage crisis with Iran. That would be tantamount to isolationism and, he pointed out, even the Swedes, the Austrians and the Swiss did not hold back on such issues.[37]

The political implications of the policy, however, were made clear by Lynch in 1979 when as Taoiseach he had just returned from a visit to the United States. In the course of discussions between himself and the US President, he claimed that what he called 'the fundamental identity of interest' between Ireland, the EEC and the US 'was clearly apparent'. This formulation was not in itself novel, although it should be noted that Lynch regarded this agreement as significant because Ireland was shortly to hold the presidency of the European Council.[38] What was new was the extent to which neutrality was increasingly and explicitly fitted into, and interpreted in terms of, the common identity of Irish, European, US and Western interests. For example, speaking in 1981 in the debate on neutrality and Northern Ireland, Haughey stated that the

> the question of our neutrality also arises in another context, our membership of the European Community. Let us be clear about one thing. This country stands for certain values, enshrined in our Constitution. Our place is with the Western democracies, and we share common concepts of human rights, freedom under the law, individual liberty and freedom of conscience. Our economic interests are also tied in with the Western industrialised world. We are, therefore, neither ideologically neutral nor politically indifferent.[39]

Neutrality, therefore, had to be fitted into this pro-Western orientation articulated by Irish governments for their foreign policy. They did this by attempting to separate the ideas of military and political neutrality. Lenihan, for example, made a distinction between 'security as such' and 'defence'. The former was a 'wider concept' which involved Ireland's 'relations with the United Nations, international relations generally, political relations and all that area other than defence'.[40] It was in these terms that Haughey could speak of Ireland's 'political commitment to Europe and the Western democracies' and its ...military commitments to the UN' and could claim in 1981 that, 'Political neutrality or non-alignment is incompatible with our membership of the European Community, and with our interests and ideals'.[41]

Irish neutrality had always been defined primarily in military terms. Whatever the political, moral and military explanations and objectives for the policy, its practice had involved the refusal to participate in military alliances. When the policy had been originally formulated, however, this military emphasis had not been offered as a qualified or technical definition. Military neutrality had constituted the starting-point for thinking about the security, the survival and the independence of the state. With the articulation of a broader conception of Irish security, to which military policy constituted only one aspect, however, two things followed. An attempt was made to 'shrink' neutrality into a place within Ireland's European policy in the sense that it was interpreted to fit in with what was presented as a broader, more important commitment. Secondly, in being fitted in in this way, the attempt was made to render neutrality – once the code-word for Irish independence – both harmless and useful with regard to Ireland's European interests.

According to the utility argument, neutrality contributed to making Ireland acceptable or trustworthy to a wide range of countries on a number of international issues. Since Ireland was the only country in the EEC which enjoyed this status, it could provide a useful bridging role between them and, for example, the countries of the Third World or the Soviet bloc. This claim suggests two questions. First, were neutrals actually capable of performing communication roles where others were not and, hence, did the rest of the Community need or value Ireland's status in this respect? Secondly, was it possible to give neutrality a pro-Western articulation in the EEC, while at the same time convincing external and domestic audiences that it was still a fundamental principle upon which Irish foreign policy was based?

The success of the policy in terms of the first question is hard to assess. While Irish governments have played a part in contacts between the EEC and ACP states and the countries of the Soviet bloc on the basis of their neutral status, it is impossible to say whether this part was indispensable. Clearly, the policy was not a success in that East–West or North–South problems have not been 'solved' as a consequence of Irish participation in their management. It is possible to say, however, that whatever progress has been made on the issues which divide these groups has been achieved with Irish involvement on the side of facilitating solutions, and that this involvement has been accepted by other governments, out of politeness at the very least, on the basis of claims by Irish governments to a neutral status.

With regard to the second question, however, it may be seen that Irish governments experienced considerable difficulty in reconciling their narrow EEC articulation of neutrality in military terms with their traditional claims for influence based upon that policy. Rather, their definition of the meaning of Irish neutrality has tended to alter in response to the demands of the context in which it was being articulated. In their claims for a bridging role between EEC and ACP countries, for example, it was Ireland's past as a colony, its present as a developing country and its consequent feeling for and sharing of the underdeveloped states' view of the world which were emphasised. This shared identity continued to be expressed primarily in liberal economic terms. Imperialism or the economic policies of the advanced capitalist states, for example, were faulted for their obsolescence, short-sightedness and immorality. They were not regarded as systemic properties of a world economy serving particular interests. This economy was still regarded as being reformable by the efforts of clear-sighted people of goodwill. At the very minimum, however, this involved a view of Ireland's 'separateness' from the EEC that went beyond the purely military distinction, and that might become increasingly politicised as Ireland was seen to be excluded from its 'fair' share of Community prosperity.

The military definition of Irish neutrality was most successfully utilised in the process of East-West contacts initiated by the Conference on Security and Cooperation in Europe (CSCE) held at Helsinki in 1973.[42] This process is open to all European countries including the USSR and also involves the United States and Canada. Increasingly, the members of the EEC have attempted to establish their own joint position for discussing the relaxation of military, economic, social and cultural relations, prior to each round of negotiations. According to Keatinge, Irish governments have made a number of substantive contributions to CSCE. Along with the governments of West Germany and

Spain, they managed to get the Helsinki Declaration to regard frontiers as 'inviolable' rather than 'immutable', and they expressed a concern for the recognition of religious freedoms. It is also likely that the difficult political circumstances in which subsequent meetings were held, provided the Irish government with opportunities for playing the role of an organisation (or conference) maintainer. Indeed, the CSCE process provided Irish governments with a number of opportunities for successful international role-playing, even if progress on objectives of substance was very limited. They consistently articulated an 'active' role for Ireland working both with the rest of the EEC and the other European neutrals such as Austria, Finland and Yugoslavia,[43] and seem to have allocated considerable resources to the preparation of their position at forthcoming conferences. Speaking before the Madrid meeting in 1980, for example, Lenihan informed the Dáil that eight members of the Department of Foreign Affairs in Dublin and several abroad were working on preparing Ireland's position and that the delegation in Madrid would have four permanent members with up to six participating in the main meeting.[44]

The reasons for Irish enthusiasm for the process are straightforward. Irish governments strongly supported the formal principles upon which CSCE was based. While it did not exhibit the characteristics of a rule-governed regime, the CSCE process at least provided Irish governments with a direct and alliance-free line of input into European security questions. Whether Ireland had any substantial impact or not, it was with evident relish that one ex-Minister for Foreign Affairs discussed his own experience with CSCE in the following terms:

Take the whole policy in regard to reducing tensions in middle Europe...Genscher [the West German Foreign Minister] asked for my support, the Germans were very anxious to get it going, and we were an accepted country right across the board in Europe, and ironically the Germans and ourselves and the Eastern European countries had to get that going.[45]

The attraction for the Irish was that they could become heavily involved in an important area of policy where success would be well worth the effort and where failure carried very little immediate risk at all. As Lenihan pointed out on a number of occasions, the success or failure of CSCE meetings was largely a function of the existing state of East–West relations, rather than the efforts of the Irish delegations at them.[46] Even the need to coordinate Ireland's position with that of other members of the EEC could be cited as a constraint upon Irish efforts. For example, in discussing the way in which the Irish presidency might be used in CMEA–EEC talks to expand East–West trade links in accord with the Helsinki Final Act, in 1979, Lenihan stated that because most economic issues were Community matters there was 'little room for initiative by individual states'. As President, however, Ireland would 'seek to further as far as possible Community preparations for the Madrid Review Meeting'.[47] This touched on the larger problem of the way in which working with the rest of the EEC might jeopardise Ireland's independent foreign policy. As a member of the opposition put it in 1980, what was the point of obtaining a seat on the UN Security Council if Ireland was always going to 'tie into an EPC line, which is the lowest common denominator', or only going to have an independent foreign policy when it was endorsed by the rest of the Community? He then went on to say that Ireland should just send a foreign affairs official from the Commission in Brussels to the UN since such a person would 'do the job just as well and cost us less money'.[48]

In replying, Lenihan acknowledged that Quinn had raised a 'very fundamental point concerning our role as an independent country' in relation to 'our role as a member of the Community' which participated in EPC.[49] The point was, he continued, that Ireland carried 'far greater weight' in the EEC than as a 'voice crying in the wilderness', and that its influence was enhanced by the fact that Ireland was accepted by the others as a 'disinterested country'. Ireland was disinterested, however, 'in the sense that we do not have any major economic or political involvement'. It had no empire, wealth or military involvement and that 'was our major source of strength'. Lenihan conceded that participation in EPC did 'inevitably' lead to a 'certain dilution of capacity to act completely independently' and he said that Ireland went along with 'consensus decisions' unless they were against the 'fundamental interests of Ireland' but, he added that Ireland had always managed to maintain 'an independent role at the UN'. This was important because, as he went on to say,

There are many areas in which we do not agree with the European view. We would not, for instance, agree with some of the military or disarmament views of most of our colleagues within the Community and we will continue to hold very strong views on that subject and speak on it in a reasonably independent and disinterested manner.[50]

Even on the issue of East–West security relations, therefore, the Irish government experienced difficulty in restricting itself to the narrow, military definition of neutrality. The reason for this was that not only did they wish to demonstrate to other governments that Irish neutrality posed no problems for Ireland's full participation in the EEC, but they also wished to show that it was an asset to both the Community and their own attempts to perform an active role within it. The problem was that a claim to a bridging role between North and South, and even East and West could not rest on the narrow definition of military neutrality set within the articulation of a pro-Western political, economic and ideological orientation. Instead, government spokesmen tended to drift back to a broader, more orthodox version of neutrality when laying claim to these roles. For example, in the passage above, Lenihan began by acknowledging the tension between Ireland's independent, neutral policy and participation in the EEC, went on to say that there was no tension at all – Ireland's neutrality was the basis of its effective EPC performance – and concluded by detailing how the country preserved its independent foreign policy despite the pressures of membership of the EEC. Ireland, he said, pursued

> an independent role in the area of European political cooperation and within the UN, seeking at the same time to go along with consensus decisions when there is no vital interest involved or a matter about which we feel very strongly such as disarmament.[51]

On other occasions he added that the 'major part' of preparatory work for CSCE contacts was carried out in conjunction with other members of the EEC,[52] and that only when the Irish were particularly concerned about progress on a certain point would they work through bilateral contacts with European neutrals.[53]

This is probably an accurate account of the way in which the tension between Irish neutrality and participation in EPC, and the confusion between military neutrality and broader conceptions of it were resolved in actual diplomatic practice. So long as the Irish government's perceptions of the EEC were correct and so long as EPC achieved very little, the Irish could accommodate themselves to it. They could make their own contribution to or departures from the joint line, emphasising European solidarity or Irish independence as the occasion demanded. In so doing, however, they left the status of Irish neutrality unresolved, trimmed down to compatibility with EEC membership on some occasions, proclaimed enhanced or untouched by its consequences on others, and at all times the government asserted that the two posed no real problem for one another. As such, the policy was exceedingly vulnerable to developments in the EEC or events to which the organisation had to respond, which forced Irish governments to change their perceptions of the character of the organisation.

In their efforts to resolve, or at least manage, the tension between Irish neutrality and membership of the EEC, Irish governments were forced to redefine their conceptions of the latter as well as the former. Their policy consisted of an elaboration of the Lemass position offered during the first period to the effect that the EEC was not currently an organisation with military functions, that this might change in the future and that Ireland had some sort of commitment to supporting the security of the present Community. Speaking as Foreign Minister in 1978, O'Kennedy said that when they had joined the EEC, the Irish had maintained that they would not become a member of a military alliance. However, citing Sean Lemass as his authority, he went on to say that should the Community come under attack, then the Irish would 'face our obligations as a member of the Community'.[54]

While the extent of the 'obligations' was itself ambiguous, domestic debates focused upon the question of whether Irish military commitments were conditional upon the political evolution of the EEC.[55] The standard response of the government was to the effect that while there had been no changes in Ireland's defence commitments at the present time, they might change in the future. In 1978, for example, O'Kennedy said that while there was no reason to suppose that change was likely in the near future, Ireland remained committed to European integration leading to some form of 'European Union'.[56] Ireland remained a neutral, although this might change as a consequence of future 'political developments' and it would meet its existing obligations should the EEC be attacked.[57] As a consequence of both choices made by the Irish government and developments in the EEC during the second period, however, the Irish position on the non-military character of the EEC was forced to change. Increasingly, the claim with regard to the EEC's lack of a military role was transformed from what had been a statement of fact to a particular view of the Community that had to be actively defended. While spokesmen for the government offered stronger declarations of Ireland's commitment to the principle of European defence, they made it clear that Ireland could permit such developments only 'in the context of a political union in Europe', and that movement in the latter direction was not currently taking place.[58] For example, in 1979, responding to a question regarding the attendance of Irish officers at NATO manoeuvres in Germany (in accordance with the Helsinki Final Act), O'Kennedy was more categorical. Ireland had not joined NATO in 1949 and, he said, it was 'not the policy or intention of the Government to reconsider that decision'. Further, he continued,

> There are no proposals within the European Community to create an EEC defence force.... The European Community has no function in relation to defence and there is no question of a common defence policy among the Nine.[59]

The reasons for these changes have already been mentioned. Between the end of 1980 and early 1981, the Haughey government had, at the very minimum, trailed its coat on the idea of re-linking the end of neutrality with the end of Partition. This might be viewed as the logical conclusion of regarding neutrality as an instrument of policy, particularly because, as the opposition were quick to point out, it had appeared to have been introduced into the domestic discussion of Anglo-Irish negotiations (if not necessarily into the negotiations themselves) without any British concession on the status of Northern Ireland being offered.[60] While discussion of the 'totality of the relationships within these islands' may have been, in part, an exercise in short-term political opportunism inspired by domestic considerations, it should be remembered that it took place in the context of the emergence of external pressures upon Irish neutrality. The success of EPC had, by the late 1970s, rekindled an interest on the part of several EEC governments in increased security and defence cooperation.

There were few consequences of substance from this activity. Nevertheless, such as there were caused problems for the Irish government. The formal problem was that these moves were being attempted without the prior or concomitant political and institutional evolution to which the Irish had linked their taking place. Worse, the EEC was not only regarded as static in these terms, but was also seen to be failing in the light of their demand for economic convergence between its members. The EEC was asking Ireland to participate in military and institutional arrangements of which it did not approve and which eroded both the substance and the distinctiveness of Irish independence, without offering it sufficient economic or institutional incentives for its concurrence. Finally, and perhaps of most immediate concern, these moves took place in the context of strengthening and demonstrating the resolve of the European section of NATO. As such, they could be embarrassingly linked to other demonstrations of European 'resolve' such as the stationing of Cruise and Pershing missiles on European territory, a development which could be regarded as being at odds with Ireland's policy on arms control and disarmament.[61]

At the heart of the problem were the proposals made by the West German Foreign Minister at the Venlo meeting in May 1981. In these, he called for the formalising of the role of the European Council as the EEC's ruling body, a regularising of the conduct of EPC business, the establishment of a permanent secretariat, and regular consultations between the member states on defence and security policy. As with all such meetings, the appropriate ministers would attend – in this case, the Defence Ministers.[62] Of interest to the press and seized upon by the opposition, was the fact that the Irish representative, Lenihan, had apparently raised no objections to Genscher's proposals at the Venlo meeting. According to FitzGerald, speaking as Taoiseach in the following autumn, four options regarding EPC had emerged at Venlo. The governments of the EEC could do nothing, make minor adjustments, work on a new report redefining and expanding the concept of EPC, or they could sign a formal treaty of cooperation.[63] While Lenihan said that he had agreed to minor changes, FitzGerald claimed that he had, in fact, also accepted the need for a new report on EPC. It had been left to the Foreign Minister of the new government, Professor Dooge, to rectify the situation at the London summit in the autumn of 1981. According to FitzGerald again, this was achieved by insisting on a vague formula for discussing EPC which emphasised the different types of states involved, did not expand the present scope of EPC and limited talks to the political aspects of security.[64] The Economist claimed that the European declaration proposed by Genscher emphasised the discussion of cultural and security matters as a grouping because the Irish would not let it say 'defence'.[65]

There were important domestic dimensions to this issue. The Minister for Foreign Affairs, for example, had been the centre of some controversy in that initially he was a member of neither the Dáil nor the Senate.[66] A diplomatic coup associated with him, therefore, served party political purposes as well as the foreign policy objectives of the government. Further, as heirs to the pro-Treaty faction of Sinn Féin, a vulnerable foundation in the context of the political culture of the Republic, the leaders of Fine Gael were unlikely to miss an opportunity to present themselves as more trustworthy guardians of the cherished values of the Republican tradition than the party of de Valera himself. On the occasion of discussing the status of Professor Dooge, for example, FitzGerald claimed that his party had never used the Lemass formulation on the future evolution of a European Defence Community while they were in power between 1973 and 1977. His point, however, was not that Fine Gael disagreed with this position; in fact, he asked the Dáil not to make too much of the distinction. He simply wished to make it clear, he said, that Fine Gael were not the 'front-runners' on this particular piece of policy.[67]

Understandably, given his *communautaire* preferences, FitzGerald was at pains to point out with regard to Genscher's initiative that at issue were not the problems posed for Irish neutrality by the EEC, but the incompetence of the political opposition when they were in power. EPC, in his experience, had always been concerned with the 'political aspects of security' although he recalled that occasionally ministers spoke 'as though they were at a NATO meeting and I had to chide them and remind them that they were not'.[68] From the elaboration of his case against Lenihan, however, it is clear that he regarded Irish neutrality as a difficult and sensitive issue. Lenihan, he argued, by his acquiescence in the discussion of expanding the competence of EPC, had opened the door, or put Ireland on the 'slippery slope', to further developments. While there had been no substantial concessions, Ireland had signalled to the rest of the Comunity that it could be pushed further than its present position on the question of EPC. The danger was that if the momentum in the Community on EPC got under way, then Ireland could not go along with it and would be pushed into a position of isolation.

During the rest of the short life of FitzGerald's first government, the pendulum swung the other way regarding who were the true defenders of Irish neutrality. From closing the door in November 1981, opened by their Fianna Fáil predecessors at Venlo, the government had made the transition by December to enduring accusations that the Genscher–Colombo proposals (the next round of EPC initiatives) were far more dangerous than anything allegedly agreed to at Venlo. Yet according to Fianna Fáil, the government was doing nothing about them. Haughey, speaking now as leader of the opposition, reiterated what he claimed had been the Irish position. There could be no defence deal before political, economic and monetary union, and the EEC should not enter the realm of power politics.

It must be recognised that our standing in the world will be greatly changed if we are perceived to have become de facto members of the Atlantic Alliance and increasingly identified with NATO decisions, such as the Sinai force. Our ability to contribute to the UN will be prejudiced thereby, as also will our dealings with the Third World and with Arab, African and Latin American countries.[69]

Why, he wanted to know, was it being left to the Greeks to take the lead in responding to these threatening developments?[70]

The reversal of roles here may be primarily explained in terms of the respective acquisition and relinquishing of the responsibilities of office. Much of the froth of the debate, for example, with regard to which set of German proposals constituted the greatest mortal threat to the survival of the state, is attributable to the requirements of party politics.[71] This posturing, however, should not obscure the fact that the exchanges were the product of a very real and developing external problem for Irish foreign policy. At home, Irish governments were confronted by economic crisis and political instability reflected in a sequence of short-lived minority governments dependent upon the support of a variety of independent deputies whose own politics did not fall within the band of consensus represented by the principal parties.[72] The EEC was associated with these difficulties, either as the root cause of Ireland's economic problems or, at the very minimum, as an unsatisfactory solution to them. At the same time, it was making demands upon a traditional component of the external manifestation of Ireland's independence. It was in this context that in the spring of 1982, the recently elected minority Fianna Fáil government of Charles Haughey had to respond to the British effort to recapture the Falkland Islands and their attempts to use the EEC as an instrument of this policy.[73]

Kenneth Waltz has remarked that crises, like bolts of lightning illuminating a darkened landscape, tend to remove the ambiguities in which a system of power relationships may be enshrouded and expose these relationships for what they really are. This is true up to a point, although it should be remembered that most international relations take place and most outcomes are determined underneath the covers with all the benefits and difficulties which the resulting ambiguity can confer. The foreign policy of small states should not and cannot be directed solely at preparing for the great test of the day of crisis. There are other important things to do, and it is likely that, being small, no amount of preparation will see them through such a test should it eventually come. Ultimately, the fate of small states is not in their own hands. Indeed, the high politics of the small state should not be directed at preparing for such a test, but at attempting to ensure that it never comes about. The illumination of the underlying power structure, therefore, is the last thing that the government of small states want when their own survival is at stake. Their chance lies in ambiguity.

The illuminating effect of crises is not restricted to throwing power relationships between principal antagonists into sharp relief. There are peripheral consequences. Other governments are forced to develop a position with regard to the central dispute, the way it unfolds and the evolving positions of their fellows with regard to the issue. To a lesser and varying extent, they too are touched by the tension and intensity which accompanies the unfolding of events within a crisis. While few governments feel comfortable about involvement in a crisis, for a number of reasons this can be an unhappy time for the governments of small states in particular. The high policy of such states may be shifted from sustaining images and roles in the arena of international society, to making choices with regard to a distinct, unstable environment of unfolding real events with their own consequences.

Secondly, their actions may become viewed by all concerned as choices made in the context of the dispute rather than as the product of eccentric national values more or less tolerated by other governments in calmer times. The need to respond to the unfolding of these events may, in fact, involve their governments in making choices which have implications for the claims to national identity and values upon which their foreign policies are supposed to be based. While the governments of small states may have few policy options when they are directly involved in, or are the object of, an international crisis, it might be expected that they have a better chance of success in what might be termed crisis management on the periphery. In the Irish case, however, even peripheral involvement caused major problems in that it illuminated the unresolved tension between Ireland's role as an independent, good international citizen and as a *communautaire*, or at least enthusiastic, member of the EEC.

The dispute between Britain and Argentina over the ownership of the Falkland Islands was longstanding, but it had been brought to a crisis by the Argentinian invasion of the islands and their dependency, South Georgia, between late March and early April, 1982. There had followed an extended period of diplomatic negotiations in which the UN was closely involved, directed at achieving a peaceful resolution of Anglo-Argentinian differences. It is very difficult to say if these negotiations had any real prospect of success because it became increasingly clear that the survival of both governments was linked to a successful outcome for them to the dispute. It is highly likely that the extended nature of the negotiations was principally a function of the time it took the British to assemble, despatch and position a task force for the reconquest of the islands. In a campaign characterised by its drama and the spectacular, if in this case limited, violence of a modern land, sea and air battle, the British landed on the islands in the second half of May and had recaptured them by mid-June.

The problem posed for the Irish government by the Falklands War was as follows. An active, independent state with a seat on the UN Security Council at the time, Ireland could not, nor did its government seem inclined to avoid taking a position on what was clearly a threat to international peace and security. Although the UN did express an opinion on who was to blame for the crisis, however, its principal concerns were with first, preventing, and when this failed, ending the use of armed force as a means of resolving the

218

question of sovereignty. It was to these ends that Ireland's representative on the Security Council devoted his efforts. At the same time, however, Ireland, as a member of the EEC, was necessarily involved in the response of that organisation to the crisis. Despite hesitation and increasing unease with the substance of their policy, the members of the EEC acting collectively, focused upon Argentinian culpability and the need for political solidarity with a fellow member of the Community under attack. The EEC not only condemned the invasion of the islands as an act of aggression, but also, in response to British requests, imposed economic sanctions on Argentina.

This left the Irish government in the uncomfortable position of pursuing a middle power approach to the dispute in one international arena, the UN, while actively siding with one of the belligerents in another, the EEC. This situation was the embodiment of the unlikely nightmare that had been conjured up by opponents of Irish membership of the EEC since 1960 – Irish neutrality compromised by its membership of a European bloc. The discomfiture of the government, however, was compounded by the specific circumstances of the call for European solidarity. At a time of increasing domestic difficulties and Anglo-Irish tension over the handling of both the hunger-strike campaign in the North and the issue of the Community budget by the Thatcher government,[74] EEC membership appeared to be pulling the country into supporting a British war – and an uncomfortably colonial-looking war at that.

Initially, the response of the Irish government to these difficulties was to ignore them. Further, it appears that during the first phase of the crisis when attention was focused upon the Argentinian move rather than the developing British response, they were content to let the permanent foreign service handle their policy.[75] Thus at the UN Security Council on 2 April, the day after the invasion, the Irish representative, Noel Dorr, stressed that the rights and wrongs of the respective claims to the islands were not presently at issue. The important question was with regard to the attitude the Council should take

in view of the armed action taken overnight by Argentina in contravention of a unanimous call by the Council on all parties to refrain from the use of force [because this required] the Council to assert its position on a very basic matter – the effort to establish a rule of law rather than force in international relations.[76]

The following day, he added a second point of Irish concern to the effect that the use of force by one party to a dispute encouraged the other to do likewise, thereby raising the risks of armed conflict. It was on the basis of this that he justified Irish support for Resolution 502, which he characterised as condemning neither side, calling for a 'cessation of hostilities, an immediate withdrawal by Argentine forces and a diplomatic solution'.[77] Subsequently, this resolution has been regarded as a major British diplomatic success as it could be interpreted as a call by the UN for the resolution of the *status quo ante* as a precondition for negotiations between Britain and Argentina.

219

Similarly, the Irish agreed to the decision to impose economic sanctions on Argentina taken by the Community on 9 April. Speaking a month later about this decision and after circumstances had changed considerably, Haughey claimed that Ireland had gone along with it, 'despite some reservations' and 'in a spirit of Community solidarity'.[78] According to the *Sunday Times*' 'Insight' team's account of the war, however, the initial discussion of sanctions had divided the Community between six (including Britain) in favour, and three holding back for a brief time. In their account, Ireland was one of the initial backers of the idea.[79]

It seems likely that in pursuing these two diverging policies, the Irish government, like many others, were anticipating a peaceful resolution or suspension of the dispute. With either of these, political pressure from the Republican wing of Fianna Fáil or the parliamentary opposition would dissipate without the government having to make the difficult choice between European solidarity and neutrality. The military escalation of the dispute, however, starting with the recapture of South Georgia in late April and culminating in the sinking of the warships *Belgrano* and *Sheffield* in early May, made the avoidance of this choice impossible. The sinking of the Argentinian ship, in particular, precipitated a change of policy on the part of the Irish government. Speaking in the Dáil on 4 May with regard to that incident, Haughey said that Irish policy both at the UN and within the EEC had been directed at 'preventing a wider conflict and promoting a negotiated, honourable settlement by diplomatic means'. The Irish had believed that such a settlement was possible if both sides had demonstrated the necessary 'political will'. However, the government was now 'appalled' at the outbreak of what amounted to 'open war' and as a consequence of this 'serious threat to world peace', they had called for an 'immediate meeting of the Security Council' to prepare a new resolution asking for an immediate ceasefire and a diplomatic settlement of the dispute under the auspices of the UN. In addition, he said that the government considered that economic sanctions were 'no longer appropriate' and that Ireland was asking the Community to withdraw them, if not immediately, then as soon as possible.[80]

These sanctions were due to expire on 17 May, but the Irish government decided to try to have them suspended on the next scheduled Foreign Ministers meeting on 8 May. Speaking a few days after this meeting, Haughey argued that Ireland had originally supported the sanctions as a means of backing Resolution 502 (even though, as one Irish diplomat pointed out, the UN had not requested any such measures)[81] supporting a peacemaking mission by the US Secretary of State and preventing the introduction of troops into the area. He said that, in Ireland's view, the purpose of the diplomatic pressure had been to deny Argentina the benefit of a *fait accompli* and to make the further use of force 'unnecessary'. By 4 May, however, there were indications that 'diplomatic and economic pressure was simply viewed as complementary to military action'. Thus Ireland had sought an end to sanctions because

220

As a neutral country, we are not prepared to back military action. Nothing in our EEC obligations requires us to give such backing. We consider that it would be inappropriate for these measures to remain in force if they were being applied or be seen to be operating so as to reinforce a military solution to the crisis rather than to promote a diplomatic and negotiated settlement.

Indeed, he argued, the withdrawal of sanctions would contribute to 'creating an atmosphere in which UN efforts would obtain a receptive hearing on both sides'.[82]

The Taoiseach then went on to give a standard defence of Irish neutrality, the principles on which it rested and all they meant to the country. While the government had received 'considerable support', Ireland was 'not afraid to stand alone on this issue of peace'. It was unique in the Community in this respect and had been accepted by the other members as such. The people of Ireland were deeply committed to the policy and had been prepared to endure considerable external pressure in the past to maintain it. He went on to say that Ireland still supported the principles of European unity and solidarity and 'had not sought to act unilaterally'. However, the Community would do well to be more aware of the 'limitations' imposed on its ability to act by its 'true nature and ideals'. The EEC had 'no role in the military sphere', and for the sake of 'unity and solidarity' it would be better if it did nothing to complement or support military action since this would 'inevitably cause division'. Instead, he concluded, the Community should cherish its reputation as 'a peaceful intermediary'.[83]

The unfolding of events in the Falklands forced the Irish government to make a difficult decision regarding their foreign policy. What kind of decision it was is less easy to say. Speaking in the Dáil on 18 May, Haughey reiterated that Ireland's support for Resolution 502 and EEC sanctions had been given on the understanding that it would contribute to a peaceful resolution of the dispute. However, he went on to say that with the increase in hostilities this hope had 'faded' and Ireland's traditional policy of neutrality had been endangered.

We were being seen and obviously could fairly be interpreted as being associated with a serious escalation of military activity.[84]

The government made it clear, therefore, that they had seen a conflict between the demands of European solidarity and what the principles of neutrality dictated that they should do. In spite of the difficulties, misunderstandings and hostility which this might engender, they felt it was their duty to resolve the conflict in favour of the latter.

In contrast to the high motives with which the government explained their decision, however, the political opposition at the time and much subsequent comment suggested that more base considerations shaped the policy. In these perspectives, the emphasis is placed upon the difficult economic and political

221

circumstances confronting the government at home and the alleged shortcomings in the personal character of the then Taoiseach, Haughey.[85] The government, it has been pointed out, was facing a critical by-election during the war and could not afford to have its Republican credentials threatened by appearing to support a British war. Because the government needed to win this by-election, because Haughey was angry at the demise of his special relationship with Thatcher and British conduct over Northern Ireland and the Community budget, and because of his own shortcomings as a statesman, so the argument goes, he was prepared to sacrifice an array of external interests for the short-term domestic gains to be made by annoying the British.[86]

Three arguments can be made in support of this view. First, there was no contradiction in Ireland's initial Falklands policy. In this view, Irish neutrality was not threatened by support of EEC sanctions or Resolution 502, and certainly did not need to be defended by upsetting the British. Secondly, breaking with the EEC over the Falklands was so obviously at odds with Ireland's 'real' external interests that only domestic motives and considerations can account for the policy. Thirdly, it may be claimed that the execution of subsequent policy was so maladroit, given the intentions for it stated by the government, that those intentions could not have been the prime concern of the government. In this view, if the Irish government were so interested in a mediating role, why did they proceed to take a series of actions harmful to British interests and helpful to the Argentinians?

With regard to the argument that there was no contradiction between support for EEC sanctions and Irish neutrality, it is clear that from the onset of the crisis, spokesmen for Fine Gael were very interested in keeping the government in step with European policy on the Falklands. This suited both their understanding of Ireland's national interests and their desire to keep the Fianna Fáil government in a very uncomfortable position *vis-à-vis* its more Republican supporters. In terms of Irish party politics, for example, FitzGerald's praise in the Dáil of the government's 'correct and wise attitude...in supporting Britain in the Security Council and the EEC in the face of Argentine aggression',[87] in late April was inspired by more than simple admiration of the government's policy. Further, he argued that this support would contribute to a solution of the Community's budget problems by having a good effect on British public opinion and by giving the British government a lesson in the importance of 'community solidarity'. FitzGerald, however, offered his own version of active, positive neutrality and argued that a strong line on Argentinian aggression was entirely consistent both with this and what he was sure that de Valera would have done in the same circumstances. He noted that there had been recent comments in the press which suggested that in addition to not participating in military alliances, neutrality involved 'actually cutting oneself off from playing any role or taking up any moral position on any world issue'. This, he said, was totally 'out of line' with the Irish tradition of neutrality. For example, de Valera when he was President of the Council of the League had taken a position on problems like Abyssinia which did not involve pussy-footing in regard to the issues but taking up a strong moral position in the face of aggression'.[88] After the change in government policy, FitzGerald extended this argument to the maintenance of sanctions in the face of an outbreak of armed conflict. The government's position that maintaining sanctions after a war had broken out was inconsistent with Irish neutrality, was itself inconsistent, he claimed. De Valera had supported the measures taken against Italy in 1935 because of the outbreak of hostilities, and the present government had followed this approach on several international issues.[89]

Underlying the claim that there was no contradiction between the demands of European solidarity and Irish neutrality was the assumption that safeguarding Ireland's European interests was more important. The Irish government should do all it could to minimise the conflict between the demands of the two, but if confronted with a choice, it should certainly not pursue a course consistent with the dictates of active neutrality to the point where it hurt Ireland's European interests. In characterising domestic opposition to the change in Ireland's Falklands policy, a senior diplomat who was closely involved in the affair put it in the following way. Being 'high-minded' was 'all very well', but 'pulling the lion's tail', 'alienating the British to the cost of our real interests' was another matter.[90] This argument was rarely, if ever, directly made. It surfaced, rather, in the oblique form of suggestions that differences existed between the government and the Department of Foreign Affairs over the change in Ireland's Falklands policy. For example, an ex-minister who had also served in the Foreign Service cited the Falklands episode as one of the few occasions on which the Department's advice had been ignored. He added, with approval, that the diplomats had proceeded to carry out government instructions 'to the letter', although no further. He felt that this demonstrated a high degree of professionalism which would do something to offset the damage to Ireland's reputation as a 'serious' diplomatic player entailed by the content of the policy.

Firm evidence of this disagreement is, needless to say, hard to find. When asked directly about it, civil servants were apt to start talking quickly about the master-servant relationship – which they present themselves as being in with their ministers – although lower-ranking officers were more willing to intimate that the Department had difficulties with the change in policy. One other source of evidence for this disagreement, however, is to be found in the behaviour of the government itself and its willingness to allow the idea to develop that a gap did exist between it and the Department on certain aspects of the Falklands policy., In particular, early on in the crisis before the change in policy, the impression was apparently given that it was the Department which was taking the lead on these aspects of policy with which the government felt least comfortable such as the EEC sanctions and Resolution 502. Thus, in congratulating the government on its initial line, FitzGerald recorded his 'regret' at the press reports which had suggested that the Taoiseach had not been in accord with a policy that 'had been derived from within the machinery of Government'.[91] Later, he noted that a press report had appeared suggesting that the decision to vote for Resolution 502 had 'been taken by our representative there without instructions and on his own initiative'.[92] The government always subsequently denied these alleged differences, but not before the doubt was sown.

The third argument regarding the questionable nature of the motives lying behind Ireland's change of policy focuses on the alleged maladroitness of what they subsequently decided to do. In this view, whatever the motives lying behind it, the objective consequences of the new policy harmed British interests and favoured Argentina. By withdrawing from EEC sanctions, Ireland weakened the solid front of European diplomatic support for Britain. By calling for a Security Council meeting, the Irish government were dragging the British back into a forum in which the latter felt that they had already achieved the best they could with Resolution 502. Beyond this point, demands for a ceasefire could only favour the Argentinians who, although likely to lose a war, were still holding the islands.

The Irish government called for a Security Council meeting on 4 May after the sinking of the first two major warships. They did so, according to their Permanent Representative at the UN, speaking to the Council several weeks later, because 'it was unthinkable in our view, at a time when other peace efforts seemed to be at an end, that the international community should accept war as inevitable'.[93]

The problem was that other efforts were not at an end; the Secretary-General had just begun a series of contacts and negotiations with the parties involved which were to run for two weeks. A parallel and public exchange between the two parties in the Security Council, complicated by the contributions and interventions by other Council members, was most unlikely to facilitate a successful outcome to the exercise in quiet diplomacy being undertaken by the Secretary-General. As FitzGerald put it, speaking in the Dáil on 11 May, into this 'carefully calculated diplomatic exercise' and without taking the advice of its own diplomats, the Irish government had chosen 'to throw a spanner'.[94] The implication was that the Irish government had called the meeting, not to ease the situation in the South Atlantic, but to serve its own purposes of distancing itself from Britain and the EEC and re-establishing its independent credentials at home.

To this the government had little reply, particularly because they had quickly deferred their call 'so as not to hinder in any way the efforts' of the Secretary-General. Haughey claimed that the Secretary General had agreed that the Irish call for a Security Council meeting 'strengthened his hand' in the negotiations which were continuing at the UN[95] (as one junior official in the Department of Foreign Affairs put it, Perez de Cuellar could hold the threat of pressure from the 'mad Irish' to hold an open meeting over the heads of the belligerents) and he said that the government were ready to reactivate their call for a formal meeting of the Security Council should this be necessary since their 'paramount concern' was to stop the fighting. This they did, when the Secretary-General reported after two weeks that his mediation efforts had been a failure. Ireland's representative on the Council justified his country's call by saying that it gave the Secretary General a chance to report on his efforts, and that the Security Council had an obligation to keep on trying so long as there was any chance of success.[96]

At this meeting, he opened by reiterating Ireland's basic position on the crisis in particular and the dangers of war in general, and he called on the Secretary-General to renew his efforts with the formal backing of the Council. Three days into the debate, however, he submitted an Irish draft resolution for ending the conflict by a graduated process leading from a short ceasefire, through limited withdrawals and negotiations to a full implementation of Resolution 502 under the auspices of the UN.[97] On 26 May, the Irish co-sponsored a 'slightly revised version of the basic text' with 'five members of the Non-Aligned Group' who were on the Council,[98] as a 'basis for common action' by the Secretary General and the parties to the dispute.

The maladroitness of the initiatives taken by the Irish government after the change in their Falklands policy is, perhaps, the weightiest evidence in the case against their motives. The original call for a Security Council meeting had been ill-timed and, despite the government's protestations to the contrary,[99] could all too easily be seen as the product of government concerns other than contributing to peace in the South Atlantic. The attempt to restore the Security Council to the centre of diplomatic activity favoured the Argentinians because of the unfolding character of the conflict. Finally, Irish policy, following the decision to reactivate their call for a Security Council meeting, seemed to contradict the principle frequently articulated by spokesmen for the government in the past, that they would not take initiatives simply for the sake of doing so.

The Irish draft resolution and subsequent deliberations in the Security Council were undertaken in the context of a British military operation to recapture the islands or to extract Argentinian concessions which would have amounted to the same thing. While the Irish representative on the Security Council could, on 25 May, give four subtle and complex reasons why, despite the Secretary-General's previous failure, it was worth pushing on with a mediation effort,[100] he summarised more accurately the limited philosophy underlying the Irish effort on 4 June. 'Someone', he said, '...must shout stop'.[101] His frustration had already surfaced, however, at the end of his speech on the original Irish draft when he had said,

If the parties do not now accept it, so be it. If they want to fight to the finish, so be it. If this Council, for whatever reason, cannot or does not wish to adopt our proposal, so be it. If a better formula can be found, so be it – we will welcome anything that will work in the present situation and bring peace while maintaining the principles I have mentioned. Whatever happens in the face of this tragic conflict, Ireland will continue to believe that it was at least right to have tried. Whatever the outcome it will not be said at the end of our short term of membership of this Council that we did not even try.[102]

However, all these shortcomings have explanations which are simpler than the hunt for questionable motives on the part of the government. The call for a Security Council meeting was ill-timed because it was the hurried response of a surprised government to an event which forced them to make a difficult choice very quickly. The attempt to use the Security Council favoured the Argentinians in the way that all UN decisions with regard to a dispute are bound to favour the interests of one party over another. The remoteness of the Irish initiatives on the Council from any prospect of success on the substantive issue was nothing new. Dorr's comments to the effect that it was important to try to avert or limit armed conflict even if the chances for success were slight, were the product of a philosophy which had sustained Irish activism on much more than just the Falklands war. The core of the opposition's criticism was that the government had put important external relationships with Britain and the rest of the EEC in jeopardy by dropping sanctions and initiating an ineffective and mischievous mediation role at the UN. While one may wish to question the motives of the government in changing their Falklands policy and fault their handling of the initiatives subsequently taken, it is very difficult to reach any conclusion other than that they were absolutely right to break with the EEC if they wished to preserve a claim to Irish neutrality beyond this point. The Haughey government was caught by its own failure and that of other governments to resolve the tension between its claims to neutrality–independence and Ireland's membership of the EEC. It is likely that had the Fine Gael–Labour coalition been in power, they too would have been pushed in the same direction by the way the Falklands crisis evolved.

While this claim cannot be proved, it can be given some weight by an examination of the character of the opposition to the government's policy on the Falklands. Much was made, as has been shown above, of the dubious motives of the Haughey government. Substantial long-term external interests, it was claimed, had been sacrificed or, at least, put at risk for short-term, domestic political considerations. The opposition, however, rarely if ever spelt out the nature of these long-term interests. They could not because what they would have had to say was that Ireland's real interests were served by cooperation with the EEC and Britain, up to and including avoiding doing anything that might get in the way of Britain's military operation in the Falklands. This, and not the minimal prospects for its success, was at the heart of the argument that Ireland's first call for a Security Council meeting constituted a terrible *faux pas*. They dared not say this, however, for it would

226

have been tantamount to accepting either that Irish neutrality had become a complete myth that could be ignored, or that it should be abandoned forthwith.

Instead, the opposition's accusations of maladroitness, while hinting at profound and substantive disasters flowing from the government's opportunism, remained precisely that, and in doing so, they focused upon the old theme of the country's reputation and the international role which it had to play. For example, according to FitzGerald, as a consequence of the call for a Security Council meeting, 'Ireland's stock at the UN has rarely been as low as at the moment'. This 'shot gun' diplomacy had entailed, he went on, that the 'respect' won by Cosgrave, Aiken and others over the years had been 'dissipated overnight'. For a 'short-term gain', to produce a 'domestic reaction', the government had been prepared to contribute to the erosion of the key paragraph in Resolution 502 demanding an Argentinian withdrawal from the islands.

Nothing more unlike the traditional professional and skilled approach of Ireland to problems at the UN could be imagined, and it has left many friends of Ireland there bemused and disappointed.[103]

There was, however, a measure of ambiguity in this return to the familiar ground of belabouring a government for its failure to live up to the high standards of morality and skill established by its predecessors with regard to the country's status. In the same speech, FitzGerald claimed that the government had failed both to act with sufficient disinterest and to live up to the expectations of its friends. Which friends and which expectations he was thinking about were clarified when he went on to say that the withdrawal from EEC sanctions had destroyed what he called the 'delicate exercise' in leverage with which the rest of the Community had been attempting to get British movement on the budget.[104] The ambiguity was succinctly summed up in a further criticism of the government which he offered a week later, on 18 May:

We have thrown away our traditional role as a peace-maker, damaging, moreover, perhaps irretrievably, so far as this Government is concerned, our relationship with Britain.[105]

These criticisms may or may not have had a measure of truth to them. They rested, however, upon assumptions about the nature of Ireland's external interests which remained unarticulated by the opposition. While the government may have been caught unprepared by the crisis, and its response may have been both clumsy and opportunistic in part, it was at least consistent with the claims for international status as an independent neutral made by all Irish governments since the late 1950s. The criticisms of the Fine Gael opposition, by comparison, were far more convoluted[106] and, ultimately, dishonest because they would not openly articulate the understanding of Ireland's external interests which made the government's policy so disturbing to them.

Initially, the policy of the Irish government towards the Falklands crisis was reactive, multilateral and ambiguous. They were content to remain part of a European and, hence, generally pro-British approach which emphasised the fault of the Argentinians in committing an act of aggression. While the Argentinians clearly remained the transgressors of international conduct and the British remained the injured party, it was possible to reconcile Ireland's roles as an enthusiastic European and as an active, independent neutral. Supporting sanctions was consistent with both roles and the Irish could also claim that their UN reputation and place on the Security Council, in that they were both useful to the EEC, were evidence of the continuing importance of Ireland's distinctive independent identity as an instrument of its foreign policy. What was left unclear, however, was whether it was the political centre of gravity of the policy – support for the British position – or its organizational manifestation in an active, independent role for Ireland, to which the government was principally committed. Had the crisis been resolved, it is possible that the ambiguity could have been maintained, with the policy meaning all things to all people and being cited as an excellent example of what a neutral Ireland could do within the EEC.

As events moved from crisis to war in the South Atlantic, however, they forced the Irish government to make a difficult choice. The Community's economic sanctions could no longer be viewed as a collective, punitive response to Argentina's decision to use force. Increasingly, they became the contribution of allies to a British policy directed at recovering the islands primarily by military means.[107] In theory, this left the Irish government with four options. They could have taken the opportunity to abandon neutrality in order to secure more effectively the substantial interests they pursued through their participation in Community solidarity. There is little evidence to suggest that this final, explicit bartering of neutrality was ever seriously considered, even by those elements of the opposition who went to some length to emphasise that 'real' Irish interests were best served by not complicating Britain's policy on the Falklands. It is difficult to envisage precisely what they would have obtained from Britain or the rest of the Community in return for such an offer.

Secondly, the government could have done as the opposition were essentially arguing, and attempted to preserve the increasingly shaky fiction that Community solidarity over the Falklands and Irish neutrality were not incompatible. While a government dominated by Fine Gael might have managed this, it was impossible for a Fianna Fail government occupying the tenuous parliamentary position which it was, and dependent upon Republican support, to attempt such an exercise. Besides, not only would such a policy have been difficult to carry out, it would also have been deceitful. Irish neutrality had already been reduced by the principal parties to a narrow military definition. Surrendering that without giving up the formal status of a neutral state could

228

only have been regarded as a shallow exercise. Thirdly, the Irish government could have withdrawn its support for EEC sanctions but done nothing else, in particular, at the Security Council. This again would have been a difficult policy to pursue in that it would have epitomised the negative neutrality or 'opting out' policy to which both the government and the opposition were opposed. It would have also been a clear indication of the extent to which membership of the EEC acted as a constraint upon Irish foreign policy. In a sense, backing off like this would have been as hard to undertake as a formal renunciation of Irish neutrality.

The final option was that of dropping out of EEC sanctions and undertaking a policy of initiatives at the UN independent of the collective effort of the EEC. Given that they could not maintain their solidarity with the rest of the EEC, this active role was the natural one to take. The government and the party they represented felt that the Falklands were not worth the fight, and its attendant costs. They saw the British response as essentially of the same character as the original Argentinian act of aggression as far as principles were concerned, and they completely lacked any emotional identification with British military enterprises of the kind which enabled others to support Britain in spite of their doubts. They opted, therefore, for this active UN role and, between early April and late May of 1982, their policy moved from supporting Resolution 502 and EEC sanctions, to withdrawing from sanctions and co-sponsoring Security Council resolutions with members of the Non-Aligned Movement.

The magnitude of this shift in policy should not be overemphasised. The government never abandoned their support for Resolution 502 as they understood it, and they continued to condemn Argentina as the country primarily responsible for the present threat to international peace and security. Further, Ireland was by no means alone within the EEC in being unhappy about the British response to the Falklands crisis. According to one serving minister, 'at heart' most of the other members of the EEC agreed with the Irish position and offered 'qualified support' to Britain only because it was a member of the EEC.[108] Indeed, Italy had joined Ireland in arguing for an early end to the Community sanctions against Argentina and, eventually, like Ireland, had dropped out of them. The change in policy, therefore, is probably more accurately viewed as the arresting of a drift rather than a complete somersault or new departure in Ireland's policy of neutrality.

There has been, however, a tendency to underemphasise, rather than to exaggerate, the significance of the change in Irish policy during the Falklands War. As far as commentators and the political opposition are concerned, it has been regarded as an anomaly, like the war of which it was a small part, or the product of the character failings of the Taoiseach at the time. Their focus has been upon the failure of the government to manage the issue and not upon the character of the circumstances which put the government in a very difficult position. Even spokesmen for the government have tended to understate the significance of the shift, in particular, by attempting to emphasise the extent to which sentiment within the EEC favoured their position rather than that of the British and that, hence, their change of policy was not quite the act of isolated courage which it appeared to be.

This is because neither the political elite nor the attentive public have resolved the problem of the place of neutrality in Irish foreign policy. It is significant that the internal debate is about the 'problem' of neutrality, whether what was once considered the foundation of independence is a problem or not. However they decided on this question, policy-makers and commentators have been uncomfortable with neutrality. The latter group of people may be seen to be operating in the context of an Irish intellectual tradition of shattering the illusions nurtured by ideologues and clung to by the 'common people'. Neutrality, in these views, is a myth bereft of moral consistency and not borne out by either Ireland's material circumstances or its 'real', as opposed to its declaratory, foreign policy. And like so many Irish myths, it is seen as feeding a constraining obsession with the past which prevents the Irish government and the Irish people from getting on with sorting out the problems of the present and the future.

If neutrality could not be removed altogether, then the task is now to defuse it and make it safe. In this enterprise, the external counterpart to shattering domestic illusions has been to explain Irish neutrality in terms which would offend no one and convince a few of its continuing utility. In addition, it is difficult to overemphasise the extent to which policy-makers and commentators in both private and public stressed that neutrality was not a problem. One commentator, for example, regarded it as 'a non-issue pretending to be an issue', said that there was no external pressure on Ireland regarding its neutrality and, as has been noted above, said that most of Ireland's external difficulties were of its own making. Domestic debate on neutrality was interpreted in party political terms and even one serving minister who had been closely involved in several such debates stated that neutrality

> has tended from time to time to get involved in internal, domestic political argument, debate, sometimes point-scoring. It is a rock to throw. Mr. A. appears to be departing from this; well then, Mr. B. in opposition will throw a stone and vice-versa... [It is] fair game.[109]

On the part of commentators, this minimising of the significance of neutrality has been unfortunate. The issue should be addressed four-square, for or against. The oblique approach, particularly when minimising the significance of the domestic debate on Irish neutrality, has tended to shade off into deprecating the issue from the lofty and traditional perspectives on the study of foreign policy. These perspectives miss the point of small state foreign policy, and in adhering to them, Irish commentators have distanced themselves from their subject in a way which is unhelpful for a full understanding of it.

Caution on the part of policy-makers, however, is more understandable. For them, Irish neutrality remains a difficult issue and talking about their approach to the Falklands War, for example, could conceivably have implications for present external relationships. In connection with this, it may be noted that each of the political leaders and members of the foreign service interviewed for this book emphasised that it was the relationship with Britain, and not with the other EEC countries, which had been shaken (mildly) by Ireland's change of policy during the war. Troubles with Britain, presumably, were something everybody could understand as being as much a product of the history of Anglo-Irish relations as anything else. Troubles with the EEC, however, and Ireland's place within it, led very quickly to the vexed question of the relationship between Irish neutrality and membership of the EEC, and this was territory over which none of them wished to linger.

This, however, is the question which remains unanswered, and while the Falklands War may have been an isolated incident, the trends within the EEC and the debate on Western security policy would seem to be increasing the tension between Ireland's roles as an active neutral and as an enthusiastic member of the EEC. Ireland, the Irish, remain committed to some form of neutrality. The latter is still built into the meaning of Irish independence, and impractical and inconvenient though neutrality may be for other purposes at times, the rewards of the EEC are not sufficient to permit any government to abandon it and all that that would entail. The policy of Irish governments has reverted to ambiguity on this difficult choice, trusting to the inability of the Community to build upon EPC, thereby enabling the Irish government to maintain its claim that no contradiction exists between membership of the EEC and its instrumental version of neutrality. This may be a fairly shrewd bet, although it would seem that very little in the way of Community developments in this respect can cause quite a lot of trouble for Irish governments.

It should also be remembered that while Irish governments may seek to preserve domestic tranquility for a time by maintaining this claim, external perceptions of Ireland's international role and external expectations for Irish international behaviour do shift with the active encouragement of the Irish government to this end. The problem here is that if Irish neutrality is presented externally as a useful instrument of policy, then it is reasonable to expect a degree of flexibility with regard to it. That is, it should serve policy as an instrument, not constrain it as a 'permanently operating factor'. Starting principles of national independence, however, cannot or should not have this degree of flexibility. The result is, in times of crisis, that external expectations of what an Irish government can and will do may jar surprisingly and unpleasantly with what domestic public opinion expects of them. The degree of distance between the two was generally in evidence during the Falklands War. In particular, however, it may be seen in the way in which every one of the options confronting the Irish government after the sinking of the *Belgrano* was viewed as a political choice, both by foreign governments and by much of domestic public opinion. Even the UN option subsequently taken by the government, one of the less political options, presumably, was so regarded. The political nature of UN decisions or actions was not new in itself. What was new was that the Irish government could no longer use the UN for cover from the political hostility generated by its part in mediatory activities. As a consequence of its membership of the EEC, foreign policy behaviour associated with neutrality and international role-playing in the past, was increasingly understood by other governments to be the product of political choices made in the present, and it was judged accordingly.

Notes

1. O'Brien, interview.
2. See, for example, MacQueen, op. cit.; Dennis Driscoll, 'Is Ireland Really "Neutral"?' in *Irish Studies In International Affairs* (ISIIA), Vol. 1, No. 3, 1982. Patrick Keatinge's, *A Singular Stance: Irish Neutrality in the 1980's,* Institute of Public Administration, Dublin,1984, provides an excellent historical and comparative analysis of Irish neutrality taking as its focus the domestic debates about the policy in the early 1980s. While disavowing that he is taking any stand for or against Irish neutrality, the author is evidently doubtful about what he calls the 'fundamentalist' version of the policy, i.e. equating it with Ireland's independence and national identity.
3. Ronan Fanning's 'Irish Neutrality, An Historical Review' provides a useful account of these in *ISIIA*, ibid.
4. See, for example, 306, 343 (O'Kennedy); 337, 1393 (Haughey); 327, 1420 (FitzGerald). In a 1984 opinion poll, 77 per cent of those asked said that Ireland should remain neutral in a war and 84 per cent said it should remain so in peacetime. Cited in Patrick Keatinge, 'Irish Neutrality' in *Ireland Today*, November/December 1984.
5. 'Fanning', *ISIIA*, op. cit., p. 28.
6. 306, 342.
7. See Keatinge (1984), op. cit., pp. 113–14, for an account of 'heretics and agnostics' who doubt the policy of neutrality to varying degrees.
8. 'Fanning', in *ISIIA*, op. cit., p.30.
9. Interview.
10. 334, 815.
11. A deputy in the Dáil, 322, 1354 (20 June 1980).
12. 327, 1394 (11 March 1981).
13. Interview.
14. 'Fanning', in op. cit., p. 31.
15. Ibid. See also Ryle Dwyer, op. cit., passim, for details of this policy and the attempts of the American government to deal with it.
16. 'Fanning', ibid., p. 34.
17. Ibid., p. 35.
18. O'Brien, interview.
19. 'Fanning', in op. cit., p. 31.
20. For details of this see 325, 968–75 (8 December 1980).
21. Ibid.
22. 327, 1392 (10 March 1981).
23. Ibid., 1394.

232

24. See Keatinge (1984) for the attitude of other European neutrals (Sweden, Switzerland, Austria and Finland) to EEC membership, and the problems created by Article 224 of the EEC treaties which says that the organisation should continue to function during time of war.

25. There is evidence that Aiken was sympathetic with this line of argument when it was applied to the question of EEC membership.

26. The attempts to organise defence procurement on a Community basis enjoyed little success, and the Irish rejected that the Sinai force constituted an exercise in 'European' peace-keeping. Keatinge (1984); pp. 90-1.

27. For details of this, particularly the Genscher-Colombo proposals of 1981, see ibid., p. 88; and *The Economist*, 16 May and 21 December 1981.

28. See the earlier discussion of Lemass and the EEC.

29. See 318, 340 for Lenihan on the EEC's 'gradual' response to Afghanistan and attendance at the Olympics (21 February 1980). Also 320, 252 and 321, 1611 (4 June 1980). The Irish government shifted over this period of time from a 'wait-and-see' attitude as pressure to boycott the Games increased, to leaving it to the Irish Olympic Committee to decide what to do and then finally supporting the boycott. On being asked about the French intervention in Shaba province, Zaire, in 1978, the Foreign Minister, O'Kennedy, said that Ireland had not been consulted before the action was taken and, hence, had no comment to make about it. 307, 1103-4 (21 June 1978).

30. 322, 1360. See 313, 767 for O'Donoghue's defence of Ireland's adherence to the European Space Agency Convention in 1979. In response to concerns about the military applications of a space programme, he claimed that if Ireland was going to prevent the manufacture of anything with military potential then it would have to 'stop a substantial fraction of all the industrial production of the country'.

31. This suggestion was put forward from time to time in the Dáil, but there is no evidence that it was countenanced as a serious foreign policy option for Ireland by the government.

32. 316, 2131-2. He said Ireland was in regular contact with India, Tanzania and Zambia.

33. 319, 468 (25 March 1980).

34. 327, 1465.

35. 327, 1465 (11 March 1981).

36. Lenihan, 319, 466 (25 March 1980).

37. 1320, 442-3 (1 May 1980).

38. 316, 1991.

39. 327, 1395.

40. 327, 1466 (11 March 1981).

41. Ibid., 1399.

42. For details see Keatinge (1978), op. cit., p. 167 and chs 2 and 5 of Keatinge (1984).

43. See 314, 30-1 (8 May 1979) for references to working with these countries by Lenihan.

44. 323, 849.

45. Interview.

46. See, for example, 314, 1922 and 323, 849-50.

47. 314, 31.

48. Deputy Quinn, 323, 1152 (30 October 1980).

49. 323, 1168-70 for all this section.

50. Ibid.

51. Ibid.

52. 322, 724-5 (17 June 1980).

53. 314, 30-1 (8 May 1979).

54. 306, 424.

55. See, for example, 309, 1799 (2 November 1978).

56. 306, 367.

57. 309, 1799. What these existing obligations were was not made very clear.
58. 325, 820-22, Lenihan (10 December 1980).
59. 316, 82.
60. See 327, 1430 for FitzGerald making this point.
61. See Haughey's address to the UN General Assembly's second special session on disarmament, New York, 11 June 1982, in which he called for a two–year freeze on adding to the existing number of warheads or delivery vehicles. Cited in *Statements and Speeches*, 3/82.
62. *The Economist*, 16 May 1981.
63. 330, 310 (21 October 1982).
64. Ibid., 315.
65. *The Economist*, 21 November 1981.
66. For debate on this see 330, 238. Also Keatinge (1984), p. 105, argues that this exchange was a classic case of neutrality being used for the purpose of domestic party politics. He states that it was seen as such by the press at the time, and this point is corroborated, in part, by the comments of those interviewed regarding the role of neutrality as a 'political football'.
67. 330, 306.
68. Ibid., 309-15 for the rest of this exchange.
69. 331, 992 (2 December 1981).
70. Ibid., 921.
71. I shall further discuss this willingness below.
72. Notably Sinn Fein-The Workers' Party (descended from the old 'official' wing of the IRA) and the Socialist Labour Party representative, Dr Noel Browne.
73. For an account of Irish policy during the Falklands war, see Norman MacQueen, 'The Expedience of Tradition: Ireland, International Organization and the Falklands Crisis', in *Political Studies*, Vol. 23, No. 1, March 1985.
74. In addition, during the crisis a Royal Navy submarine had become entangled in the nets of an Irish trawler and had pulled the vessel along until it sank.
75. Interview with senior official of the Irish foreign service and see also FitzGerald, 333, 1690 (28 April 1982).
76. Press release from Ireland's Permanent Mission to the UN, 2 April 1982 covering Ambassador Dorr's statements on the Security Council. This section utilises press releases from the same source over the next few days of the crisis.
77. Ibid.
78. 334, 800 (11 May 1982).
79. *Sunday Times of London Insight: War in the Falklands*, Sunday Times, London, 1982. The tenth member is not accounted for.
80. 334, 35.
81. Interview.
82. 334, 800-4 for Haughey's announcement of the change in Irish policy.
83. Ibid., 804.
84. 334, 1425.
85. When Haughey received the nomination for Taoiseach in 1979, the opposition, including FitzGerald in particular, did not confine the comments in the Dáil to policy, but rather criticised him in terms of his personal character. Haughey had been a central figure in the arms scandal of the early 1970s and his government acquired a reputation for questionable practices in its conduct.
86. The by-election in Dublin was lost. Keatinge (1984), pp. 116–17.
87. 333, 1686 (28 April 1982).
88. Ibid., 1690. In an interview O'Brien also argued that de Valera would have probably supported the British military effort to counter aggression. There is no answer to this and

hence no profit in seeking one. The Falklands War offered two images. The first was of Britain stubbornly clinging to territory acquired in the days of empire for reasons of prestige and sentiment using the wishes of colonists to justify their position. The second is of the principle of self-determination confronting an expansionary dictatorship. The first is at least as powerful as the second, and my guess is that the parallels with Northern Ireland would be too compelling to have allowed a Republican leadership to ignore them.

89. 334, 1428 (18 May 1982). He cited Iran, Afghanistan and Poland.
90. Interview. He stated this as an argument made at the time without claiming it to be his own position.
91. 333, 1690 (28 April 1982).
92. 334, 807 (11 May 1982).
93. Statement by the Irish representative in the Security Council, 21 May 1982. Cited in a press release.
94. 334, 807.
95. 334, 802 (11 May 1982).
96. Press release, 21 May 1982.
97. Ibid., 25 May 1982.
98. Ibid., Resolution 505.
99. For example, see 334, 804 (11 May 1982), Haughey.
100. Ireland's representative in the Security Council cited in a press release for 25 May 1982. The reasons he gave for persisting with the initiative were: to give the Secretary General a formal mandate to continue with his efforts; to preserve anything which had already been agreed to; to give an opportunity to the belligerents if they were looking for a way out of the conflict; and to produce a series of steps by which confidence might be gradually built between the belligerents.
101. Ibid., 4 June 1982.
102. Ibid., 25 May 1982.
103. 334, 809-19 (11 May 1982).
104. 334, 1430.
105. 334, 1430.
106. See, for example, FitzGerald, 334, 812 (11 May 1982). After arguing that the Irish initiative at the UN was inconsistent and ill-timed, he then faulted it for destroying the EEC's leverage over Britain, failing to support an EEC partner under attack and letting the British 'off the hook on the issue of the avoidance of further violence'. It is not altogether clear whether the EEC's leverage was over the British use of force in the Falklands or their holding up an agreement on CAP prices.
107. This is an important point because critics of the change of policy on sanctions claimed that neutrality was not inconsistent with sanctions even after the fighting started. See Keatinge (1984), op. cit., p. 106.
108. Interview.
109. Interview.

12 Conclusion and postscript

My purpose in this book was to answer two sets of questions: why, and with what consequences did the Irish governments pursue a policy of international role-playing after Ireland became a member of the UN in 1956, and why, and with what consequences, did they continue this policy after Ireland became a member of the EEC. The form of this policy – the international good citizen role – may be explained in large part by reference to the fundamental national values articulated by Irish governments and the opportunities provided by the international system to act on those values. I have argued, however, that the full significance of international role-playing may be understood only when it is treated as a status policy, a response to problems with the credibility of Ireland's formal standing in international society as a sovereign, independent state.

During the first period, between 1956 and 1966, Irish governments pursued a foreign policy which was, according to their own pronouncements, organised around the idea of presenting Ireland as a coherent and distinctive personality in international society, both as an expression of the values of its people and in an attempt to secure prestige and influence. In terms of the internal resources which they mobilised and the external costs which they were prepared to sustain, this policy was important to Irish governments but it was kept separate from other aspects of Ireland's external affairs. In effect, the government treated the international system as two separate realms, one of

236

'political' foreign policy and the other of 'economic' external affairs, and they approached their policy to each realm in a very different manner. With regard to the former, Irish policy was assertive, reformist and practised on the basis of emphasising Ireland's contribution as a nation to resolving problems of war and peace. In contrast, the approach of Irish governments to the conduct of their economic relations, largely with Britain, was piecemeal, conservative and concentrated upon responding, where necessary, to events. This separation was explained partly in terms of the individual preferences of people in the government and partly in terms of the fact that assertive action in the economic realm courted more immediate costly consequences than activity in the political realm. However, it was also shown that key members of the government had clear views about the different nature of economic and political activity and that on the bases of these, they worked consciously to keep them separate.

This worked until Ireland was confronted by the probability of major charges in the trading system of which it was a part. The efforts to create some kind of European community caused problems for Irish governments in two ways. First, they emphasised the extent to which the Irish people were still not masters of their own affairs. In the face of uncertainty about their external trading position in the early 1960s, the government of the day thought it necessary to direct their efforts to securing and, for a time, deepening their links with Britain. This was an emphasis with which the image of Ireland as a modern, progressive republic, embodied in the active-independent foreign policy, jarred badly. The government attempted to deal with this problem by re-emphasising the separation between political and economic affairs; the former was the realm of the possible, perhaps, but the latter was the realm of necessity for certain. In this they were reasonably successful. Whatever disappointments Irish politicians and diplomats may have experienced as a consequence of the failure of the diplomatic prestige which they acquired through role-playing to convert into influence in other areas of external policy, was compensated for by the success of the policy in its own narrow terms. Further, if virtue perforce had to be its own reward abroad, then it was a source of considerable popularity and support for Irish governments at home. Nevertheless, by the late 1960s, the insulation and circumscribing of Ireland's active foreign policy into a narrow and detached effort to improve the peacekeeping procedures at the UN, indicated the diminished importance of Irish foreign policy to the pressing external concerns of the period.

The decline of the significance of Ireland's foreign policy during the 1960s was also related to a second problem which moves to create a new European organisation caused for Irish governments. It was clear that these moves did not conform to the distinction which Irish governments attempted to maintain between political and economic affairs. This raised the possibility that Ireland's foreign policy, based as it was upon an independent and neutral orientation, would not merely be irrelevant to the pursuit of objectives in the

Anglo-Irish and European contexts, but positively harmful. During the period, the Irish government dealt with suggestions to this effect by denying that membership of a European grouping of states would pose political problems for Ireland, and by suggesting that the future evolution of such an organisation as the EEC might make necessary certain changes in Irish policy which were, nevertheless, still consistent with the basic principles upon which it was based. Neither of these claims was put to the test at the time, although it may be seen that, in the formulations of Lemass in particular, the foundations of the future debate in terms of trading neutrality for the benefits of Community membership were laid down.

The evolution of Irish foreign policy during the first period can be interpreted in terms of both a realist and an interdependence conception of what is important in international relations and the foreign policies of small states. In the context of the former, it is possible to argue that international role-playing was never very important to Irish governments and, hence they attempted to rid themselves of it as soon as it became a liability. From an interdependence perspective, it is possible to regard Aiken's activities at the UN as the last, fairly wild, fling in the story of the achievement of an Irish independence which was based upon little real contact with the outside world. 'Europe' abroad, the Whitaker 'revolution' at home and the 'de-politicisation' of policy towards Northern Ireland, signalled a new period of increasing external involvement. For this, new external strategies would have to be fashioned in the course of which the luxury of a foreign policy which did not address concrete Irish interests, annoyed Ireland's friends, consumed scarce resources and was based on an increasingly untenable conception of Irish independence and sovereignty, would have to be abandoned.

This did not occur. Membership of the EEC resulted in many changes in Irish foreign policy, notably in terms of the volume and scope of the activity. It did not, however, result in any de-politicisation of policy, nor in any reduction of the effort to portray Ireland as a distinctive national actor through the performance of its international role, quite the reverse. During the second period, between 1977 and 1983, Irish governments took advantage of the increased opportunities for international role-playing which EEC membership opened to them and, indeed, because of the absence of any clear distinction between economic and political affairs in the EEC, they extended the role-playing approach into areas of policy which they would previously have handled on a more pragmatic and less assertive basis.

There are several possible explanations for this. The central issue in theoretical terms, however, is whether the persistence of this form of foreign policy behaviour was to be accounted for in terms of inadequacies in the interdependence thesis or the failure of the EEC to constitute a fair test of its predictions. This is a difficult question to answer but the position taken in this book has been that whether it has succeeded or not, the EEC represents the most explicit and large-scale attempt to build a system of relations between states and peoples on the proclaimed implications of their mutual need. On the basis of this argument, the impact of EEC membership on Irish foreign policy was examined as a test of two predictions made by the interdependence thesis for foreign policy behaviour: that prestige policies emphasising national identity would decline, and that small states would reap the benefits of certain 'equalisation' effects which were said to accompany an increase of interdependence.

The first prediction was shown to be completely wrong. Irish governments maintained a distinctive approach to arms control, disarmament and peacekeeping, and extended the projection of an Irish role into the issues of development assistance and a Middle East peace settlement. The EEC, according to Irish governments, served as both a source of support and an arena for their international role-playing efforts and during the course of the second period, their emphasis shifted from the former to the latter conception of the Community. Indeed, at times this emphasis shifted from the idea of the rest of the EEC as an audience before whom Ireland performed to impress and lead, to using them as a group, in contrast to which Ireland defined itself. It is with regard to the extension of Irish international role-playing into the areas of high policy with which the members of the Community concerned themselves, that the argument that the EEC constitutes a bad test of interdependence is at its most compelling. The EPC process between governments can be regarded as an inadequate substitute for the failure to integrate policy-making on internal Community to issues. By the same argument, Irish international role-playing on issues external to the Community may be interpreted as compensation for Irish disappointment at the EEC's failure to evolve.

The problem with this, however, is that it was demonstrated that role-playing and the emphasis on a distinctive national identity were extended by Irish governments into internal Community policy-making, even on those issues where the EEC made some progress in achieving common policies. This can only partly be explained by the fact that internal policy-making largely remained a matter of inter-governmental bargaining on the basis of the power and influence of the individual national actors. Critical to any Irish success, especially in the more regime-governed aspects of Community policy-making, was the emphasis that these rules put upon the formal equality of the sovereign states as the major actors in the policy process. Irish governments began the period attempting to exact benefits from the Community on the basis of their 'special status' as an economically disadvantaged participant and their whole-hearted commitment to the evolution of the Community. It was Ireland's standing in this regard, they claimed, which enabled them to profit from the policies of the EEC to the extent which they did. As they became increasingly disturbed by the performance of their own economy and dissatisfied with the direction of Community developments, however, this *communautaire* role was supplemented and increasingly replaced by a *demandeur* posture. The latter combined threats of disrupting Community processes, rather than protestations of Community 'spirit', with the details of Ireland's economic predicament as the basis of claims for special treatment by the rest of the Community. Common to both approaches, however, was an emphasis on Ireland's distinctiveness as a means of obtaining what Irish governments wanted from the Community.

With regard to the second prediction of the interdependence thesis, that regime politics would have an equalising effect on the power of big and small countries, this too was not verified by Ireland's experience in the EEC. Clearly, the Irish government participated in more external decisions which had domestic consequences for Ireland than ever before as a consequence of EEC membership. However, after Ireland joined the EEC, many more external decisions had an impact on Ireland than had been the case in the past. Further, this involvement in decisions and, in particular, the use of linkage threats which was characteristic of Ireland's *demandeur* role, was capable of obtaining only side-payments as the price for Irish participation in common policies which might be disadvantageous to it. They had played no part in the creation of the CAP, the Community policy from which they gained the most, and they demonstrated very little ability to defend it in the face of delays in or threats to its operation. Regime rules did not necessarily work in favour of weak states as far as Ireland was concerned, and in the case of the CFP, the structure of the regime and its procedures for solving problems worked very clearly to Ireland's disadvantage. The most obvious gain within the Community that could be associated with EEC membership was the ability, for the first time, to diverge in a significant manner from British economic policy. Even this new room for manoeuvre, however, was largely the product of Britain's decline and the opportunities for diplomatic diversification provided by EEC membership, rather than the existence of rule-governed politics. Further, it may be that the consequences of this diversification will remain both limited and ambiguous.

The most spectacular gains from any equalisation effects of EEC membership were with regard to Ireland's part in the Community's external political policy. It provided opportunities for coordinating the Community's position, speaking on behalf of it to other governments and in international fora, and on occasions, taking a diplomatic lead for the Community to follow. These developments, however, did not conform to the predictions of the interdependence thesis because they involved, for the most part, issues of high politics and entailed an involvement on the part of the Irish which emphasised their distinctiveness and suitability for the role which they performed, typically, according to them, as a bridge between other governments and the members of the Community. By the end of the second period, it was the national distinctiveness of role-playing, rather than the service which Ireland performed for the rest of the Community by such a policy which was being emphasised by the government. This coming full circle and, in particular, the re-emergence of the neutrality debate within Ireland in the early 1980s pointed the way to the real significance of EEC membership for Ireland and the impact of an increasing involvement with the international system for small states in general.

To talk about a transformation of international relations on the basis of conditions of increasing interdependence is, for small states at least, wrong. Critical to the predictions of the interdependence thesis regarding foreign policy behaviour is the idea of a measure of power equalisation between weak and strong actors. This equalisation is derived from either the existence of regime politics or the objective facts of mutual need. There is little evidence of this in the Irish case. Regime politics or the existence of rules in themselves neither necessarily hurt nor hindered the pursuit of Irish interests. In the case of the EEC, the form and operation of these rules reflected the underlying power structure and the way in which the major actors lined up on an issue. Sometimes this favoured Irish interests, on overriding the British 'veto' in 1982 for example, and sometimes, as in the cases of the implementation of the CFP and the EMS, it forced them into positions which the Irish government did not like.

With regard to the posited beneficial effects of 'objective' mutual need upon the affairs of the weak, there is no evidence to suggest that Ireland gained from EEC membership in this regard, either. It is here that the interdependence thesis is at its weakest because it is unable to suggest why the symmetries of mutual need override the asymmetries which must nearly always accompany them. Within the EEC, the strong remained strong, the weak remained weak, and the fundamental constraint under which any Irish government attempted to play regime politics was that Ireland needed the rest of the EEC far more than any of them needed Ireland. Thus, while the interdependence thesis is correct in suggesting that the involvement of national societies with one another is becoming intensified, it was the asymmetry of need which determined the character of Ireland's involvement in the process. It was for this reason that Irish governments had very little real choice about whether they became members of the EEC, and why for them an intensification of international contact took the form of an intensification of their degree of dependence upon the world outside, both in the general terms of the performance of the international economy and the more specific terms of their own decisions becoming contingent upon decisions made in the policy processes of the EEC.

International role-playing was primarily a response to a sense of credibility problems with Ireland's formal status as a sovereign, independent state, to a sense that the facts of Ireland's external circumstances posed a continuing threat to any Irish government's claim in this respect, and hence to its legitimacy. As the Irish economy and the EEC experienced increasing difficulties in the late 1970s, so the negative consequences of a more intense involvement with the outside world were experienced within Ireland, and the credibility problems of the state intensified. The Irish government responded to this by making the most of the opportunities provided by membership of the EEC for pursuing an active foreign policy emphasising Ireland's capacity to perform as a distinctive, independent entity on the international stage. There was, however, one major problem with this strategy in the EEC and this resulted from the collapse of the distinction between economic and political activity. The neutral, independent orientation upon which Ireland's distinctive international role was based became increasingly threatened by the demands of EEC membership; their realm of necessity extended from economic matters into what had once been regarded as purely political questions. This more than anything else should have underlined for Irish governments that the 'choice' offered to small states by processes of integration and interdependence is not between living with the political symbols of the past or participating in an increasingly apolitical future devoted 'simply' to economic development.

Membership of the EEC provided the specific form of the process by which Ireland became increasingly integrated into the international economy. Since 1983, the end of the second period examined here, this process and the stresses and strains of 'adjustment' which it imposes upon Irish society continued, exacerbated considerably by the general recession of the early 1980s. Indeed, it is possible to argue that Ireland underwent a continuous and growing economic crisis after 1983. Between its election in 1982 and its defeat in 1987, the coalition government led by Garret FitzGerald presided over the continued growth of Ireland's export industries and a continued decline in the importance of Britain as a trading partner.[1] However, these successes and the reduction of inflation were achieved only at the cost of very high levels of unemployment and taxation, and the revival of emigration. Further, by 1986 the country was burdened with a budget deficit and an exchequer borrowing requirement respectively estimated to be equal to 8.5 and 13 per cent of GNP. In 1987, Fianna Fail led by Charles Haughey were returned to power without an overall majority. They quickly developed a mixed strategy of public expenditure cuts, public sector wage freezes, tax reforms and government department reforms combined with an attempt to stimulate economic development in new areas such as financial services, horticulture and maritime resources.[2]

These economic difficulties, however, did not give rise to a political crisis or upheavals in Irish foreign policy of the order of the one produced by the Falklands War. One reason for this, was that the period between 1982 and 1987 was one of political and governmental stability within the Dáil. More importantly, the dominant partner in the coalition government, Fine Gael, was not ideologically inclined to meet economic difficulties by invoking nationalist sentiments. In large part, therefore, its foreign policy consisted of 'business as usual'. The Irish continued to contribute to the UN force in the Lebanon, and the anniversaries of Ireland's entry into the UN and first major peacekeeping contribution were duly noted.[3] In July 1984, they assumed the Presidency of the Council of Ministers for the third time. The Council met in Dublin in September 1984 and established its joint position which Ireland's Foreign Minister, Peter Barry, presented to the UN General Assembly later that month.

In December of that year, the third Lomé agreement between the EEC and the ACP states was concluded under the Irish presidency.

However, the 'practical' and 'non-ideological' approach of the coalition government was most evidenced by its national policy. In 1983 it announced the establishment of a 'New Ireland Forum' and invitations were issued to political parties on both sides of the border to participate and hear submissions from concerned groups. Only those who unequivocally renounced violence were invited to participate and only the parties of the Republic and the Social Democratic and Labour Party from the North actually did in drawing up the recommendations of the hearing. A report was issued in 1984 and the following year the Anglo-Irish Agreement was concluded. In this, both parties agreed that there could be no change in the status of the North without the consent of the majority of the population, but that if this consent was forthcoming, then both countries would do what was necessary to effect the change. Further, the Irish 'conceded' the importance of recognising the existence of two traditions within Ireland, in that the government argued that it was not only impossible, but also not right, to attempt to ignore the Unionist-Protestant position with its attendant aspirations and fears.

In return for this and increased security cooperation, the British accepted that there was, in fact, an 'Irish dimension' to the affairs of the North. The practical consequence of this was the establishment of the Anglo-Irish Inter-governmental Conference within the framework of the Council of the same name set up in 1981. This body is jointly chaired by a British and Irish representative and meets frequently in Dublin, Belfast and London. While it deals chiefly with such matters as attempting to coordinate security and judicial efforts against the IRA, Irish supporters of the agreement have stressed the way in which it permits the Irish government to represent interests and concerns of the nationalists in the North to the British government. To date, those aspects of the agreement concerned with improving Anglo-Irish cooperation along the border appear to be of more consequence than those which recognise an 'Irish dimension' to the problems of the North, unless one accepts the anger of the Unionists at this as evidence of its importance. Further, the agreement in all its aspects seems to pale into insignificance as a determinant of what happens in the North when compared to the conflict's own dynamics. The Anglo-Irish Agreement represented a considerable diplomatic achievement in inter-state relations on the part of the Irish government, but it also serves as a clear reminder of the very limited influence Irish governments enjoy even on issues of critical concern to them.

Of more direct importance to the argument of this book, it may be noted that developments in the EEC since 1983 continued to pose problems for Ireland and underlined the limited capacity of its government to shape international events even in an increasingly regime-governed environment. Speaking to the Dáil in July1983 about the recent 'Solemn Declaration on European Union', Peter Barry, the Minister for Foreign Affairs in the coalition government, argued that Ireland's traditional policy of 'military neutrality' would not be changed by developments in the Community. His conception of the neutrality policy, which he claimed had been shared by all governments since the state came into existence, was to the effect that it was a pragmatic choice. Neither the level of security enjoyed by Ireland nor the 'physical safety' of its people would be markedly improved by its becoming a member of an alliance, but not joining allowed it a 'modest but constructive diplomatic role'.[4] This modest view of the policy notwithstanding, however, Ireland would oppose any attempt on the part of other members of the Community to move it beyond coordinating the 'political and economic aspects' of security. These efforts belonged in the EPC process, and decisions made there had to be unanimous. Hence, he argued, Ireland had a 'veto' both 'at all stages of discussion' and over the 'conclusions arrived at'.[5]

By the summer of 1985 and the meeting of the European Council in Milan, however, efforts to coordinate European security policy within an EEC framework had become part of a broader process designed to reform the EEC and bring the Rome treaties 'up to date'. By that time the EEC had set itself the task of achieving a genuine single 'internal market' by 1992, reforming its institutions and decision-making processes and discussing two draft treaties, one British and one Franco-German, for establishing common foreign and security policies.[6] Since Ireland was so dependent on trade, both the coalition government and their Fianna Fáil successors could only welcome movement in the Community towards a common internal market. Nevertheless, these changes presented a series of problems for Irish foreign policy which went beyond the possible threat to Irish neutrality.

They were linked to developments in the perennial debate about the Community's finances and common policies. The system by which the CAP produced food surpluses and guaranteed incomes for Irish farmers, among others, became increasingly threatened. In particular the Irish were unable to prevent the imposition of a super-levy reducing milk production in the Community. By the spring of 1987, the new Taoiseach, Charles Haughey, was making it clear that Ireland's agriculture and food industries would have to undertake more processing of their production in Ireland since the 'intervention inputs' of the Community could no longer be relied upon.[7] A few days before this, his Foreign Minister, making a statement on the thirtieth anniversary of the signing of the Rome treaties, declared that membership of the EEC had been beneficial to Ireland and had not compromised its neutrality. Nevertheless, the EEC was still not doing enough to develop 'economic and social cohesion' among its members. The preamble to the original treaties had referred to reducing regional differences in standards of living and this, he said, had to be a 'major goal' of the Single European Act by which the members assented to Community reforms.[8]

Ireland was the last member of the EEC to ratify this Act because the Irish Supreme Court had decided that a national referendum was required before changes with constitutional implications could be implemented.[9] The vote in favour was clearly in accord with the preferences of the government. Ireland, they claimed, continued to favour any kind of movement towards a genuine European community which could act as a vehicle of economic prosperity and a force for international peace and stability. This is why they had supported the admission of Spain and Portugal the previous year. Such progress would necessarily entail the surrender of a measure of national sovereignty to a joint authority. Only by this, for example, could strong regional and social policies directed at ending regional imbalances be established. According to Michael Hoey, the Executive Director of the Irish Council of the European Movement, proposals for doubling the EEC's structural spending by 1992, the date for achieving a single market, were of critical importance for Irish participation in the next stage of Community-building.[10]

Thus the depositing of Ireland's instrument of ratification of the Single European Act in Rome in June 1987 was presented as evidence of its continued *communautaire* commitment. Nevertheless, accompanying it was a formal declaration by the government which referred to both the old Protocol 30 of Ireland's accession to the EEC back in 1973 and to Title III of the present Act. With regard to the former, the Irish government noted that the completion of the internal market would have 'full regard' to the protocol's recognition of Ireland's 'special problems' and the Community interest in fostering Irish economic development in order to

align the standard of living in Ireland with those of other European nations and to eliminate underemployment while progressively evening out regional differences in levels of development.

With regard to the provisions of Title III, they declared that this 'did not affect Ireland's long-established policy of military neutrality'. The coordination of policy positions among the members applied only to political and economic aspects of security. It did not include

the military aspect of security or procurement for military purposes and does not affect Ireland's right to act, or refrain from acting in any way which might affect Ireland's international status of military neutrality.[11]

While the period since 1983 did not produce a political crisis of the order suggested in the original argument of this book, therefore, it may be seen that the potential external causes of such a crisis were not diminished. As Frances Cairncross suggested in an article on Ireland in January 1988, the country remained, after fifteen years in the EEC, one of the 'poorest of the rich' with a GDP equivalent to 64 per cent of the Community average.[12] The gap had not been narrowed and yet, significantly, Irish governments remained committed to fostering development by attracting more capital-intensive export industries dependent on external investment and markets. Clearly, their implicit bargain with the rest of the EEC still held good, if less from conviction than from the lack of an acceptable alternative. If Ireland could secure unambiguous economic benefits from membership, then the government remained prepared to pay a price for this in terms of its own sovereignty and established components of the country's national identity as these had been traditionally articulated.

To judge by the severe cuts in public expenditure instituted by the Fianna Fáil government which took office in the spring of 1987, it would appear that even the more republican of the two principal political parties was still prepared to take this approach, albeit with its reservations written into Ireland's acceptance of the Single European Act. However, this is a political party which is both vulnerable to and tempted by the demands of republicanism for a more radical, nationalist approach when 'respectable' and 'responsible' behaviour fails to yield results. Like the semi-developed countries of Latin America, Ireland is currently berated by economic orthodoxy both for its low standard of living *and* for using the easy credit thrust upon it in the 1970s to try and do something about that and minimise the social dislocation caused by the process of integration into the international economy. However, if further integration translates into merely a smoother flow of locally generated capital and educated young people out of the country, complicity in the inertial character of Britain's crisis management policy in the North and no clear redressing of regional imbalances, then it would be unlikely that the present government could hold to its course even until 1992. It is also highly unlikely that Ireland's problems of economic development can be solved by the efforts of its own government or the collective effort of its Community fellows. This being so, the fate of their policy and much else depends on something over which the government exercises no control, the ability of the international economy to recover to a point at which Irish industries start to benefit and revenues become available for a revival of expenditure on social policies. Their predicament in this regard is a direct consequence of the character of the international regime into which Irish governments have seen no alternative but to try and integrate their country over the last 25 years.

Notes

1. Various sources suggest that export industries directly provide some 80,000 jobs with another 80,000 indirectly dependent on these. See, for example, Michael Hoey, 'Ireland and Europe: A Changing Relationship', in *Ireland Today*, 1038, June/July 1987. He cites predictions that by the end of the century Irish exports to the rest of the EEC will exceed those to Britain by a factor of 2 or 3. Nevertheless, in an economy where trade accounts for over 50 per cent of GDP, Britain still accounts for nearly as much of Ireland's trade as the rest of the EEC combined (*IT*,1010, July/August 1984).

2.   For details, see Charles Haughey speeches in the Dáil, 'The Path to Recovery', 8 April 1987 and 'Restoring Confidence', 25 April 1987. The centrepiece of the government's strategy was public expenditure cuts, a policy of 'Hack and Pray' as Frances Cairncross put it in *The Economist*, 16 January 1988. It is a mixed strategy in that three generations of industrial policy may be detected in it. First, and most importantly, the strategy involves cutting public expenditure, largely on social programmes and removing barriers to economic activity, for example, in developing a financial services industry. Secondly, it maintains the older Fianna Fáil conception of industrial policy as a business of picking winners and negotiating agreements with what Haughey calls the 'social partners' (the Irish Congress of Trade Unions, the Confederation of Irish Industry and the Construction Industry Federation). Thirdly, and intriguingly, some of this economic development, notably in horticulture and forestry is justified in terms of import-substitution.

3.   *IT*, 1018, 1985. Thirtieth anniversary of UN membership and 28th anniversary of sending troops to the Congo.

4.   *Statements and Speeches*, 4/83.

5.   Ibid.

6.   *IT*, 1020, November 1985.

7.   Charles Haughey, 'Restoring Confidence', speech to the Dáil, 25 April 1987. For analysis of Irish foreign policy between 1983–7 which investigates the questions raised in this book see Paul Sharp, 'External Challenges and Domestic Legitimacy: Ireland's Foreign Policy 1983–7' in *Irish Political Studies* 4, 1989 pp. 100–120.

8.   *IT*, 1036, April/May 1987.

9.   The Supreme Court had decided this in April 1987. The referendum took place on 26 May; 44 per cent of the electorate voted and just under 70 per cent of these were in favour of the change. *IT*, 1037, May/June 1987.

10.   'Hoey', in IT, June/July 1987.

11.   *IT*, 1037, May/June 1987.

12.   *The Economist*, 16-22 January 1988.

Index